W9-DBW-493

RELIGION AND
THE CHALLENGE
OF PHILOSOPHY

200.19
B26

RELIGION AND THE CHALLENGE OF PHILOSOPHY

by

J. E. Barnhart

1975

LITTLEFIELD, ADAMS & CO.
Totowa, New Jersey

Copyright © 1975
by
LITTLEFIELD, ADAMS & CO.

All rights reserved. No part of this book may be repro-
duced in any form without permission in writing from
the publisher except by a reviewer who wishes to quote
brief passages in connection with a review written for
inclusion in a magazine, newspaper or broadcast.

Library of Congress Cataloging in Publication Data
Barnhart, Joe E.   1931–
  Religion and the Challenge of Philosophy
  (A Littlefield, Adams Quality Paperback No. 291)
  Includes bibliographical references and index.
  1. Religion—Philosophy.   I. Title.
BL51.B245   200'.19   75-16364
ISBN 0-8226-0291-1

PRINTED IN THE UNITED STATES OF AMERICA

To James R. Barnhart—my brother.

123999

123333

Contents

PREFACE ix

INTRODUCTION 1

PHILOSOPHY AND RELIGION 1

FAITH AS COMMITMENT AND FAITH AS
OBJECT OF COMMITMENT 3

THE CHALLENGE OF PHILOSOPHY 4

   I   IS RELIGIOUS EXPERIENCE AN
      EXPERIENCE OF GOD? 7

   II THE QUESTION OF REVELATION
      THROUGH SACRED SCRIPTURE 36

  III CLASSICAL THEISM AND THE
      TELEOLOGICAL ARGUMENT 61

  IV CLASSICAL THEISM AND THE
      COSMOLOGICAL ARGUMENT 80

   V CLASSICAL THEISM AND THE
      ONTOLOGICAL ARGUMENT 96

  VI GOD, EVIL, AND SUFFERING: TWO
      VERSIONS OF CLASSICAL THEISM 111

 VII GOD, THE ABSOLUTE, AND THE PROCESS .. 134

VIII PANENTHEISM AND
      PROCESS PHILOSOPHY 150

  IX NATURALISM AS AN ALTERNATIVE
      TO SUPERNATURALISM 166

   X MORALITY WITHOUT
      SUPERNATURALISM 190

  XI MIRACLES, SUPERNATURAL HEALING,
      AND PRAYER 212

 XII MYTH AND SALVATION 239

XIII IS THERE LIFE AFTER DEATH? 262

EPILOGUE 280

SUBJECT INDEX 303

NAME INDEX 309

Preface

No one approaches the study of religion in a wholly impartial and unbiased manner. Fortunately, in a somewhat open society it is possible to establish lines of communication among various groups. This encourages religious convictions not only to be expressed, but also to be critically debated in a lively manner. In this book I have endeavored to formulate in readable style some of the most fascinating and creative interchanges between religion and philosophy.

A leading philosopher and spokesman of atheism once visited with my wife and myself at our home. A few months later, a Baptist minister and his wife visited with us. What struck us was not the great differences between the atheist and the Baptist, but the profound similarities. Recently, I visited with another Christian minister in his home, having only the day before had a profitable discussion with a student of Buddhism. Again, I was impressed with the compassion and insight of both individuals with whom I ate and talked. In Boston, I met a professing Marxist who seemed very much like some angry fundamentalist radio preachers I had heard in Tennessee. What I am trying to say is this: religion and philosophy are very rich and subtle, and it is often misleading to divide people and their views into the simple categories of "believer" and "unbeliever."

In this book I hope to share some of the influence that other persons and books in philosophy and religion have had on my own life. But it is not my job to please you by reinforcing you in your convictions; neither is it my concern to uproot your convictions. Rather, I wish to pursue the issues and ride the currents wherever they lead. You will have to take your chances as to how you fare in this venture. Thinking profoundly, especially on questions of vital religious concern, takes as much courage as brains.

Writing a book is one quick way of discovering how much one needs both the criticisms and the encouragement of others. I am pleased to express my appreciation for the work of Juanita M. Putnam and Robert Gregory Dresh. The skills of Jane Sells, Betty Johnson, and B. K. Brown, as well as the courteous assistance of the library staff of North Texas State University, have helped make it possible for me to enjoy writing this book. Patricia White of Littlefield, Adams & Co. made numerous useful recommendations; I am grateful for her professional contributions. My wife, Mary Ann, despite having her own work, was ready to come to the rescue when certain details of the book had to be attended to without delay.

In the course of more than two decades I have had the good fortune of being challenged by the personalities and writings of some remarkable scholars. While they are not to be held responsible for the limitations of this book, nevertheless apart from them it would be considerably less informed than it is. Hence, my sincere appreciation goes especially to the following: Eric Rust (Old Testament scholar and proponent of Christian theism), Kai Nielsen and Anthony Flew (proponents of atheism and humanism), John Lavely and Peter Bertocci (expositors of personalism), Charles Hartshorne (defender of the ontological argument and process philosophy), and T. C. Smith (New Testament scholar and model of intellectual courage).

While I have never met Sir Karl Popper, the influence of some of his philosophical works will be apparent to some of my readers. D. J. Harris, Richard M. Millard, and Robert C. Tucker are former instructors to whom I am indebted for their noble example of religious and intellectual sensitivity. My very tolerant colleagues in the Philosophy Department of North Texas State University provided a generally peaceful and encouraging environment for the writing of this book.

J.E.B.

Acknowledgments

The authors and the publisher gratefully acknowledge the following sources for permission to quote passages from the works indicated.

Doubleday & Company, Inc. for an excerpt from *Myth of Christian Beginnings* by Robert L. Wilkens, Doubleday, Anchor, 1972.

William B. Eerdmans Publishing Co. for an excerpt from *Scripture, Tradition, and Infallibility*, William B. Eerdmans, 1973; and for an excerpt from *Thy Word is Truth* by Edward J. Young, William B. Eerdmans, 1957.

National Council of the Churches of Christ for quotations from *The Revised Standard Version Bible*.

Presbyterian and Reformed Publishing Co. for excerpts from *Religion, Reason, and Revelation* by Gordon Clark, Presbyterian and Reformed Publishing Co. 1961.

RELIGION AND
THE CHALLENGE
OF PHILOSOPHY

Introduction

PHILOSOPHY AND RELIGION

Illusion and Disillusion.   It is hoped that in this book philosophy and religion will be seen, not as natural enemies, but as two profound dimensions of vital human existence. It is too simple to say that religion produces illusions whereas philosophy produces disillusionments. Traditionally, people have turned to both religion and philosophy in order to find some meaningful response to certain contingencies of life.

But if philosophy and religion are not natural enemies, neither is one to be reduced to the other. Like science, philosophy is passionately committed to the ideal of truth. But contrary to the proverb that the possession of truth will make people free, there are many who find at least certain truths to be almost incapacitating. Philosophy is sometimes called upon to help people to learn how to gain perspective on those truths that seem so hard to bear.

Science's major commitment is to knowledge or truth for its own sake, while religion's primary commitment is to some version of salvation. Philosophy often stands between these two profound human concerns. When science would seek to transform all human values into one value (namely, the search for truth), philosophy must join religion in opposition to such tyranny. And when religion would seek to subvert truth and turn it into a handmaiden of religion's own pronouncements, then philosophy must join with science in defending the search for truth for its own sake.

Religion is likely to condemn what it sees in philosophy as doubt and disbelief. But philosophy's major commitment is not to doubt for its own sake, but to doubt for the sake of more rational belief. This is not to say that the "nonrational" depths

1

are to be somehow rationalized away; rather it is to say that even the nonrational depths must be seen in perspective. One need not respond destructively to destruction. Nor need one respond irrationally to either irrationality or nonrationality. Indeed, philosophical analysis would teach us to perceive some differences between the *ir*rational and the *non*rational.

If philosophy does sometimes serve to disillusion the true believer, it need not do so with a vengeance. Disillusionment is a serious condition, and philosophy is obligated to help the disillusioned to recover from the blow. It is hoped that the illusions of the new faith will not be so great or so harmful as those of the old. But philosophy cannot guarantee that they will not be. Philosophy cannot provide salvation. It can, however, throw a beacon light on the territory and thus help determine what the new path of salvation will be, or at least will not be. But this is to speak in too general a manner. Let us pursue further this matter of religious belief and the challenge of philosophy.

Doubt and Faith.   Philosophy requires of religion that it take doubt to be, not a moral weakness, but an essential ingredient of rational thought. Many religious spokesmen have, however, classified doubts under the heading of temptations. They have warned their readers and followers not to yield to doubts but to overcome them.

But *how* are doubts to be overcome? That is a crucial question. It is often answered that doubts must be overcome by increasing one's faith. This raises the question as to which specific actions count as faith. For some spokesmen, faith includes the practice of putting away reading materials that are not in agreement with one's professed view, turning away from discussions with those who call attention to what they regard as contradictions within the view, and in general refusing to bring one's view out into the open for careful analysis and scrutiny. Paradoxically, this kind of faith seems to indicate a *lack of faith* in one's view or position.

A strong faith is one that can better endure the scrutiny of rational inquiry, whereas a weak faith is one that collapses under fire. The strength or weakness of a faith, however, must not be confused with how an individual *feels* about his faith or what he *does* about it. Here we can see that the word 'faith' has at least two meanings. There is no paradox in having a faith that is both strong and weak when we grasp the distinction between these two meanings of 'faith'. This distinction is worth pursuing.

FAITH AS COMMITMENT AND FAITH AS OBJECT OF COMMITMENT

Faith As Object of Commitment. In religious discourse the term 'faith' is often used to refer to *that which is believed in*. If someone asks you, "Do you have the faith?", you may be reluctant to answer him. Your reluctance rises out of the simple fact that he has not informed you of the particular faith he has in mind. If a conservative Roman Catholic speaks of "the Church," he will more than likely have in mind the Roman Catholic Church, whereas a Lutheran will probably have something else in mind. Similarly, if a Mormon asks you if you are of "the faith," he may be referring to the Mormon faith. But in Iran "the faith" will more likely be the Muslim faith.

Now, the Muslim faith includes such putative objects as one God (Allah), Muhammad as his prophet, the Qur'an as the revelation of God in a written document, angels, heaven, hell, and a long list of other things that Muslims regard as true and worthy of commitment. So, I ask you, "Do you adhere to the faith?" In this context I am asking you whether you are a Muslim.

The point here is that there are many "faiths" or objects of commitment. Sometimes to ask whether or not your faith is strong is to ask *not* for information about yourself, but rather about the object of your belief or commitment. If you are a Muslim, I want to know whether the Muslim teachings are credible, not whether you personally are strong in your commitment to them. My question has to do, not with you, but with the Muslim teachings and doctrines. I am also asking whether the Muslim beliefs are consistent with one another. Furthermore, is there evidence to support the Muslim faith or teachings?

If the Muslim faith (i.e., beliefs, teachings, etc.) can hold up under scrutiny and inquiry, then it is a *strong faith*. Whether or not the faith in this sense is strong does not depend on the strength or weakness of the believers. Indeed, the believers may be very weak in their commitment, even though the *object of their commitment*—the Muslim faith in this case—

might prove to be quite strong when put to the test of critical inquiry.

Faith As Psychological Commitment.   In this book your psychological states of mind and behavioral responses are not the immediate concern. What is the immediate concern is the object or objects of your commitment. It cannot be denied, however, that the object of commitment would be of little human concern unless eventually it involved the psychological dimension. If belief in God were of no human concern for good or ill, then this book would not discuss the arguments for and against belief in God.

The object of one's commitment might be very *weak*, depending on what it is. That is, under careful examination it might prove to be filled with contradictions, misleading in its assertions, lacking in evidence, and in general unable to withstand logical analysis and empirical investigation. (A more rigorous analysis would distinguish the *claims* of one's commitments from the objective *referents* of the claims. I have temporarily blended them together under the heading "the objects of one's commitment.") Furthermore, the object of one's commitment might even be morally inferior and unworthy of human commitment. Nevertheless, despite this, it might very well elicit from someone a strong faith in, or commitment to, it. If so, then the appeal of the faith doubtless lies not in its intellectual or moral strength, but in some other dimension.

On the other hand, a person may have a very weak commitment to a faith that is very strong intellectually and morally. Why would someone manifest such a weak commitment to such a strong faith? Well, that is a matter of empirical observation and investigation. It may be that a particular faith, while very strong intellectually and morally, is lacking at the emotional level. It does not reinforce the believer in terms of community support and other powerful elements classified under the heading of the "emotional dimension."

THE CHALLENGE OF PHILOSOPHY

Ideally, the best faith would be the one that is strongest intellectually, morally, emotionally, and in other relevant dimensions. A number of people—perhaps most—agree that some faiths are not worthy of human commitment, although these people will sometimes disagree sharply as to which particular faith is most worthy and which is least worthy. The task of philosophy is to challenge religious faiths (as well as nonreligious faith). Philosophy must cross-examine them, explicate their claims, and check them out for evidence and consistency.

But the motive of philosophy need not be to destroy religious commitment per se, but rather to help it seek out the faith that genuinely deserves honest commitment and moral dedication. So long as human beings die and suffer outrageous fortunes, religion will remain a part of the human condition and response. Hopefully, philosophy, too, will be on hand to help keep the religious response from becoming still another outrage instead of a true help in the time of profound human need.

CHAPTER I

Is Religious Experience an Experience of God?

INTRODUCTION

The systematic study of religious experience and conversion began in the twentieth century with the fascinating book *The Varieties of Religious Experience,* published in 1902 by the American psychologist and philosopher William James. A few decades later, studies were made of conversion experiences occurring in psychoanalysis. Referring to his own personal experience of therapy under Sigmund Freud, a client wrote:

For the first few months I was able to feel nothing but increasing anxiety, humiliation and guilt. Nothing about my past life seemed satisfactory any more, and all my own ideas about myself seemed to be contradicted. When I got into a completely hopeless state, he [Freud] then seemed to piece everything together in a new setting.[1]

Students of Christian religious conversions are familiar with the phrase "under conviction," which describes the state of mind of individuals who are on the verge of being converted. Christians who use this phrase hold that just before the conversion takes place a person will often feel himself to be terribly "convicted" of his own sinfulness and worthlessness. The picture that the sinner has of himself is a dismal one indeed, as the Christian hymn entitled "At the Cross" indicates:

> Alas, and did my Savior bleed,
> And did my Sovereign die.
> Would He devote that Sacred Head
> For such a worm as I!

The apostle Paul, John Bunyan (author of *The Pilgrim's Progress*), and many other Christians have each referred to themselves as "the chief of sinners." "Sinners under conviction" have suffered overwhelming thoughts of self-depreciation, guilt, dis-

7

gust with their whole lives, and abject despair. Some have been tormented with the thought of having "committed the unpardonable sin." Billy Graham's father was one such person.

In his *Varieties of Religious Experience*, William James distinguishes the "once born" believer from the "twice born." The former absorbs his religion in a rather gradual and undramatic manner. His religious life is more an evolutionary development than a dramatic conversion. The "twice born" individual, by contrast, is described by James as a "sick soul" because he feels himself to be a miserable creature totally cut off from the only way of life that he regards as secure and valuable. He believes that he is suffering what may best be described as a spiritual plague, which must be cured if he is to know genuine happiness. He sees himself in some sense as in the throes of a sickness unto death, which is an alienation or separation from that which makes life meaningful and worthwhile.[2] Being born into the natural world is not enough. He must now be "born again" if he is to move into the kingdom of salvation, where he will no longer feel himself to be an alien and an outcast.[3]

Religious conversion of the more intense and dramatic type has some close parallels in numerous psychoanalytic experiences. Some of Freud's clients were declared to be "cured" by his method of the rehearsal of significant past events in the clients' life combined with an intense emotional buildup and release called "transference."[4] Before experiencing his cure, the previously mentioned client of Freud confessed that "nothing about my past life seemed satisfactory any more." Nevertheless, despite this "completely helpless state," he eventually found, through the guidance of Freud, a radically new life and orientation.

The author Arthur Koestler speaks very frankly of his own dramatic conversion to militant Communism. Like the apostle Paul, Charles Finney, and many other noted Christians, Koestler's conversion was very sudden. And again like many Christians, his sudden conversion had a special background or staging. Some years later as he looked back over his conversion experience, Koestler wrote that it came on the heels of a cluster of profoundly disturbing personal experiences during the Depression in 1931.[5]

The point that Koestler wishes to make is that a combination of miserable factors—including guilt, shame, and self-reproach —set him up for a conversion experience. In short, he was in need of undergoing a dramatic change in his whole life.

The pattern of his life from that day forward became drastically different from what it had been. Many years later he was radically converted again, from Communism to political liberalism. The setting and immediate background of his second conversion were even more shocking: imprisonment during the Spanish Civil War, fears of being executed in the way that some of his friends had just been executed, and an intense recalling of a childhood trauma.

It would be a mistake to think that most conversions come at the close of calm discussions. Perhaps they ought to come in that way, but mostly they do not. Koestler's intense subjective experience of conversion had strong elements of fear, humiliation, mental torture, and eventually mystical feelings, as if the self were not located anywhere. According to Koestler, this mystical experience induced an "inner peace which I have known neither before nor since."[6]

Koestler did not believe, however, that his transforming experience was an experience of God. Nevertheless, there are many people who assert that it was through a powerful conversion experience that they came to know without doubt that there truly is a God. To provide a philosophical examination of this claim will be a major objective of this chapter.

CLARIFYING THE ISSUE

The modern philosopher C. B. Martin has offered a forthright and hard-nosed critique of the claim that religious experience is "direct evidence" of the existence and reality of God. As was seen in the paragraphs immediately above, very moving, radical, and lasting conversion experiences do take place in the lives of individuals. But in many, perhaps most, cases no claim is made that the Jewish or Christian God has been encountered or experienced. Indeed, one of the problems of the "argument from religious experience" is that it seems to open up the floodgates for all sorts of spirits and deities to enter into human experience. Not only the orthodox Christian's God, but various other rival divinities, demons, spirits, deceased ancestors, and other supernatural beings are strongly believed to be "visiting" the subject in some very special way.

Before considering one of Professor Martin's critical objections, you must fix in your mind what the issue at hand is and is not. First, it is *not* a question of the intensity, vividness, or powerful influence of the extraordinary experience in the life of the individual. Second, the debate is not concerned to deny the conspicious fact that conversion often does change the individual's life in a drastic and significant manner. Third, there is no concern to deny that the believer undergoing this profound experience often ends up with strong convictions that previously he did not embrace. Indeed, in many cases the believer, once converted, for the rest of his life never seriously doubts or gives up his new convictions.

The central question of this chapter may be stated very simply: *Does the believer's religious experience or conversion provide evidence for, or a basis for, belief in the existence or reality of God?*

In this chapter we will focus primarily on the Jewish and Christian understanding of God, although in most cases the arguments set forth will have some bearing on other views of God.

ON NOT SEEING GOD

Believers in God sometimes say that they know that he exists because they have experienced him personally. They claim to have had a direct experience or apprehension of him. A noted theologian states this position crisply when he writes the following: "It is not as the result of an inference of any kind . . . that the knowledge of God's reality comes to us. It comes rather through our direct, personal encounter with Him in the Person of Jesus Christ His Son our Lord."[7]

In making the assertion that the knowledge of God's reality is not an "inference," the theologian means that the assertion does not come through a process of reasoning. It is not a conclusion drawn from a set of premises. Rather, the assertion is taken to be a confession of an immediate experience of God. It is not taken to be a *hypothesis about* God.

If you were born blind, you would have no direct acquaintance with anything visual. Similarly, believers in God sometimes assert that people who do not experience God are simply "deity-blind," just as some people are blind to certain colors. When you experience the color blue, for example, you do not have to say, "Well, I shall make a hypothesis that I am experiencing the color blue." Presumably you simply report your immediate experience without making any inferences or going through any reasoning process. If you do not experience the color, then something is wrong. Perhaps you are not in the proper position. Or perhaps you are color-blind.

IN WHAT SENSE IS GOD REAL?

C. B. Martin holds that this argument advanced by believers in God is fundamentally misleading. It takes for granted what needs to be substantiated. The mere fact that a person has certain experiences is one thing. It is another thing to make an assertion as to what these experiences are *of*, or what they *refer to*.[8]

If one of your friends tells you that yesterday he saw a blue and pink cat, you do not necessarily take his word. Yet in another sense you might take his word, for there are at least two ways in which you could or could not take it.

Assuming for the moment that he is not lying, you may ask him about the conditions under which he saw this unusual cat. What time? Where? Who was with him when he saw it? Were there other witnesses? And so on. It is very possible that he actually did see the blue and pink cat in his dreams. In ordinary conversation you will tend to say that the cat in the dream was not "real." But if your friend persists, you might even agree that it was real, but only in another sense of the word. The blue and pink cat was real only as a character in the private dream experience of your friend. You might even be able to explain some of the processes by which the dream experience of this cat came about. But what you will not accept from your friend is that the blue and pink cat in the dream experience has the *same sort of reality* that the black cat of your neighborhood has.

The theist who claims to have experienced God "directly" will not agree that God is real merely in the sense that the blue and pink cat in your friend's dream is real. You might condescendingly tell your persistent friend that his dream cat is real *to him*, but in making this concession you are not conceding very much. And certainly the theist does not want to be reduced to saying that God is real to him as a believer but not in any other way.

What the theist claims is that God exists *objectively*. If God is no more than an item in the believer's personal experience, then God would be merely a *subjective* phenomenon, just as your friend's blue and pink cat is merely a subjective phenomenon.

When awake, you do not buy cat food for the cats of your dreams, no matter how vivid your dreams are or how much they do for you emotionally and in other ways. In other words, when you wake from your dream, you do not attempt to relate to your dream cat in the way that you relate to your neighbor's cat. To be sure, the cat of your dream may prove to be very significant in your life. But it is not significant *as a cat* but as a symbol of something else in your life when you are awake. In other words, it is taken as a symptom of something else, whereas your neighbor's cat is at least a real cat and not merely a symbol or symptom. (In a later chapter we will explore the view that the alleged experience of God is in reality a symptom or symbol of something that is not a God at all.)

FEELING CERTAIN OF GOD'S EXISTENCE

If a theist says that he has had a powerful religious experience, he usually means at the very least that he has had "certain sorts of emotions and feelings."[9] But he also means more than this. What is presently important to grasp, however, is that having an experience does not guarantee that one's *interpretation* of the experience is beyond question. Even when awake, a person may see blue, but it is still open to question as to *what* it is that he sees as blue. In other words, he may be altogether certain that he has an experience of blue, and he may even feel certain that it is a blue *flower* that he sees across the street.

You might not be disposed to question that he is experiencing blue, but you might easily raise the question as to whether the blue belongs to a flower. After a more careful inquiry, you might be able to show him that what he has just judged to be a flower is in actuality a piece of crumpled blue paper. To be sure, at the time when he said he saw a blue flower, he was very *certain* that it was a flower. But of course the feeling of certainty has little to do with what is or is not the case. The used-car salesman may in his own mind be absolutely certain that the car he longs to sell you has a clean motor and an excellent crankshaft. But his feeling of certainty is, strictly speaking, irrelevant to the actual condition that the car is in.

You do not examine the salesman to see whether he is telling you the truth. Rather, you examine the car itself. Similarly, the believer's convictions and feelings or absolute certainty about experiencing God are not relevant to the question of the existence or reality of God. These feelings merely tell you about the believer, not about God. The fact that an atheist feels absolutely convinced that there is no God is, strictly speaking, of no importance when we are trying to determine whether there is or is not a God. (Naturally, if you wish to study either human believers or unbelievers, then their personal feelings of either certainty or doubt would be relevant. But that is not the topic of concern in this chapter.)

MISTAKING THE STIMULUS

It is sometimes said that human beings would not have the longing for God unless there was in reality a God to satisfy this longing. Some theists argue that certain religious emotions exist in people because God has stimulated those people. The religious emotions are their human responses to God's stimulation. For example, some theists hold that when human beings feel *awe* as a very powerful experience, they *apprehend it immediately and without question as God confronting and encountering them.*[10]

Unfortunately, this claim is not self-validating, for it is quite possible to say that the experience of awe is *mis*apprehended as being of God. The experience of awe might well be a response to stimuli that are not supernatural but, rather, natural and cultural. The sight of the very beautiful, but quite natural, Grand Canyon may indeed stimulate powerful feelings and emotions—including awe—within us. This does not, however, necessarily entail that the feelings and the awe are stirred up by a supernatural divine Being. Within some cultures the wind at night will sometimes stimulate awe and even terror in the people. Why? Well, from childhood they have been taught that sometimes the wind is really spirits or ghosts passing through the night.[11] But this experience of awe, no matter how real and intense it is *as an experience*, is not necessarily an experience *of* spirits or ghosts. If a person experiences awe, or some very profound experience that he classifies as a religious experience, his opinions as to what generates the experience in him are not infallible. People sometimes are in intense and prolonged pain, but merely because they are the ones suffering the pain does not entail that they are authoritative in diagnosing all the conditions bringing their pain into being.

There may be a God or ghosts, but someone's having an intense and powerful experience of awe (or some other kind of moving experience) is not in itself convincing evidence that God or ghosts are in fact a reality. Religious experience (in whatever way defined) provides no compelling evidence to support the conclusion that only God could be the true stimulus of religious experience.[12]

THE RELIGIOUS LONGING

Some theists have argued that the world would make no sense if our religious longing were left unsatisfied. Hence, they conclude, it makes more sense to hold that God does exist and that he does satisfy the restless heart of human beings when they open their hearts to him.[13]

According to most Christians, human life would be meaningless without the God revealed in Christ. The following quotation expresses this faith rather well:

A life without Christ is scarcely worth living. He who is not a member of Christ wanders about in darkness. It is only through Christ that you realize what it is that you have to live for. He who wishes to become a member of Christ must say good-bye to life as he has lived it hitherto and be born afresh.[14]

It would be intellectually dishonest to deny that many Christians have found "meaning" for their lives by accepting what they call "Christ." They have said good-bye to a life that they have come to regard as unrewarding and have found in Christianity a new way that gives them a sense of direction and meaning. The above quotation describes accurately what many Christians believe that Christ has done for them.

The quotation above does not, however, in fact come from a Christian at all. It is a description of what the God *Poro* means to members of a tribe in West Africa. I simply substituted the word 'Christ' for 'Poro' in order to indicate some psychological similarities between Christianity and this African religion (and perhaps most religions claiming to believe in a God or Gods). In the initiation rite of the West African religion, the initiates come to believe that they have been visited by a demon who has virtually destroyed them. But fortunately the end of them is not final, for they come to believe also that "Poro has raised them to new life," just as the apostle Paul came to believe that Christ had raised him to a new life.[15] In other words, members of the West African tribe experience a very moving and powerful conversion that greatly changes their lives. But most Christians are not willing to let the undeniably powerful conversion experience of this West African religion count as a "direct apprehension of" or "immediate encounter with" the God Poro. No matter how moving the testimony of these African believers may be, Christians will not themselves believe that Poro is a reality.

John Wesley's Methodist movement in eighteenth-century England, Billy Graham's contemporary evangelistic crusades, and the West African tribe all make use of the follow-up program for their new converts. In West Africa the converts are given direction and instruction in their faith and are also trained to have additional moving emotional experiences in the future. Many Christian groups have periodic revivals in order to develop the emotional dimension of their faith, and some groups lead their members to experience a "second work of grace" and sometimes a "third work."[16] It would seem to be the case that the emotional experience must be *explained* as being an experience *of God*—Christ for Christians, and Poro for the African Tribe.

The point to be made here is that the "religious longing" (or whatever else it may be called) is apparently satisfied in a great variety of ways. At least the believers testify to a certain satisfaction in the many dimensions of their lives. Unfortunately, this variety in the ways of finding satisfaction for the religious longing seems seriously to weaken the claim that profound religious experience is a self-validating proof of the existence of God. In other words, the argument from religious experience is so liberal that it "proves" more than its proponents desire to prove. Christians who use the argument seem to want to prove the existence of their God alone, but the argument from religious experience opens the gates for every religion to get into the act. Christians, Jews, so-called pagans, and even atheists could use the argument from religious experience to "prove" their case.

The founder of Buddhism, for example, apparently found peace without belief in God at all. His religious longing seemed to find a level of satisfaction that few individuals find for theirs. But he seemed not to take his profound conversion experience of "enlightenment" to be an experience of God. For him, the question of God was insignificant. A meaningful life did not include finding a relationship with God, and the Buddha seemed inclined to believe that there was in fact no everlasting God.[17]

A THREEFOLD DISTINCTION

The development of this chapter thus far suggests the following threefold distinction: (1) There exists some intense dissatisfaction or longing that is classified as religious in nature. That is one thing. (2) The report that this longing has been, or is being, satisfied is a second thing. (3) And designating what it is that brings about this satisfaction is a third thing. The great disagreement about especially this third point should make people more cautious in making cosmic claims about the source of the satisfaction.

It is fruitful to divide this third point into two parts. The first has to do with *procedure*, the second with the *referent*. This needs to be spelled out. There are procedures that the believer must go through—or be led through—in order to obtain satisfaction of the religious longing. Certain conditions have to be met. Almost all religions require faith or belief as a necessary procedure or condition. (Unfortunately, this is not as simple as it at first sounds, for belief must have a *referent* of some sort, even if the believer is sometimes mistaken about what the referent is.) Some Christians insist on the procedure of baptism as essential to knowing God. And "believing in Christ" often turns out to be a kind of code-phrase to cover a whole repertoire of practices, "services," activities, duties, rituals, verbal confessions, and even new associations.

But a procedure presupposes that there is something more than the procedure. There must be something at the other end of the line, so to speak. The procedure of dialing a phone would not be meaningful if there were no one to answer. Hence, to claim that the religious satisfaction has come about is almost invariably to make some further claim about the existence of some "objective reality," some *referent*, that has brought about the satisfaction.

The atheist or nontheist claims that the "objective reality" is not a supernatural Being but, rather, is a vast network of the variables of nature and of human culture. Physiology, chemistry, biology, and the like seek to understand the natural variables. Psychology, sociology, anthropology, history, linguistics, and philosophy study the vast sea of cultural variables, from systems of ideas to attitudinal variables and indoctrination techniques. Some theists assert that the religious experience is brought about supernaturally and that in this religious experience the "objective reality" is immediately and unquestionably apprehended as none other than God.

Both the theist and the nontheist alike are tied to *hypotheses*, although some nontheists or atheists think it is simply self-evident that there is no God. Some theists, equally confident, take God's existence to be self-evidently confirmed by religious experience. But in either case, theist or nontheist, the claim is one that must be subjected to more precise formulations and more severe testing. (In the next three chapters, additional arguments for the existence of God will be carefully formulated and critically examined. Following that, certain other claims and views will also be examined with regard to their bearing on religious issues.)

People sometimes take their beliefs and convictions for granted to the extent that they resist thinking of them as hypotheses. During World War II some people were satisfied by horsemeat, which they honestly but mistakenly supposed to be beef. A person might have said that only a good beefsteak could satisfy his great hunger, but his butcher would have known better. A person may be satisfied religiously without having a clear understanding of what it is that has satisfied him.

DRUGS AND OTHER INDUCEMENTS

Usually those who claim that God exists believe also that he possesses certain attributes. Moreover, they believe that he is without certain other attributes. If God were a cosmic sponge absorbing every character and trait of whatever description, he would not qualify as the God whom Jews, Christians, and Muslims claim to know and worship. Their God is not viewed as a grand glob. They regard him as having distinct attributes that set him off from other views of God.

Usually, to believe in a God of certain distinct attributes is to believe also that there are at least some distinct minimal procedures that one must go through in order to "encounter" this God. The question of taking a drug as a procedure for experiencing God has been largely frowned upon by the major streams of Christianity, Judaism, and Islam. Consider the following first-hand report:

All at once, without warning of any kind, I found myself wrapped in a flame-colored cloud. For an instant I thought of fire . . . the next, I knew that the fire was within myself. Directly afterward there came upon me a sense of exultation, of immense joyousness accompanied or immediately followed by an intellectual illumination impossible to describe. Among other things, I did not merely come to believe, but I saw that the universe is not composed of dead matter, but is, on the contrary, a living Presence; I became conscious in myself of eternal life. . . . I saw that all men are immortal: that the cosmic order is such that without any preadventure all things work together for the good of each and all; that the foundation principle of the world . . . is what we call love, and that the happiness of each and all is in the long run absolutely certain.[18]

This experience reported above was not brought about by a drug. But the following one was, or at least the person who had the experience believed that the drug he had just taken was instrumental in bringing it about:

Suddenly I burst into a vast, new, indescribably wonderful universe. Although I am writing this over a year later, the thrill of the surprise and amazement, the awesomeness of the revelation, the engulfment in an overwhelming feeling-wave of gratitude and blessed wonderment, are as fresh, and the memory of the experience is as vivid, as if it had happened five minutes ago. And yet to concoct anything by way of deception that would even hint of the magnitude, the sense of ultimate reality . . . this seems such an impossible task. The knowledge which has infused and affected every aspect of my life came instantaneously and with such complete force of certainty that it was impossible, then or since, to doubt its validity.[19]

What is significant is that drug-induced experiences seem to be similar to religious (or at least mystical) experiences that are not drug-induced. This would seem to give some weight to the naturalists' claim that religious or mystical experiences come about by natural and cultural stimuli rather than a supernatural Presence.

There are some Christian or quasi-Christian groups, however, who believe that a drug may help open the way for apprehending the supernatural Presence.

Some Christians and Jews have charged that drug-induced experiences of a religious nature are too wild and bizarre to be taken seriously as genuine religious experiences. But this charge overlooks the fact that even drug-induced experiences vary greatly from group to group. In fact, one of the most noted students of "consciousness expansion" through the use of drugs claims that the "set" and the "setting" determine to a remarkable degree the subject's reaction to the drug.[20]

Consider the following report by an observer of a group of people in a religious setting:

Men saw Christ on the cross with blood running from his wounds. They cried aloud and fell upon the ground, sometimes a great number being so affected simultaneously. Hands were clenched, the flesh became cold, persons leaped in the air "with all their might," and "it seemed to the person as if soul and body would, as it were of themselves, of necessity mount up, leave the earth, and ascend thither." In overwhelming weakness men saw the flames and "the piercing all-seeing eye of God" with such vividness that the body was overcome. In at least one instance a man was driven to suicide by cutting his throat.[21]

This above scene took place without the use of drugs. The eighteenth-century Calvinist preacher Jonathan Edwards was simply using very forceful and vivid sermons in seeking to convert the citizens of New England to Christianity. Indeed, the setting became so excessive that great numbers in surrounding New England towns were seized with the compulsion to cut their own throats. According to Edwards' own report, people began hearing voices, " 'Cut your own throat, now is a good opportunity,' " and they "were obliged to fight with all their might to resist it."[22]

In his book *The Nervous System*, Dr. Peter Nathan (research neurologist at the National Hospital for Nervous Diseases, London) argues that people who "hear voices"— whether of God or of Satan—are talking to themselves. Prayer is a kind of inner dialogue. Nathan explains that those

who hear voices or hear people talking about them, are actually saying the words they hear but enunciating them without forcing air through the vocal cords. Microphones placed over the larynxes of such patients detect the words enunciated though they detect no sound. These otherwise inaudible sounds have been recorded on tape, amplified, and then played back to the patients. These patients then recognize them as the voices they heard.[23]

Apparently, sometimes the stimuli of extraordinary experiences are located on the inner side of the individual's own skin. The seventeenth-century philosopher Spinoza wrote:

No one has thus far determined what the body can do. . . . For no one has yet had a sufficiently accurate knowledge of the construction of the body . . . and the many things which sleep-walkers do. . . . All of which sufficiently shows that the body can do many things by the laws of its own nature alone at which the mind is amazed.[24]

The Old Testament states that the prophet Elijah heard "a still small voice," which he took to be the voice of God.[25] If Professor Nathan is correct, the prophet might have been talking to himself without being conscious of doing so. The stimuli or cues came from within his own organism. To be sure, this does not rule out the likelihood that the cues inside the organism were themselves conditioned and reinforced by phenomena outside the body. Nevertheless, Professor Nathan notes that after a very special operation on some of the patients in Lyons Hospital, they ceased to have hallucinations and they no longer heard the voice of the deity or his messengers.[26]

This, of course, does not prove conclusively that communications from God are in reality not divine visitations at all, but rather the product of changes in the individual's physical and social set and setting. A philosopher, however, taking the new research that physiology and other sciences offer, might wish to argue that the theist's case has been seriously damaged by recent research on the brain. The evidence is rather clear that the individual's religious outlook can be greatly modified by the use of such "unspiritual" means as drugs, electrical stimulation of the brain, surgery, and other procedures.

PHYSIOLOGY AND GOD

Perhaps the most disappointing case for Christian revivalists and evangelists is the unresponsive melancholic who seems unable to receive divine grace and thus be cured of his intense guilt and grief. Sometimes about all the evangelist can recommend is patience and prayer: wait until God's favor comes around again; perhaps the next time his grace will come even to the melancholic. Where preaching fails, however, drugs and electrical stimulation of the brain often work surprisingly well to rid the melancholic of his burden of guilt.[27] The descriptions of former melancholics who have, by these new methods, had their burden of guilt lifted may fruitfully be compared to the testimony of John Bunyan in his books *The Pilgrim's Progress* and *Grace Abounding to the Chief of Sinners*.

The philosophical and religious implications of research development in physiology are enormous. If experiences of the supernatural seem to be brought about, not by so-called "spiritual" procedures, but by scientifically observable procedures, then the question that eventually must be answered is this: "Are the experiences of the supernatural to be seen as no longer supernatural either in their *procedures* or in their *referents*? In short, has the supernatural become demythologized and naturalized?" The theologian Rudolf Bultmann thought that Christianity must not try to hold on to the supernaturalistic cosmology of the New Testament. For him, the essence of Christianity lies in the direct encounter between God and man. But now it seems that even this theological fortress might be dismantled by the steady advance of the science of physiology and the behavioral sciences. Bultmann's existential Christianity would seem to be threatened by a more recent attempt to demythologize.

The accounts of religious persons going through such procedures as fasting, retreating to the desert, and losing sleep are too numerous to mention here. It used to be thought by many that these procedures were necessary to prepare the soul for God's special revelation, or for God's special presence. But the study of physiology seems to demonstrate that the impact of these procedures is more on the brain than on the soul.

During his conversion experience, the apostle Paul, after a hot trip from Jerusalem to Damascus, was three days and nights without sight, food, or water. Physiologists and psychologists are familiar with the powerful effects on the individual when he is placed in a position of sensory deprivation. Hallucinating becomes a common phenomenon. Anthropologists are aware of the solitary "vision quest" of American Indians. After being deprived of sleep, food, and drink for a few days, the young Indians began to be visited by supernatural beings. In other parts of the world the individual deprived in this way frequently came to regard himself as possessed by spirits.[28]

Admiral Byrd, isolated in his South Pole hut, tells in his book *Alone* of his experiences with the uncanny. Captain Slocum, who sailed alone around the world, was visited by supernatural helpers whom Slocum hallucinated.[29] Weston La Barre cites similar instances:

Another well-known example of the mysterious stranger is the presence that haunted Sir Ernest Shackleton and his companions in the Antarctic. Vast empty areas like snow-fields and deserts and featureless open sea seem especially evocative of hallucinatory projection. Like Admiral Byrd, Christina Ritter had similar experiences during her long winter isolation. Stypulkowski, a Russian prisoner in Lubianka Prison, experienced such hallucinations; so did Jan Baalsrud, a Norwegian resistance-fighter, who spent twenty-seven days alone, injured on a mountain plateau, before rescue.[30]

It is pretty well documented that among brainwashing techniques the use of sensory deprivation in solitary confinement is a major tool of political conversion. A number of comparisons between political and religious conversions have recently been researched.

THE EVANGELICAL REAR-GUARD

Evangelical Christians today who play down what they regard as the excess of certain forms of intense experience, especially visions and voices, are frequently critical of pentacostal Christians and enthusiasts. Evangelicals seem to have developed a kind of "rationalism" that suppresses both experimental and experiential religion. They prefer a more print-oriented religion, with the Bible as the norm and standard of faith. But what these Evangelicals have not faced up to is the apparent fact that the Bible is riddled through with prophets, priests, and apostles who experienced all sorts of visions and voices. It looks as if Evangelicalism will have to fight another rear-guard battle by selecting the "inspired" Biblical personalities to be sealed off in some religious vault. For Evangelicals, what we learn about physiology and the other sciences pertaining to conversion and extraordinary experience will presumably be seen as relevant to *contemporary* human beings, but not to those *ancients* who contributed to the production of the Bible.

Evangelicals are already convinced that the "revelations" that came to Isaiah, Ezekiel, John, and the like were supernatural in *content*. Furthermore, they assume that the super-natural content came in a supernatural *way*. Unfortunately, they are not clear as to whether this entails that God simply bypassed the physiology and other natural and cultural conditions of the prophets, or whether God "made use of" these natural and cultural conditions in the way that, say, a hypnotist might make use of them.

In any case, even the hypnotist and his activities may be detected and observed as themselves natural and cultural phenomena. Evangelicals seem committed to the view that the *means* of divine revelation are supernatural in some sense, but they seem to be not committed to trying to discover at which precise point the natural ends and the supernatural begins. Indeed, what exactly is meant by 'supernatural' is not always clear. This, of course, raises the question of what a miracle is; we will deal with this issue in a later chapter.

THE INDISCRIMINATE APPROACH

Individuals who have little love for systematic thinking might choose to accept indiscriminately all extraordinary experiences, in which all sorts of alleged supernatural beings and messages present themselves. Unfortunately, such a position of total inclusiveness must fail to take seriously all the *claims* of the putative supernatural visitors and messages, for the assertions of many putative supernatural visitors and messages contradict those of the others. For example, the traditional Christian view is that not all supernatural beings are what they appear to be; and any spirit or message that does not harmonize with traditional Christian doctrine runs the risk of being branded as stemming from Satan. All forms of sorcery and witchcraft are strictly forbidden in the Old Testament, and the people of Israel are commanded to execute all sorceresses.[31] The New Testament promises that sorcerers will be punished in hell.[32] One of the letters of the apostle Paul heatedly condemns drugs and potions in connection with sorcery.[33] Today, Evangelical Christians differ among themselves as to whether any human being who is not a Christian can in fact communicate with the dead or have supernatural powers.

Many Christians who hold that the visions of Isaiah in the temple, or John on the island, or Peter on the rooftop, or Paul in bed were supernatural in some special sense are absolutely insistent that the visions of Joseph Smith, the nineteenth-century founder of the Church of Jesus Christ of Later-Day Saints (Mormons), were not supernatural, unless, of course, they were stimulated and directed by Satan.[34]

STAGING AND INTERPRETING
RELIGIOUS EXPERIENCE

According to the first chapter of 1 Samuel, a woman named Hannah was married but could have no children. The Lord, so the Old Testament account alleges, "had closed her womb." Now, Hannah's husband loved her dearly; but she felt that, nevertheless, he loved his other wife, Peninnah, much better, inasmuch as she had given him sons and daughters. To make matters worse for Hannah, Peninnah used to ridicule her for being "barren." So after many days and nights with tears, and even fasting, Hannah went to the temple and "vowed a vow." She made a deal with the Lord: if he would open her womb and give her a son (her husband serving as the natural means of impregnation), then she would give up her son to be a priest of the Lord.

While she was praying and making this promise in the temple, the priest Eli noticed her. Because she was mumbling rather than praying openly and clearly, he thought that Hannah was drunk, and told her so. Fortunately, this gave her the opportunity to tell her problem to the priest, and he in turn assured her that the God of Israel would grant her a positive response to her petition. Whereupon she, no longer carrying a sad countenance, left the temple in good spirits.

In due time she became pregnant and gave birth to Samuel. Shortly after the child was weaned, his mother faithfully kept her promise and took her firstborn to the temple to live with Eli the priest and to be raised by him in order that the boy might eventually become himself a priest of God. Eli did his job well, and the boy "grew both in stature and in favor with the Lord and with men." According to the third chapter of 1 Samuel, Hannah's son spent his time helping Eli with the priestly duties and in the process doubtless learned a great deal about the role of a priest. However, it seems that Eli had all but ceased having visions.

Then one evening while lying down within the temple where the sacred Ark was located, Samuel heard a voice calling him. Apparently thinking it was Eli, Samuel answered and went to the side of the aging priest. But Eli told him to return because he had not called him. This happened three times, and each time Eli sent him back. On the third time, however, the priest told the boy not to return to him but to answer the voice because it would be God's voice.

After all, "Samuel did not yet know the Lord, and the word of the Lord had not been revealed to him."[35] Hence, Eli had to tell his young assistant what was going on and even how to respond to the voice. Well, when the voice came a fourth time, it was accompanied by visual sensations. "The Lord came and stood forth, calling as at other times, 'Samuel! Samuel!.' " When Samuel answered, then God gave him the message.

On the following morning Eli asked for the content of the message. When Samuel complied, the old priest then informed him that the message was truly from God.

My reason for presenting this account is to call attention to the staging and learning process that Samuel underwent. The Old Testament notes that there were various bands of prophets here and there in Israel. There were even schools of prophets —as if the vocation had to be learned. In order to become a priest, Samuel had in effect to study with Eli, in the way that a practicing physician used to have an assistant who learned the profession from him.

But as the author of 1 Samuel points out, Eli did not have many visions and revelations from God during the time when Samuel was studying with him.[36] Hence, while the boy could learn many of the details of the routine priestly job by imitation, he could not learn by observing in Eli much of the details of how to receive visions and revelations from God. That was apparently why Eli had to teach him not only to classify the voice as being God's voice, but what to say in reply. In short, the assistant did not know how to behave when addressed by the deity. Eli then even had to assure Samuel that he had in fact received a revelation from God. The author of 1 Samuel designates it as a "vision." A vision might be interpreted in a variety of ways, but apparently *Samuel was quite prepared to trust without question Eli's instructions and interpretations*—at least until Samuel became somewhat more skilled on his own in this new dimension of his vocation.

As is well known, Freudian psychoanalysis is greatly concerned with (1) dream experiences, (2) confessions, (3) in-

tense emotional experiences, and (4) the psychoanalyst's interpretations of the dreams and confessions. Moreover, the
therapist might in various subtle or not-so-subtle ways recommend new avenues and categories of thinking and behaving.
In a very similar way, religious experience is often staged and
interpreted. In fact, this is what any culture or subculture
tends to do to, or for, its new members.[37]

Those who have been impressed with Carlos Castaneda's
stories of the Yaqui Indian, Juan, will note that with words,
sounds, body cues, etc., Juan stages extraordinary experiences
for Castaneda and insists that he accept Juan's own *interpretation* of them. Furthermore, when Castaneda reports his new
and extraordinary experiences to his teacher, Juan then *selects
for Castaneda* those experiences that *Juan himself* thinks are
most important, significant, and *real*.[38] The following quotation from Castaneda is very revealing:

After ten years of apprenticeship with don Juan my mind could no
longer uphold my ordinary criteria of what is real. . . . Under the
pressure of don Juan and don Genaro's acts my mind had entered
into an impasse.[39]

If one can appreciate the influence of don Juan on his disciple's
way of seeing the world, then he ought better to appreciate the
influence of Mao or Joseph Smith on their disciples' ways of
seeing the world. A comparison between the methods of don
Juan and John Wesley would make a fruitful study also.

A careful study of the relationship between Juan and Castaneda reveals Juan's use of standard techniques of dramatic
conversion and brainwashing.[40] This is not to say that some
beliefs are somehow "pure," whereas all others are staged and
interpreted. Rather, it is to say that *all* beliefs are staged and
interpreted. This is no innocent point to make, and it has very
disturbing implications for those who think that their own
world-view is somehow "given" as some kind of epistemological Garden of Eden.

The role of the philosophy of religion, then, is not to escape
to some primitive Garden of Eden and pretend to live as
epistemologically innocent noble savages. Rather, the philosophy of religion is, first, an attempt to establish and maintain
communication among the various systems or schools of interpretation. Second, it is a commitment to learn whatever can be
learned from other world-views, or, on a more limited scale,

from various schemes of interpretation. And, third, the philosophy of religion helps to develop critical inquiry. That is, no scheme is given immunity from cross-examination. (To be sure, even the practice of cross-examination must itself be cross-examined.)[41] And the cross-examination dialectic may continue, hopefully with progress, so long as people find the need, interest, and desire for it.

When young Joseph Smith had what Mormons, and some others also, believe was an intense religious experience, he, like Samuel, went to his father to report the contents of his vision. Joseph relates his father's response: "He replied to me that it was of God, and told me to go and do as commanded by the messenger."[42] In short, Smith's father helped to give him an *interpretation* of his experience.

EXPERIENCE IS THEORY-LADEN

A noted modern philosopher of science, Karl Popper, argues that all human observations and experiences are theory-laden. That is, all experiences that claim to provide knowledge, or a resolution to some problem, are shaped to some extent by a prior theoretical framework.[43] This is to say, then, that no perception, observation, or experience is infallibly given knowledge. Every claim—whether verbalized or not—is conjectural and hypothetical. Professor Popper does not intend that his view be taken to mean that no assertion is any more reliable or credible than another. His point is that not even experience can be taken as immediate or raw *knowledge*. Knowledge also involves judgment; but where there is judgment, there is also the possibility of either true or false judgment, and degrees of falsity and truth.

Popper goes on to argue that even the *languages* that people use are pregnant with theory, even when the users of a language are unaware of the theoretical background. The point here is that no language—not even biblical language—is immaculately conceived or born into a pristine environment. Languages grow and develop out of the background of problems, frameworks, settings, and sets. Whatever is described by any language will, therefore, be somewhat affected by this background of anticipations and expectations out of which the language grew.[44]

Mystics have often insisted that their mystical experience of

God must not be talked about because the experience is ineffable. Unfortunately, such mystics break their own strict code when they assert that their experience is *of God*. As soon as they say this, they are making a knowledge-claim that may or may not be warranted. One of the most noteworthy students of mysticism and religious experience remarked, "What has generally been a characteristic of the mystics is their copious eloquence."[45]

Religious converts to theism sometimes say that they are not interested in theorizing and arguing about the existence of God. They merely want to give their witness and testimony regarding what God has done for them. Unfortunately, every religious "testimony" is already a mental suitcase loaded with theories, conjectures, arguments, claims, and hypotheses, which the believer innocently forgets that he is carrying around with him. Merely to mention the word "Christ" in a testimony is to presuppose an entire repertoire of hypotheses—e.g., that there actually was a Jesus of Nazareth, that he actually rose from the grave (bodily? spiritually? as a hallucination of the disciples?), that he is the cosmic Son of God, that he works miracles in the lives of people under certain conditions, that he was born of a virgin, and so on.

Hence, when someone says that he wants only to give you his witness, he is like a person, suitcase in hand, telling you that he is just dropping by to say "Hello!"

PHILOSOPHY, CONVERSION, AND BRAINWASHING

Conversion and brainwashing are alike in some ways, but unalike in others. There have been conversions that have come without the conditions of either (1) excessive sensory deprivation and physical and emotional weariness, or (2) the overstimulation of the brain that comes in such settings as terror, fear, anger, or excessive emotional agitation. (These conditions may be compared to the overload of an electrical circuit.) Despite the tendency of laymen to regard philosophers as disembodied minds, there is a good physiological basis for thinking of *philosophical activity* in terms of calm thinking, deliberation, critical acumen, and keen sensitivity to argument and evidence. Philosophers as individuals—or individuals who engage in the philosophical activity—will, of course, only *approximate* to varying degrees this ideal of critical acumen, etc.

People must not imagine that they can become supermen impervious to the bombardment of their senses or to the opposite technique of depriving their brains of external stimulation. If people are to engage in philosophical activity, they must be trained and disciplined for it. Furthermore, in the battle for the mind the courageous warrior is not one who runs headlong into an all-out assault that will render him helpless.

Brainwashing seems to be most effective when either or both of the two extreme states of the brain are present. In the "ideal" setting, the victim is placed in solitary confinement only to be brought out later to be assaulted with words, other sounds, visual shocks, and other devices for bombarding the brain to the point of vulnerability or exhaustion.[46] The fact that both dramatic conversion and brainwashing take place more readily under conditions of extreme brain states cannot, however, be taken as evidence counting for the falsehood of the *views or beliefs* received through either dramatic conversion or brainwashing. The test for determining the falsity of a claim or assertion is not a brain condition or state. Furthermore, there are many ridiculous and false assertions that have been arrived at in a calm, dispassionate, and deliberate setting and brain state.

It is a mistake to insist that all ideas accompanied by strong emotional behavior *must* be false. It is also a mistake to insist, as some religionists do, that truth cannot be approximated except through intense emotional experience. The task of the philosophy of religion is to work to keep in good repair the lines of communication between believer and unbeliever, or between believers of different persuasions. The aim of the philosophy of religion is that of continuing the growth of inquiry through both understanding and critical evaluation. To the degree that conversion and brainwashing repress the mutual and continuing interchange of information and argumentation, they are to the same degree in serious conflict with the aim of philosophy.

How you happened to have arrived at where you are in your present thinking on religious matters is, from a philosophical standpoint, not as important a question as whether you will maintain or develop both an open mind and a critical mind. It is difficult to be both open and critical, but that is what the standard of philosophy requires.

BELIEVING IN ORDER TO UNDERSTAND

Many Christian scholars have argued that they believe in order to understand.[47] This attitude has been criticized as reversing the proper order. The critic asks how you could possibly believe, for example, a lecture that is delivered in the Turkish language if you do not first understand the language.[48] Even if the lecture were translated into your language, you still could not believe it unless you had sufficient background and training making it possible for you to understand it. So, how could you be expected to believe?

This debate might be scaled down a bit. Suppose that you understand *some* aspects of a religious faith, but not all aspects. If the religious issue seems momentous to you, then you might, for important experimental reasons, *act* in some ways as a believer might act. That is, you might associate with those who do believe in this religion, you might read some of the literature, and you might perform some of the rituals up to a point or at least observe them with an open mind.[49]

However, this is a double-edged sword cutting both ways. Those who are involved in a particular religious commitment sometimes overlook a simple but crucial fact: namely, that the unbeliever is also a believer. That is, merely because a person does not believe, for example, that there is a God does not mean that he believes nothing. In fact, the very logic of belief entails some *un*belief. If you are a convinced and believing orthodox Roman Catholic, you are not a believing orthodox Muslim. The Muslim may call you an unbeliever, and you may call him an unbeliever. You may both refer to the nontheistic naturalist as an unbeliever. But by the same token, he may classify both of you as unbelievers, inasmuch as neither of you believes in his nontheistic naturalism.

Those standing outside one particular persuasion sometimes charge that those standing inside it are biased. And in reply, the insiders sometimes charge that the outsiders are uninformed and closed. In this case a philosophical attitude might begin to develop in an individual when he comes to realize that with regard to some views he is an outsider. Everyone is in some respects both an insider and outsider—with all the risks and limitations of each. The important thing, therefore, is for insider and outsider to keep in communication with one another and to avail themselves of the opportunity not only to give witness to their views and convictions, but also to place them on the witness stand where they may be severely tested and cross-examined. Indeed, whenever a person is able to carry on this dialogue in an informed and fruitful way with others and within himself, he has more fully approximated the philosophical ideal. In that sense, philosophy is not the exclusive property of any profession, but is available to anyone who will train himself in the discipline to whatever degree it is open to him.

To have a point of view and to believe in it strongly is not dogmatism. But to refuse to submit one's view to critical evaluation *is* a case of dogmatism. Hence, dogmatism is seen primarily in the *way* we hold our beliefs rather than what we believe. We do, however, risk having our belief revised or even dismantled if we dare to transcend our dogmatism. On the other hand, a belief may have already been discredited and rendered incredible, but the dogmatist may refuse to face it— like some of the passengers on the *Titanic* who could not bring themselves to understand that the ship was sinking. They had faith in the *Titanic*. But it sank nevertheless. There is always the danger that we may place our faith in one belief-system in order *not* to understand any competing belief-system.

NOTES

1. Cited in William Sargant, *The Battle for the Mind* (New York: Perennial Library, Harper & Row, 1959), p. 123. Also by the same author see "The Mechanism of Conversion," *British Medical Journal* 2 (1951): 311.
2. See Søren Kierkegaard, *Fear and Trembling and The Sickness Unto Death*, trans. Walter Lowrie (Garden City, N.Y.: Doubleday, 1941, 1954).
3. See James, *The Varieties of Religious Experience: A Study in Human Nature* (New York: Modern Library, 1902), pp. 125–138, 143, 153, 195.
4. The role of the rehearsal of alleged significant events in the history of the community or group is a powerful means at the group's disposal for generating strong emotional experiences and behavior. One of the sensitive issues in both psychoanalysis and religion has to do with whether these rehearsed central events did in fact happen as remembered. For discussions of some of the issues involved in a religion that depends on a "salvation history," see Ronald W. Hepburn, *Christianity and Paradox: Critical Studies in Twentieth-Century Theology*, rev. ed.

(New York: Pegasus, 1966), chaps. 6 and 7; and also Robert L. Wilken, *The Myth of Christian Beginnings: History's Impact on Belief* (Garden City, N.Y.: Doubleday, Anchor Books, 1972).

5. This account is found in his book *Arrow in the Blue* (New York: Macmillan, 1952), pp. 349–351.

6. The account of his second conversion and the profound mystical experience that accompanied it is found in his book, *The Invisible Writing* (New York: Macmillan, 1954), pp. 348–353, and in his article "The Initiates," in *The God That Failed*, ed. Richard Crossman (New York: Harper & Brothers, 1950), chap. 1. Koestler's "inner peace" came upon his release from prison. At that time he also gained new freedom of mind, enabling him to criticize some of the inconsistencies of the Communist Party, from which he officially resigned a few months after his prison release.

7. John Baillie, *Our Knowledge of God* (London: Oxford University Press, 1949), p. 132.

8. See C. B. Martin, *Religious Belief* (Ithaca, N.Y.: Cornell University Press, 1959), p. 72.

9. Ibid., p. 261.

10. See Rudolf Otto, *The Idea of the Holy*, trans. John W. Harvey (New York: Oxford University Press, Galaxy Books, 1958).

11. See Mircea Eliade, *Rites and Symbols of Initiation*, trans. W. R. Trask (New York: Harper & Row, Harper Torchbooks, 1958), pp. 68, 87, 91.

12. See Raziel Abelson, "The Logic of Faith and Belief," in *Religious Experience and Truth*, ed. Sidney Hook (New York: New York University Press, 1961), p. 127.

13. See Etienne Gilson, *The Christian Philosophy of St. Augustine*, trans. L. E. M. Lynch (New York: Random House, 1960), pp. 101, 103–105, 238–243.

14. See Gustaf Bolinder, *Devilman's Jungle*, trans. M. A. Michael (London: Dennis Dobson, 1954), cited in Sargant, *Battle for the Mind*, p. 171.

15. See Romans 6.

16. The pentacostal Christians have found that "speaking in tongues" not only provides an intense emotional "transference," but also makes subsequent instruction much easier. The physiology of this method is treated in Sargant, *Battle for the Mind*.

17. For a useful interchange between an imaginary Christian and an imaginary Ceylonese Buddhist, see Ninian Smart, *World Religions: A Dialogue* (Baltimore: Penguin Books, 1969), pp. 51–66. Professor Smart is a liberal Christian whose version of Christianity would probably be much too broad for most Christians.

18. James, *Varieties of Religious Experience*, pp. 390 f.

19. Anonymously related in "The Issue of the Consciousness-Expanding Drugs," *Main Currents in Modern Thought* 20 (September-October 1963): 101 f. Both the above accounts are discussed by Huston Smith in "Do Drugs Have Religious Import?" *Journal of Philosophy* 61 (1964): 517–530.

20. "Set is a person's expectations of what a drug will do to him, considered in the context of the whole personality. Setting is the environment, both physical and social, in which the drug is taken" (Andrew Weil, *The Natural Mind: A New Way of Looking at Drugs and the Higher Consciousness* [Boston: Houghton Mifflin, 1972], p. 29).

21. Elmer T. Clark, *The Small Sects in America*, 2d ed. (Nashville: Abingdon Press, 1949), p. 89. Clark is drawing from and quoting Jonathan Edwards, *Narrative of Many Surprising Conversions*, 3d ed. (Boston: S. Kneeland & T. Green, 1738), p. 73; and idem, *Thoughts on the Revival of Religion* (Boston: S. Kneeland & T. Green, 1742).

22. Clark, *Small Sects in America*, pp. 88 f., quoting Edwards, *Narrative of Many Surprising Conversions*, p. 74.

23. Peter Nathan, *The Nervous System* (Philadelphia: Lippincott, 1969), p. 307.

24. Spinoza, *Ethics*, rev. ed., trans. Andrew Boyle (New York: Everyman's Library, 1959), pt. 3, prop. 2, note.

25. See 1 Kings 19:12.

26. See Nathan, *Nervous System*, p. 308.

27. See Sargant, *Battle for the Mind*, p. 193. Since the time when Sargant wrote his book, advances in the science of brain physiology have refined considerably the procedures of electrical shock of *specific areas* of the brain. Unfortunately, this refinement has not yet reached every mental hospital. Cf. Jose M. R. Delgado, *Physical Control of the Mind: Toward a Psychocivilized Society* (New York: Harper & Row, 1969). Methodists may be surprised to learn that in the eighteenth century their founder, John Wesley, said of electrical treatment "that it is the most efficacious medicine in nervous disorders of every kind, which has yet been discovered" (Sargant, *Battle for the Mind*, p. 189, n. 3). Both electrical stimulation and medicine left much to be desired in the England of Wesley's day.

28. See Weston La Barre, *The Ghost Dance: Origins of Religion* (New York: Dell, Delta Books, 1972), p. 43.

29. See ibid.; S. J. Freedman, H. Gruenbaum, and M. Greenblatt, "Perceptual and Cognitive Changes in Sensory Deprivation," *Journal of Nervous and Mental Diseases* 132 (1961): 17–21; C. A. Brownfield, *Isolation: Clinical and Experimental Approaches* (New York: Random House, 1965).

30. La Barre, *Ghost Dance*, pp. 53 f.

31. See Exodus 22:17; Leviticus 20:27; Deuteronomy 18:10–12.
32. See Revelation 22:15.
33. See Galatians 5:20. Paul uses the term *pharmakeia*, which is probably a sorcerer or sorceress who uses drugs in his procedures.
34. An excellent contemporary example of this is found in Jerald and Sandra Tanner, two former Mormons who came to reject Joseph Smith as a prophet of God but nevertheless still believe that such men of the Bible as Paul, Isaiah, and Peter did receive supernatural visions and information from God (see Tanner and Tanner, *Mormonism: Shadow or Reality?* enl. ed. [Salt Lake City: Modern Microfilm Co., 1972]). For an account by a former Mormon who has ceased to believe in the supernatural content and means of both Joseph Smith's and the biblical writers' visions, see Fawn M. Brodie, *No Man Knows My History* (New York: Knopf, 1945).
35. 1 Samuel 3:7 (RSV).
36. 1 Samuel 3:1 (RSV).
37. See Peter Berger and Thomas Luckmann, *The Social Construction of Reality: A Treatise on the Sociology of Knowledge* (Garden City, N.Y.: Doubleday, Anchor Books, 1967); and Erving Goffman, *The Presentation of Self in Everyday Life* (Garden City, N.Y.: Doubleday, Anchor Books, 1959). Goffman's work first appeared as a monograph at the Social Science Research Center at the University of Edinburgh in 1956. See also J. E. Barnhart, "Is One's Definition of 'Religion' Always Circular?" in *International Yearbook of the Sociology of Knowledge and Religion*, ed. Günter Dux, vol. 9 (1975), pp. 122–135.
38. See Carlos Castaneda, *The Teachings of Don Juan: A Yaqui Way of Knowledge* (New York: Ballantine Books, 1969), pp. 41–45, 59, 99, 119, 130, 133, 145 f., 158, 172, 191, 220, 229, 231, 233, 236, 239, 257–264, 271. (Originally published by University of California Press in 1968.)
39. Castaneda, *A Separate Reality: Further Conversations with Don Juan* (New York: Pocket Books, 1972), p. 262. (Originally published by Simon & Schuster in 1971.) Whether Castaneda did in fact study under don Juan, as he claims he did, is a matter of debate. In any case, there is little doubt that Castaneda is keenly sensitive to issues of epistemology (the theory of knowledge). At the very least, it may be said that he has written a significant four-volume epistemological novel that pricks the naiveté and smugness of the world-view of North Americans and Europeans.
40. See Sargant, *Battle for the Mind*, p. 144 f., 151–158.
41. See Søren Kierkegaard, *Philosophical Fragments, Or a Frag-*

ment of Philosophy, trans. David F. Swenson (Princeton, N.J.: Princeton University Press, 1936), pp. 36–38, 47.

42. Joseph Smith, "Origin of the Book of Mormon," in *The Book of Mormon* (1830; reprint ed., Salt Lake City: The Church of Jesus Christ of Latter-Day Saints, 1950), p. iii.

43. See Karl Popper, *Objective Knowledge: An Evolutionary Approach* (New York: Oxford University Press, 1972), pp. 9, 30, 135–138, 258 f.

44. See ibid., p. 146. On the linguistic component of especially the experience of seeing, consult Norwood Russell Hanson, *Perception and Discovery: An Introduction to Scientific Inquiry* (San Francisco: Freeman, Cooper & Co., 1969), pp. 124–127. Doubtless many languages began as pictures or pictograms.

45. Otto, *Idea of the Holy*, p. 2.

46. Cf. J. A. M. Meerloo, *The Rape of the Mind: The Psychology of Thought Control, Menticide and Brainwashing* (New York: World Publishing Co., 1956); Bao Ruo-Wang (Jean Pasqualini) and Rudolph Chelminski, *Prisoner of Mao* (New York: Coward, McCann & Geoghegan, 1973); I. P. Pavlov, *Lectures on Conditioned Reflex*, trans. Horsley Gantt (New York: International Publishers, 1928). Richard Cavendish in *The Black Arts* (New York: Putnam, 1967) explains how sorcerers and the like have used various devices for producing in their own brains either of the two extreme states mentioned above.

   A profound religious conversion is not always brought about solely by extreme brain states. In his critique of Sargant's book *Battle for the Mind*, D. Martyn Lloyd-Jones points this out. Only by ignoring the vast sea of social and cultural influences in the world, however, does Lloyd-Jones feel free to jump to the conclusion of supernatural intervention (see *Conversions: Psychological and Spiritual* [London: Inter-Varsity Fellowship, 1959]).

47. See Augustine, *On the Freedom of the Will*, trans. Francis E. Tourscher (Philadelphia: Peter Reilly Co., 1937), bk. 2, chap. 2.

48. See Arthur C. Danto, "Religious Faith and Scientific Faith," in *Religious Experience and Truth*, pp. 143 f.

40. Anthropologists, sociologists, and philosophers are currently debating the meaning and value of participant observation and *Verstehen* (understanding). See Michael Martin, "Understanding and Participant Observation in Cultural and Social Anthropology," in *Boston Studies in the Philosophy of Science: Proceedings of the Boston Colloquium for the Philosophy of Science 1966/1968*, vol. 4, ed. Robert S. Cohen and Max Wartofsky (Dordrecht, Holland: D. Reidel Publishing Co., 1968), pp. 303–330.

CHAPTER II

The Question of Revelation Through Sacred Scripture

PRELUDE

In Chapter I you saw that experiences that are taken to be religious have to be *interpreted* if they are to have any cognitive meaning. One of the knotty problems with "religious experience" is the fact that there are so many different interpretations.

In the attempt to cut this knot, various traditional religions assert that God reveals in a special way what the religious experience means. Or to state the matter somewhat differently, they claim that God has provided a special revelation that informs people regarding the proper way to relate both to him and to their fellow men. Of course, this claim that there is special revelation recorded in Scripture is itself an interpretation, hypothesis, or conjecture. Whether it is a warranted conjecture or assumption is a matter of dispute.

In this chapter you will be introduced to various views of the inspiration of the Bible. As you know, various traditional religions have reached the conclusion that there is a God who has provided them with a set of written documents that they take to be holy Scripture. Inasmuch as we will not be able to examine all these various Scriptures, I have chosen to deal with the claim that Christians make that God inspired the Bible to be written and that he preserved it as a written record of his self-revelation.

The Jews had earlier made this claim for the Hebrew Bible, which the Christians call the Old Testament. Christians add the New Testament as the final books of the Bible. Followers of the Islamic faith regard the Old Testament, the New Testament, and especially the Qur'an as divine revelation. Those who follow the Mormon faith accept the Old Testament and

New Testament as holy Scripture. In addition, they believe that God has revealed himself in the Book of Mormon, but not in the Qur'an.

In this chapter the question to be dealt with is this: "What do Christians mean when they say that the Bible—the Old and New Testaments—was inspired by God and given as trustworthy revelation of his will?" In dealing with this question about the Bible you will be able to take much of what you learn and apply it in understanding the claims about various other Scriptures in both the East and the West.

We turn now to explore some of the more explicit views pertaining to the Bible as "inspired revelation." The first two views take the Bible to be infallible and inerrant in the original documents or autographs. To say that Scripture is infallible means that it has the "quality of never deceiving or misleading and so [is] 'wholly trustworthy and reliable.'" Thus, an infallible and inerrant Bible would be one in which "all its teachings are the utterance of God." This is not to say that the Bible sets forth opinions on every topic. Rather, "it claims in the broadest terms to teach all things necessary for salvation."[1] Those affirming that the original documents of the Bible are inerrantly inspired are making a very bold claim: namely, that every writer in the Bible is considered "free of logical, historical, psychological, theological, and philosophical mistakes."[2]

THE BIBLE
AS A PERFECTLY WORDED DOCUMENT

The Infallible Terms of Salvation.   A great number of Christians believe that the human race is in deep trouble. The most desperate need that people have is to gain salvation. The whole human population is declared to be suffering from "soul-sorrow."[3] In other words, everyone is "lost" and in need of direction by which he may be reconciled to God and gain entrance to heaven. There are all sorts of opinions as to how to gain this "salvation" and "reconciliation," but numerous Christians believe that God has graciously revealed "the exact terms which must be met for our own reconciliation."[4]

However, if these terms are not perfectly spelled out and are not written down infallibly (i.e., without error), then people might be misled as to what they are. Those who regard the Bible as a perfectly worded document believe that because

God is perfect, he would certainly not set forth his divine document in an imperfect manner. Hence, they regard every word in the Bible to be exactly and precisely as God intended it. This means that there is nothing trivial or incidental in the Bible. Every syllable is as God designed it. To be sure, those holding to the *Perfect Wording theory* agree that God used human prophets, apostles, and the like to write the Bible; but God, they insist, was the real author. He simply selected various individuals and controlled them in such a way as to obtain his desired end, namely, a Scripture that reveals inerrantly the road to salvation and the truths necessary for the development of Christian doctrines. It turns out that these doctrines have to do with a great number of topics, ranging all the way from the nature of God and Satan to the outline of things to take place at the end of the world.

Not One Error Can Be Admitted.   Those defending the Perfect Wording theory of the Bible contend that if Christians admit that the Bible asserts even one false statement, then they are faced with the possibility that the Bible asserts *numerous* false statements. Indeed, where would the line be drawn between truth and falsity? To be sure, there are false statements throughout the Bible, and the Perfect Wording theorists acknowledge this fact. But what they deny is that these statements are *asserted as true.* They are, rather, simply recorded and *exposed* as examples of false statements.[5] The point that the Perfect Wording theorists wish to emphasize, however, is this: "If the orginal manuscript [of the Bible] already had mistakes in it, who can say now how far this element of error goes, and how are we to get the errors sorted out? We would be in complete confusion."[6]

The Perfect Wording theorists utilize many analogies in order to get their point across that a perfect God would provide a revelation free of all errors and mistakes in the original documents or autographs written down by the prophets and apostles. What could be said of an expert who engineers the construction of a great dam whose very foundation has a few small cracks in it? The trouble with small cracks in a dam is that they may become major cracks. A Scripture that has some mistakes in it is compared to a dam with cracks or to a scale that is inaccurate. Or it is like a legal contract that omits a few words here and there and even contains improper wording. A God who permits errors to creep into his Scripture is regarded as being a thousand times more irresponsible than, say, a man who, desiring to control the size of his family, neglects now and then to use the proper contraceptive device, or a woman who is negligent about taking her pill.

God's Honor and Human Dignity Are at Stake. God's honor is declared by the Perfect Wording theorists to be at stake. They insist that a perfect God simply would not reveal himself in a Scripture containing errors. "We believe," writes a Perfect Wording theorist, "that it is in keeping . . . with the nature and honor of God . . . that in inspiring each sacred author, He jealously guarded His original manuscript to preserve it from error."[7]

Not only is God's honor thought to be at stake, but man's dignity also. In the words of one defender of the Perfect Wording theory,

God has revealed to us his word. What are we to think of him if this word is glutted by little annoying inaccuracies? Why could not the omnipotent and omniscient God have taken the trouble to give us a Word that was free from error? Was it not a somewhat discourteous thing for him to have breathed forth from his mouth a message filled with mistakes? Of course, it was discourteous; *it was downright rude and insulting*. The present writer finds it difficult to have much respect for such a God.[8]

Now, a person tends to feel insulted if he has certain expectations, the satisfaction of which he thinks he has a right to. Indeed, in the above quotation the writer seems to *demand* that God give him a Scripture free of all errors. Of course, demands, rights, and expectations do not exist in the abstract. They develop according to certain concrete conditions and circumstances. We will postpone discussing the question as to whether the circumstances of life can justify the Perfect Wording theorists' demand for an infallible Scripture whose very wording is precisely as God would desire it.

Some critics of this theory might say that God simply could not give this kind of infallible revelation to finite and fallible human beings—whether they be prophets like Jeremiah or apostles like Paul. Once God created human beings to be finite, he ruled out the possibility of giving them infallible revelations free of all error. God could no more give us an infallible Scripture than he could make a circle into a square without simply eliminating the circle.

Some Christians try to meet the criticism by saying that God could give infallible information to fallible and finite human beings without overriding the unique personality of each individual person who receives God's special revelation. So, we turn now to consider the theory that allows for more flexibility in the process of divine inspiration. Most Christians who hold that the Bible is God's infallibly revealed revelation seem to move back and forth between the view presented above and the one that we are now going to explore.

THE BIBLE AS A PERFECTLY REVEALED MEANING

One Message with Many Arrangements.   It is important to keep in mind that those who hold the Bible to be infallible revelation presuppose not only that there is a God interested in revealing an infallible document, but also that there is a crucial *need* for such a document. The assumption is that people are on their way to hell and therefore need some kind of information that will show them how to avoid eternal damnation. Of course, if this assumption of everlasting torment is not warranted, then the need for an infallible Scripture is reduced considerably. Indeed, it is certain portions of the Bible itself which assert that people are going to hell. It is the Bible which informs them that they absolutely need divine special revelation to save them from everlasting torment. We will consider later whether there is any good reason to regard as trustworthy those parts of the Bible that speak of hell. Indeed, we will consider whether—or to what extent—we can regard as trustworthy any of the Bible's claims regarding various religious topics.

More than the Perfect Wording theorists, those Christians who affirm what may be called the *Perfect Meaning theory* are prepared to say that the wording in the Bible might have been somewhat different from what it in fact is. What is important, they claim, is that God's meaning or message did come across without error. They believe that there was some flexibility in the way the message was set forth. This Perfect Meaning theory tries to make greater room for the personal background and traits of the individual writers of the Bible. The theme of Salvation as well as doctrinal and moral teaching are regarded as expressable in a great variety of forms and styles.

A piece of music may be set forth in a number of different

arrangements, according to the unique personalities of the arrangers. According to proponents of the Perfect Meaning theory, if one musical theme can have many arrangements, then God's message can have been arranged in a variety of ways. Indeed, some of the writers of the Bible apparently used bad grammar, or less-than-elegant sentence structure, or even imperfect literary style. Nevertheless, according to this view, the message came through without error or loss of meaning. The gospel of salvation and the great theological doctrines shine forth despite the weakness of the human writers. God is thought to have used imperfect human beings as instruments to produce a Scripture free of error and sufficient to inform the human race of salvation, morality, and theological truths. This view is sometimes called the "Dynamic theory" of inspiration, because it emphasizes that the Biblical writers were able to write according to their own special talents and weaknesses. But the theory does "not mean to say [of the Bible] that there is falsity or error here."[9]

In a number of ways a woman may tell a man that she loves him. Similarly, those holding to the Perfect Meaning theory reason that God could have revealed his message in a variety of literary arrangements and forms so long as the essential message was not lost.

Emphasis on the Whole of Scripture.   No musical composition or literary work can be judged by isolated passages taken out of context. The composition must be judged as a whole. Similarly, the Perfect Meaning theorists insist that the Bible is infallible as a whole work. But the Perfect Wording theorists, while agreeing with this point, are eager to add that a perfect whole cannot be made of imperfect parts. A chain can be no stronger than its links, a building no stronger than the bricks and beams that compose it.

Perhaps these two views of the inspiration of the Scriptures differ mostly on the weight to be given to the various parts of the Bible. Both regard the Bible as infallible, but not exactly in the same way. Because of its emphasis upon every word in the Bible being exactly as God intended it to be, the Perfect Wording theory tends to draw more detailed revelations from the Bible than does the Perfect Meaning theory. While the former theory sees the Bible as a whole, it also tends to see within this larger whole a number of smaller systems of revelation. Everything in the Bible must have some very significant truth. As might have been expected, great theological disputes have erupted among those who strongly emphasize the Perfect Wording theory. After all, if God himself is the author of every single word, then it is important not to overlook the significance of each word.

By contrast, the Perfect Meaning theory stresses that the Bible has a few major and crucial truths to get across. Everything else in the Bible is subservient to these major truths. Hence, it is not so important to worry about certain minute details, which may be simply the *human* aspects of the Bible. To worry about such insignificant details is to fail to emphasize the broader and loftier message of God that comes through human means. "Cultic mentality" is the title that one Christian writer attaches to those who he thinks emphasize the minor parts of the Bible at the expense of the major infallible message.[10]

The Debate regarding the Nature of the Unity.　　It is one thing to claim that the Bible is infallible revelation. But it is another to know how to interpret it infallibly. Protestant Christians do not profess to have infallible interpretation, although it is fair to say that many of them seem to take for granted that in practice their own interpretations are mostly infallible. Even among those Christians, whether Protestant or Catholic, who emphasize the overall unity of the Bible and underplay the sub-unities within the totality—even among them, a considerable amount of debate continues regarding what exactly the unifying message of the Bible is. They agree that whatever it is, it is infallibly revealed in the Bible, but they cannot agree as to what it is.

The reason for regarding the Bible as an organic unity is that it is supposed to reflect the harmonious mind of God. God's mind is thought to be a perfect and rich organic unity. The apostle Paul is thought to have identified the Old Testament with God. "Paul not only personifies the Old Testament but he hypostatizes it."[11]

Unfortunately, even if the "mind" of the Bible is taken to be one infallible whole or unity, the fact remains that there are all sorts of claims as to what exactly the unity is. Can all the sub-unities be worked together into one overriding unity? Various sub-unities have been set forth—for example, structural unity as well as historic, dispensational, prophetic, personal, symbolic, and organic unities.[12]

If we take one of these sub-unities and examine it, we find that it is in fact a source of great *disharmony and disunity* among Christians. The "dispensational" unity has created enormous conflicts among and within Christian churches. In 1913 one of the foremost dispensationalists had worked out an ingenious scheme of what he took to be the Bible's clear teaching regarding what would happen near the "end of time." Fifteen years later, this same author repudiated all his former dispensational views. He is quoted by a later Christian as saying:

It is mortifying to remember that I not only held and taught these novelties myself, but that I even enjoyed a complacent sense of superiority because thereof, and regarded with feelings of pity and contempt those who had not received the "new light."[13]

This is certainly not to criticize Christians or anyone else for changing their minds; changing one's mind is a mark of intellectual growth. The point here is that among those Christians who speak glowingly about "infallible revelation" and the "unity of the Bible" we may discover a large amount of disunity and conflict of opinions. Such disappointment is to be expected among Freudians, humanists, and others, for they boast of no infallible Scripture to guide them. But Christians are as divided among themselves as if they had no infallible Scripture, which raises the possibility that perhaps they do not.

There is a multiplicity of "unities" that Christians see in the Bible. In addition to the structural, historic, dispensational, prophetic, personal, symbolic, and organic unities mentioned above, the following may be added: "the mediational unity of Scripture" (i.e., Christ); "thematic unity" (including such motifs as man, creation, providence, sin, etc.); "conceptual unity"; and "formal unity."[14] All these unities presuppose the "unity of the life of God," which the Bible is said to reveal to some extent.[15]

Why Are Christians Concerned about the Nature of the Unity of Scripture?   It is crucial for many Christians to identify the highest unifying theme of the Bible, because that unifying theme will touch the Bible's every verse and chapter. That unifying theme will be the tinted glasses through which each passage is read and understood. One set of glasses will see the people of Israel as God's select people serving the cause of Jesus Christ, whom present-day Jews do not even regard as their Messiah. The sensuous poetry of the Song of Songs will be seen, not as the utterances of human beings making love to one another, but as an allegory of the spiritual relationship between Christ and his church.

The gist of the issue is this: even among those who take the Bible to be an infallible message, great disagreement exists as to how to *rank* the various parts and themes of the Bible. All Christians inevitably give greater weight to some parts of Scripture than to others. But by what higher principle or standard is this done? Usually the answer given is that either the Bible itself indicates how to rank its passages or the Holy Spirit gives directions to the sincere believer. Unfortunately, those who *differ* in the weight that they give to the various parts of the Bible are quite eager to claim, nevertheless, that they are following the directions of the Bible and the Holy Spirit. There seems to be no way to resolve these controversies in any infallible way, which means that the thesis of infallibility has been made somewhat ineffective. Perhaps, then, infallibility is something that many people desire to have but never seem able to realize—not even in a book that they take to be a repository of divine truths, propositions, and utterances.

THE BIBLE
AS A REPOSITORY OF ESSENTIAL REVELATION

Defining the Issue of Infallibility.   Desiring to disentangle themselves from much of what they regard as secondary and tertiary aspects of the Bible, an increasing number of Christians seem to be moving toward a view that may be characterized as the *Essential Truth theory*. These Christians believe it is disastrous to try to defend as true those parts of the Bible that are clearly in error. In other words, the notion that the Bible is infallible or free of all errors is being given up by a number of Christians. The previous two theories (i.e., the Perfect Wording and Perfect Meaning theories) affirm that the Bible is infallible. They differ only in what respect it is infallible. But the Essential Truth theory concedes that there are errors in the Bible.

Furthermore, those advancing this Essential Truth theory believe that it is also a waste of time and effort to try to obtain divine revelation from some Biblical passages. If no divine revelation is there, then it is fruitless to "read it into" certain parts of the Scripture. You recall that those adhering either to the Perfect Wording theory or to the Perfect Meaning theory insist that the Bible is infallible and inerrant. Together they strongly attack any theory that—like the Essential Truth theory—professes to give up the notion of the Bible's complete infallibility. The Essential Truth theorists and other theorists are just as forceful in attacking the assumption of the Bible's total infallibility.[16] The question for us is, "What is this tense debate really about?"

First, something ought to be said about the word 'theorists'. There are still those in every religion who insist that they do not waste time with theories. What they want to do is to "give witness to the truth." Or, in the case of some Zen Buddhists, they want to speak simply of "facts" and not theories. What this attitude fails to appreciate is the point that every statement about facts or truth is made against a background of theory. Every claim to be experiencing God (or whatever) is riddled through with theoretical assumptions. This in itself does not make the assumptions necessarily wrong, but neither are they necessarily right. The point is that all claims, whether we call them opinions or basic convictions, are one and all convictions to be tested. This includes the conjecture just stated.

The second point about the debate is this: the contestants are trying to resolve what, to them, is a critical problem loaded with profound consequences for their lives. The problem may be stated in this way: On the one hand, if the Bible contains errors regarding some things, then how can Christians trust it to give them divine revelation regarding salvation? Perhaps the Bible is in error on this topic also. On the other hand, there do seem to be some errors that threaten the claim that the Bible is the *infallible* revelation of God. Honesty would demand that these errors be admitted.

The infallibilists usually respond to this dilemma in one of two ways. Either they assert that the errors have all been exposed as not errors at all, or they believe that the *apparent* errors will *eventually* be shown not to be errors. Speaking for the second alternative, one infallibilist states, "We walk by faith and not by sight."[17] But this is simply a way of saying that he *strongly hopes* that his belief in infallibility will pay off.

In the latter part of the nineteenth century, Pope Pius IX

arranged to get himself and every other pope declared infallible when they were speaking officially (or ex cathedra) on
matters of faith and morals. What was overlooked is the fact
that no way could be found to guarantee the infallibility of the
procedures for setting up this arrangement. The quest for infallibility in theology may be compared to the fruitless quest
for a perpetual motion machine. There seems always to be a
gap in the armor, an Achilles' heel. Pope John XXIII seemed
somewhat embarrassed about the doctrine of papal infallibility. He is quoted by a leading Roman Catholic theologian as
having said the following: "I'm infallible only when I speak ex
cathedra. But I'll never speak ex cathedra."[18] Apparently, pro-
ponets of the Essential Truth theory as well as a number of
other Christians feel equally uncomfortable in asserting the
Bible to be infallible and inerrant.

Clarifying the Essential Truth Thesis.   Professor Dewey
M. Beegle, a modern biblical scholar and leading spokesman
of the Essential Truth theory, writes: "In all essential matters
of faith and practice, . . . Scripture is authentic, accurate, and
trustworthy."[19] Whenever something is said to be "essential,"
the question implied is, "Essential to what?" The Essential
Truth theory of inspiration says that the Bible provides "sufficient truth" for directing people toward salvation and toward
love of God and fellow human beings. Combined with the
work of the Holy Spirit, the Bible is said to be sufficient to
"achieve God's purpose for each generation as well as for ex-
trapolating into the future."[20]

Of course, this presupposes that we can know what God's
purpose is. The Essential Truth theorists claim that God's purpose is revealed in the Bible. But the infallibilists ask the following embarrassing question: If the Bible contains errors regarding certain historical and other details, how can anyone be
certain that it does not contain errors regarding either what
God's purposes are or what is the true way to fulfill those
purposes?[21]

Partial Infallibilism Implied.   The answer that the Essential Truth theorists finally provide is very simple. They *assume*
that the Bible accurately reveals God's purpose (or purposes)
and gives trustworthy directions for human moral behavior.
They take for granted that "men were chosen [by God], each
one in his own particular situation, to speak, or to write, or to

do, whatever was essential to further the redemptive movement."[22] What this boils down to is a theory of the *partial* infallibility of the Bible. The Bible is said to contain some "minor errors" and various irrelevancies, but the essential truth about God's directions regarding how to obtain "salvation" and how to lead a moral life is "authentic, accurate, and trustworthy." To be sure, the *words* 'infallible' or 'inerrant' are not usually used by the Essential Truth theorists. But just beneath the surface the assumption seems to be that the Bible does infallibly reveal God's mind regarding such significant matters as everlasting salvation, Christ's resurrection and saviorhood, and certain moral guidelines for mankind. What the Essential Truth theorists are not prepared to call into question is their assumption that the Bible is free of error in what it teaches regarding such topics as the following: heaven and hell, the necessity of salvation of a special kind, views about certain moralities and immoralities, Jesus as the Son of God, and certain other "essential truths."

Let me give an example. In challenging the infallibilists to give up their insistence that every part of the Bible is infallible, Professor Beegle assures them that their new doubts will not destroy their faith. Why? Because, he says, "*the truth will always lead to Christ.*"[23] But Professor Beegle's bold assertion and reassuring words are based on the *assumption* that the Bible does reveal infallibly that "the truth will always lead to Christ." Beegle seems to realize that his position is in trouble, and he goes to great lengths to call into question increasingly more areas in which claims of infallibility have been made. He even denies that the Bible can give "certain protection against false doctrine." What is left, then? His answer is very simple: "sufficient protection for salvation."[24] In other words, the Bible is infallible revelation regarding only salvation and the things necessarily connected with it. Regarding other things, however, the Bible is apparently not infallible.

What is interesting is the fact that the way for Beegle's making this move seems to have been already prepared in his own thinking. He points out that it is very "likely that the disciples confused some of Jesus' statements about the destruction of Jerusalem with some of his remarks about the second coming." Professor Beegle acknowledges that the writers of the New Testament did not see "eye to eye in all the doctrinal details related to eschatology [i.e., the end of the world]."[25] Indeed, Beegle believes that the New Testament authors lacked perfect agreement regarding such important doctrines as Christ's atonement for sin or the nature of the Trinity.[26] However, what he cannot yet call into question is the doctrine that Jesus is the Son of God and that people need salvation if they are to avoid hell and gain heaven.[27]

One can only admire Professor Beegle's attempt to hold dearly to the basic commitment of his religious faith while at the same time seeking truth and eliminating errors wherever he finds them. In my own opinion, the infallibilists were right to fear that once the Bible is admitted to be not infallible in some minor parts, then it might very well turn out to be not infallible or trustworthy in any of its *major* doctrines. At the same time, I think that Professor Beegle and a great many other biblical scholars have pretty well shown that there are errors in the Bible. The conclusion, I regret to say, is that the Bible seems not to be authoritative as a guide to such metaphysical doctrines as salvation, life after death, God's existence, and various other matters. Indeed, Professor Beegle, desperately concerned to hold to his conviction about Christ and salvation, nevertheless seems determined not to ignore altogether what must to him be painful conclusions. Of the biblical passages dealing with the resurrection of Jesus, Beegle says plainly that they "swarm with difficulties, some details of which cannot be harmonized." He takes solace in "the historical core back of the accounts."[28] Indeed, he goes so far as to say that he cannot even assert that disbelief in Jesus' physical resurrection or in his virgin birth will exclude a person from "saving faith." He concludes that "God recognizes the sincere doubts of men and he undoubtedly saves men who do not have enough faith to believe certain teachings of the Scripture."[29]

Naturally the infallibilists will accuse Beegle of surrendering to "subjectivism." But the infallibilists have never grasped the point that they may well be the most subjective of all. To keep asserting the infallibility of a book, many of whose claims have been seriously challenged, to say the least, is to take refuge in wishful thinking, which is the essence of subjectivity. The atheist Ayn Rand boldly refers to her philosophy as "Objectivism." But this in itself does not make her view any more objective (i.e., true and credible) than any other view. Each view—including that of the infallibilists—must be tested and critically examined. If the theological and metaphysical claims of the Bible are true, then they are objective. But if they are *not* true, then belief in them is indeed only subjective—even when the believer announces three times daily that his faith is objectively grounded.

In the final paragraph of his controversial book, *Scripture, Tradition, and Infallibility*, Professor Beegle writes, "Ultimately, authority is an individual, personal matter because everyone will be judged according to his *willingness* to know God's will and to obey it."[30] This is but a short step from saying that the honest seeker of truth will not be harshly judged by God. Indeed, what could be said of a God who would damn a person for being willing to follow the evidence wherever it leads? Of course, many infallibilists hold that a person cannot be honest-minded and still disagree with them. Some of their opponents have, in turn, accused them of moral and spiritual blindness. Of more importance than these charges and counter-charges, however, is the need to keep in good repair the lines of communication between all "theorists."

Why the Last-Ditch Stand?   There is no need to hold back the hard question that Dr. Beegle must deal with. It is this: Why do the Essential Truth theorists still cling to the assumption of the Bible's trustworthiness regarding salvation? Why do they refuse to entertain the possibility that the Bible may even be mistaken about salvation or about Christ? Beegle's answer seems to be that the Essential Truth theorists simply start with the assumption that the Bible could not be mistaken in these matters.[31] The infallibilists have openly asserted that their own assumption is that *every part* of the Bible is infallible. Beegle advances a number of arguments showing why he cannot accept this particular assumption or conjecture.[32] The question, then, remains as to whether Beegle is prepared to bring his own assumption out in the open and examine it critically. Indeed, he has already admitted to "shifting the line of defense from 'absolute truth' to 'essential truth.' "[33] Acknowledging that the Bible is "fallible in minor details,"[34] he must now move to face the question as to whether it is fallible in *major* details, namely, the details about "salvation" and the person of Jesus.

THE KEY IMAGES THEORY

Very close to the Essential Truth theory is the view that in the Bible, as well as in the history of Israel and the Christian church, God has caused certain key images to emerge and to be preserved. As men and women experienced God, they came to express their experiences in certain great images or symbols. Some of these predominating images of God and his relationship with Israel and the Church are: the Kingdom of God, the Son of Man, the Suffering Servant, and the Messiah.[35]

Now, this *Key Images theory* is popular among those who are already convinced that there is a God who has been working in a special way with Israel and the Christian church. Those who are not convinced of this position, however, may take the images as tentative conjectures with which to experiment. In that sense, they may be seen as possible leads that might, for the honest seeker, open up avenues of religious exploration.

Of course, if the believer is justified in asking the seeker to think along the lines suggested by the great key images, then the seeker is justified in asking the believer to consider thinking along new lines and with fresh categories, images, and conjectures. Sometimes, new "models" or "images" do open up fresh ways of experiencing and believing. Unless it assumes its own infallibility, no one group can rightly assume that it can learn nothing by experimenting with the images and categories of other groups. In many ways, we are especially ignorant if we can never view our own dearest convictions through the eyes of at least one other perspective very different from our own.

THE BIBLE AS THE OCCASION OF THE SACRED EXISTENTIAL ENCOUNTER

The Bible As a Place in Which to Encounter God. Christians who have been influenced by the philosophical movement called existentialism tend to see the Bible as a vital and sacred temple wherein the individual sometimes meets God. It is as if the Bible contains a number of sacred cues and symbols that increase the likelihood of opening up a reconciliation between God and the human individual. According to this view, he who reads the Bible is in a sense walking through a cathedral. God's presence may suddenly become "real" to the reader. God breaks in upon him in a divine-human encounter.

Those who hold to this *Sacred Encounter theory* believe that the biblical stories, poems, teachings, proverbs, etc., focus on the essential elements of religious concern. The question as to whether Jesus did in fact rise from the grave becomes, for the Sacred Encounter theorists, a secondary question. Being concerned with the historicity of Jesus is like being concerned with the question as to whether there actually was a literal prodigal son behind the parable. To concern oneself with such questions is to miss the crucial point of the biblical stories.

What is thought to be important is that the early Christian disciples came to see "God in Christ." To read about Jesus in the Gospels, therefore, is to make yourself open to the possibility of appropriating for yourself the early disciples' sense of "new being" that came through the love and fellowship they experienced.

Hence, the stories of an alleged historical Jesus are regarded as only occasions for lifting the human inquirer to a new level of awareness of "the Christ." According to this view, Jesus is the Christ in the sense that the biblical stories open the mind and heart to the possibility of encountering God in Christ. The stories provide the occasion of experiencing forgiveness, grace, acceptance, hope, and resolution. What is significant in the stories? It is not that there once was a Jewish rabbi named Jesus, but that in the first century a community of fellow sinners were brought to the point of experiencing forgiveness, fellowship, and new courage to thrive lovingly in the face of unfavorable odds.

To be sure, there doubtless were historical realities behind what happened in the lives of those early Christian disciples. But the Sacred Encounter theorists doubt that we can ever have sufficient data to piece together the historical truth about the spatial and temporal details of the life of Jesus.[36] Nevertheless, it is often good to inquire into these details, for in doing so one often "encounters the living Christ." It is as if a repairman were going to work each day at the cathedral. He is not going there to "meet God" but rather to repair the roof. But while there one day he hears the grand organ and is profoundly moved as he has never been before.

What the Sacred Encounter theorists are implying is that the reality beyond mankind is such that human beings can be raised to new heights of love and made sensitive to new dimensions of being. They can find new hope, resolution, self-acceptance, other-acceptance, and "meaning" for their existence. The term 'the Christ' refers to that dimension of divine reality that evokes in us "new being," "new power," and greater sensitivity to a context that is infinitely wider and deeper than our everyday environment. Or, to say it in another way, our everyday reality is seen to be not a closed little drama of its own; it stands, rather, as the possibility of receiving "new power and being" and new dynamic relationships from beyond itself.

Faith beyond the Historical Jesus: Rudolf Bultmann's Program of "Demythologizing." The leading and highly controversial New Testament scholar Rudolf Bultmann believes that as a *project of historical research* the quest for the historical Jesus is quite irrelevant to Christian faith. He claims that the original Jesus is lost in the obscurities of a mixture of fact and fantasy, myth and reality. Christian faith, Bultmann holds, cannot wait around to see what the latest archaeologist will turn up, or what news will come from New Testament research regarding the person of Jesus of Nazareth. No, as existential beings we must make our decisions *now*; we must proceed to *live today*.

The Bible, thus, cannot serve as an unquestioned guide to the footprints of a Jesus of the first century. Rather, the Bible serves to expose us to ourselves. It is a challenge to see oneself as a creature "incapable of redeeming himself from the world and the powers which hold sway in it."[37] Far from taking us back to times past, the Bible, says Professor Bultmann, calls attention to our present arrogance and pride, and to the possibility of our own death at any moment. The Bible also brings us the promise of redemption and grace.

But Bultmann offers an *existential* version of "redemption" and "salvation." Hell is not seen as some final cosmic ghetto into which all sinners are herded for eternity. Nor is heaven a place where people go to eat superb food and sing hymns forever. The concepts of hell and heaven must, therefore, be demythologized. That is, they must be viewed neither as locations in outer space nor as states of being in the remote future. Instead, they are to be understood as modes of finite human existence here and now.

Similarly, redemption and salvation are, for Bultmann, the realization that a life of legalism and the treadmill can be *changed*. We are not wholly prisoners of our past. Grace is a major theme of the Bible, says Bultmann, and he sees it as a promise of a new chance to live meaningfully in the present life. Faith is the glad acceptance of this new chance—this new possibility—to live in gratitude and freedom. 'Christ' is understood to be far more than the obscure Jesus of Nazareth. *'Christ' is God in his mode of encountering the sinner and bringing into play the grace of new life here and now.*

To be sure, propositional statements may be used to describe what this new encounter of freedom means to the "redeemed" person. But that is an after-the-fact enterprise. Basically, for Bultmann, the Bible serves as the occasion by which God reveals, not so much propositional truths, as his own gracious and liberating presence. The "second coming of Christ," therefore, is not some future astronomical event, but rather is, when demythologized, an existential experience. It takes place when God as the Christ of grace breaks in upon the believer in the form of a new power to cope with the absurdities, trials, and opportunities of existence. The story of the Creation is demythologized to mean the new power that is brought into a person's life in such a way as to make it possible for him to love and to be loved, to accept and be accepted.

What, then, is the Bible's inspiration? It is its power to serve as the instrument through which people are themselves inspired, empowered, liberated, and forgiven by "God in Christ." Existential *philosophy*, says Bultmann, can teach, but it cannot empower and inspire to love. That is a matter of divine grace. It is not surprising, therefore, that Bultmann's favorite biblical passages emphasize divine initiatives in moving and motivating sinners to accept both forgiveness and new possibilites of freedom and moral responsibility.[38]

Historical Claims of the Bible.   Writing in the same existential vein as Bultmann, another Sacred Encounter theologian makes the following cryptic statement: "The truth that Jesus Christ rose from the dead is of a different order from the fact that water boils at one hundred degrees centigrade at sea level."[39] This same theologian refers to "Jesus Christ as the Word of God."[40] Sometimes the writings of existential Christians are very confusing to Christians raised in an orthodox setting. For the orthodox, to hear or see the words 'Jesus' or 'Christ' is perhaps to recall some notion of a bearded Hebrew who turned out to be far more than a great teacher. But for existential Christians, the historical Jesus and the events of his life are not very important. 'Jesus Christ' means to them what they take to be the other side of the personal and sacred encounter with God. And for those existential Christians, such an encounter is declared to be far more "real" than any Palestinian figure who might have lived two thousand years ago.

To state it bluntly, existential Christians think it is foolish to place one's deepest faith in the historical claims of a book— even the Bible. Tales and legends grow up too quickly and are soon taken to be actual facts. For all we know, say the existential Christians, most of the biblical stories of Jesus are myths, fictions, or half-truths. Trust in the biblical reports if you like, but existential Christians place their faith in what they take to be the "contemporaneous Christ" whom they meet and know here and now.

In considering the precariousness of placing your faith in reports of historical happenings, consider the following:

Mircea Eliade tells of a legend in a small village in Maramures in Romania, in which a young suitor had been bewitched by a fairy, and a few days before he was to be married, the fairy threw him from a cliff. Shepherds found the body, and when they returned it to the village, his fiancee poured out a beautiful funeral lament. Investigating the legend, a folklorist discovered that the story had *taken place only forty years earlier* and that the heroine was still alive. He spoke with her, and she described a quite commonplace tragedy. One evening, her lover had slipped and fallen off a cliff; he was not killed instantly, but was carried to the village, where he soon died. At the funeral, the fiancee participated in the customary ritual lamentations. Popular memory had stripped the story of almost all historical authenticity in spite of the presence of the principal witness and many other villagers who were contemporaries. "When the folklorist drew the villagers' attention to the authentic version, they replied that the old woman had forgotten; that her grief had almost destroyed her mind. *It was the myth that told the truth*; the real story was already only a falsification."[41]

Most Christian and Jewish believers who accept putative reports in the Bible merely *because they are in the Bible* would ask people to regard as superstitious nonsense the midrash that claims that at the Red Sea "God assumed the shape of a mare and decoyed the ruttish Egyptian stallions into the water."[42] Yet the same believers ask people to believe the following story, simply because it is set forth in the Bible:

When the ass saw the angel of the Lord, she lay down under Balaam; and Balaam's anger was kindled, and he struck the ass with his staff. Then the Lord opened the mouth of the ass, and she said to Balaam, "What have I done to you that you have struck me these three times?" And Balaam said to the ass, "Because you have made sport of me, I wish I had a sword in my hand, for then I would kill you." And the ass said to Balaam, "Am I not your ass, upon which you have ridden all your life long to this day? Was I ever accustomed to do so to you?" And he said, "No."[43]

This charming story continues by saying that the prophet Balaam finally came to see the angel, who held a sword in his hand. The angel explained that had the ass not turned aside, Balaam would now be dead because the angel had in mind to cut the prophet down.

There is no need to overreact to the Bible by insisting that every historical and geographical notation is inaccurate. The Bible is a collection of ancient pieces of literature, some of which were first formulated orally. It should not be surprising that the Bible would combine a mixture of some very accurate reports with some inaccurate ones. And, of course, there are numerous theological and metaphysical *interpretations* that, like the other Scriptures of the world, are a matter of debate and serious inquiry.

THE BIBLE AS A SEEDBED OF INTERPRETATIONS

It is easy to forget how very rich, variegated, and complex the Bible really is. In it may be found poetry, songs, historical reports, legends, myths, psychological insights, religious biography, metaphysical and theological theories, parables, predictions, dreams, as well as other forms of religious literature. It is also easy to forget the fact that the Bible was not simply written as one book. It is a collection of materials composed by numerous authors. Sometimes the materials were edited and reworked. What is crucial to keep in mind is that the Hebrews wrote a considerable amount of literature over a number of centuries, but only some of it was *selected* by later Jews to be classified as sacred Scripture.

For example, when they eventually settled on the material to be included in their Bible (which Christians call the "Old Testament") the Jews did not select materials in a random way. Rather, they took those pieces of Hebrew literature that were thought to have been written by prophets and other esteemed ancients. Furthermore, those in charge of the final judgment as to what to include in the Hebrew Bible seemed to have in mind what they wanted and did not want. They tended to select the literary materials that fitted with their assumption that throughout Hebrew history God had been providentially caring for the people of Israel in a very special way. Hence, when people today speak of the "unity of the Bible," they sometimes forget that there was a deliberate attempt to weed out materials that did not fit with the unifying theme of God's special care for Israel. The influential early Christians adopted this view of Hebrew history and added to it the qualification that the Christian movement was the true heir of the Hebrew faith.

There is no great supernatural mystery to the view that many ancient Hebrews, as well as Christians, wrote and spoke about what were crucial matters of concern to them. Like people of other religious traditions, they confronted problems, responded to them, had experiences, and wrote down some of their interpretations of what was going on about them. Indeed, like ourselves and people from every part of the globe, they believed that their interpretations were true. Some of them even felt that they were speaking on behalf of God. In many parts of the world, people have thought of themselves as receiving messages from the deity.

For example, about four centuries before the time of Moses, the noted Babylonian king Hammurabi believed that the great code of law that he instituted in his land was inspired by the deity Shamash, the guardian of law and justice. In A.D. 1901 a copy of this remarkable code was discovered 150 miles north of the head of the Persian Gulf. This sensational discovery was made by the French archaeologist Jacques de Morgan.[44] "The code was inscribed on a round-topped stele of black diorite, some six feet in height, which now is in the Louvre. At the top is a bas-relief showing Hammurabi standing before the enthroned sun-god Shamash."[45] Beneath this bas-relief is a prologue in cuneiform characters stating that Hammurabi had been divinely called to administer righteousness and justice. It would be surprising if the ancient Hebrews had not shared the rather common supposition that the leaders of the people were "called" to receive God's message and to carry out his directions.

Much of the Bible may be seen as expressions of individuals' trying to make sense of their world (or some aspect of it) and trying to respond to it in some intellectual, moral, emotional, or ritualistic manner. It may very well have been that a prophet named Balaam thought he had a conversation with his animal companion. A man who could see an angel and converse with it could probably hear an ass speak Hebrew.

But as we saw in Chapter I, people can have all sorts of extraordinary experiences. The critical question is: How are these experiences to be taken, understood, and interpreted in a broader setting? I have sometimes had very vivid and powerful dreams. But I cannot claim that they are "real" in the same sense that my neighbor's black cat is real or that Japan is real.

As for Balaam's conversation with the ass and the angel, the following tentative hypothesis is suggested: If there is any substance at all to the story, it is possible that the prophet had a vision or dream, or simply enjoyed an interesting, although hardly supernatural, hallucination. The Bible seems not always to draw a clear line between visions, dreams, and those actual events belonging to a realm wider than the individual's private experience only. Indeed, the Bible often says that the Lord came to someone in a dream or vision.

Perhaps there is more truth here than most Jews and Christians would care to admit. Indeed, orthodox Jews do not hesitate to say that the dreams and visions of the early Christian disciples and apostles were terribly *un*reliable when they claimed that God had given them special revelations. But the same orthodox Jews are quite eager to believe that numerous dreams and visions set forth in the Old Testament were and are quite reliable and trustworthy as messages from God.

A less supernaturalistic interpretation is that people have often dreamed up theological and metaphysical views of God. But Galileo and Newton also dreamed up theories about much of the universe, as did Einstein and Darwin. The issue then is not that people dream up their theories. Rather, once the dreams and visions are verbalized and made public, can their assertions be tested and critically examined? In the sixth chapter of Isaiah, the prophet Isaiah claims that he saw the Lord. Perhaps he did; perhaps he did not. If there is no God, or if God is not the sort of reality that can be seen in visions, then we must say that Isaiah only *thought* he saw God. You and I have sometimes been mistaken in what we thought we experienced, although at the time we might have been absolutely convinced that we were not mistaken. Perhaps Isaiah was mistaken in his interpretation of what he experienced.

But soon we must turn to make serious inquiry into the evidence and arguments for the existence of God (or at least of the God in which many Christians and Jews profess to believe). The prophet Isaiah may have been a very truthful person. But the issue that we must confront is *not* that of Isaiah's moral integrity. After all, he may have been very *honestly* mistaken. Our faith in *God* must be distinguished from our faith in Isaiah's opinions and interpretations. If God exists, then perhaps he will not be offended if finite human mortals are very interested in finding out whether he does exist and what he is like.

True, many people have presumed to speak on his behalf. (A couple of decades ago a Methodist bishop wrote a book entitled *Who Speaks for God?*) If we cannot simply take as infallible the word of human beings—even finite human beings of the Bible or of some other Scripture—we must look wherever we can for "signs and evidence" of God. If the Bible, the Qur'an, or any other Scripture turns out to be more-or-less accurate in its claims about the existence and nature of God, we will then have reason for learning more from it and putting its other numerous claims to the test. But if these claims fail to test out, then we will have to live our lives according to the light and evidence that we do have.

NOTES

1. James I. Packer, *"Fundamentalism" and the Word of God: Some Evangelical Principles* (Grand Rapids: Eerdmans, 1958), pp. 95 f.
2. See Edward John Carnell, *An Introduction to Christian Apologetics* (Grand Rapids: Eerdmans, 1948), p. 196.
3. Ibid., p. 63.
4. Ibid., p 291.
5. See Clark H. Pinnock, *Biblical Revelation: The Foundation of Christian Theology* (Chicago: Moody Press, 1971), p. 78.

6. René Pache, *The Inspiration and Authority of Scripture* (Chicago: Moody Press, 1969), pp. 138 f.
7. Ibid., p. 134.
8. Edward J. Young, *Thy Word Is Truth* (Grand Rapids: Eerdmans, 1957), p. 73. Italics added.
9. A. H. Strong, *Popular Lectures on the Books of the New Testament* (Philadelphia: Griffith & Rowland, 1914), p. 11.
10. See Edward John Carnell, *The Case for Orthodox Christianity* (Philadelphia: Westminster Press, 1951), pp. 54–59.
11. Bernard Ramm, *Special Revelation and the Word of God* (Grand Rapids: Eerdmans, 1961), p. 166, n. 13.
12. See Arthur T. Pierson, "Testimony of the Organic Unity of the Bible to Its Inspiration," in *The Fundamentals for Today*, ed. Charles L. Feinberg (Grand Rapids: Kregel Publications, 1961), pp. 178–184.
13. Quoted in George E. Ladd, *The Blessed Hope* (Grand Rapids: Eerdmans, 1956), p. 53. Dispensationalism has to do with special blocks of time or history that God has presumably marked off for special purposes.
14. Ramm, *Special Revelation*, pp. 102 f.
15. Ibid., pp. 17, 102.
16. For a vigorous debate between, on the one hand, the Perfect Wording and Perfect Meaning theorists, and, on the other hand, the Essential Truth theorists, see *Review and Expositor* 71 (Spring 1974): 2.
17. Pinnock, *Biblical Revelation*, p. 81.
18. Hans Küng, *Infallible? An Inquiry*, trans. Edward Quinn (Garden City, N.Y.: Doubleday, 1971), p. 87.
19. Dewey M. Beegle, *Scripture, Tradition, and Infallibility* (Grand Rapids: Eerdmans, 1973), p. 308. Italics added. The first edition of this book appeared in 1963 under the title *The Inspiration of Scripture*.
20. Ibid., p. 307.
21. See Norman Geisler, "Theological Method and Inerrancy," *Journal of the Evangelical Theological Society* 11 (1968): 143 f.
22. Beegle, *Scripture, Tradition, and Infallibility*, p. 207. Beegle is quoting Olin A. Curtis, *The Christian Faith* (New York: Eaton & Mains, 1905), p. 178.
23. Beegle, *Scripture, Tradition, and Infallibility*, p. 298. Italics added.
24. Ibid., p. 286. Professor Beegle writes: "The essential trustworthiness of the Bible is a fact, and anyone who has experienced the regenerating power of Christ comes to Scripture with the assurance that it 'has the words of eternal life.' Where new evidence proves that some statement of God's Word is inaccurate, one can readily accept the fact knowing that *the essential*

truths will not be altered" (ibid., pp. 281 f.; italics added).

25. Ibid., p. 278.
26. See ibid., p. 278, 283.
27. See ibid, p. 279.
28. Ibid, p. 61.
29. Ibid., p. 65.
30. Ibid., p. 312. Italics added.
31. See ibid., p. 19.
32. See ibid., chaps. 8 and 9.
33. Ibid., p. 290.
34. Ibid.
35. See Austin Farrar, *The Glass of Vision* (London: Dacre, 1948), pp. 36–39, 57.
36. See Rudolf Bultmann, *Existence and Faith*, trans. Shubert Ogden (New York: Meridian Books, 1960), p. 52.
37. Rudolf Bultmann, *Primitive Christianity in Its Contemporary Setting*, trans. R. H. Fuller (New York: Meridian Books, Living Age Books, 1956), p. 197.
38. See Bultmann, *Existence and Faith*, pp. 85, 93 f.
39. J. Harry Cotton, *Christian Knowledge of God* (New York: Macmillan, 1951), p. 123.
40. Ibid., p. 125.
41. Robert L. Wilken, *The Myth of Christian Beginnings* (Garden City, N.Y.: Doubleday, Anchor Books, 1972), pp. 10 f. Wilken is drawing from Mircea Eliade, *Cosmos and History* (New York: Harper, Harper Torchbooks, 1959), pp. 44–46.
42. Robert Graves and Raphael Patai, *Hebrew Myths: The Book of Genesis* (New York: McGraw-Hill, 1963), p. 12.
43. Numbers 22:27–30 (RSV).
44. See Jack Finegan, *Light from the Ancient Past: The Archaeological Background of the Hebrew-Christian Religion* (Princeton, N.J.: Princeton University Press, 1946), pp. 17–18, 47–48, and fig. 22.
45. Ibid., p. 48.

CHAPTER III

Classical Theism and the Teleological Argument

DOES THE UNIVERSE HAVE OVERALL PURPOSE AND DESIGN?

Classical Theism and Providence. Theism is the view that there is one God who creates the world and exercises providential control over it. The English word 'theism' is simply taken from the Greek word *theos,* which means "God." *Classical theism* adds that God is all-powerful (omnipotent), is all-knowing (omniscient), and is present everywhere (omnipresent). Furthermore, this God is said to be perfect in every way, everlasting, good, and in no way dependent upon the world for his existence.

According to classical theists, God made the world out of nothing. Why did he make it? Because he wanted to share his love with finite creatures. *Deism* is the view that God, once he created the world, set it to run on its own and according to its own laws, without further divine intervention. By contrast, classical theists hold that God not only created the world with a certain purpose or purposes in mind, but is actively involved in directing the world in fulfillment of his purpose or purposes. Hence, the "hand of God" is said to be seen at work in both nature and human history. The word 'providence' is often used to refer to what is taken to be God's control in the universe.

You have doubtless heard people say on various occasions that such and such a happening is the will or purpose of God. Classical theists believe that despite opposition from human sin and other evil forces, God is still carrying out his plan with providential skill and care. True, things may sometimes look bad, but God is said to be steadfastly at work directing the great historical drama and leading it toward its ultimate goal.

God's Design in Nature. One of the famous arguments for the existence of the God of classical theism is often referred to as the *teleological argument*. The word 'teleology' is based on the Greek word *telos*, which means simply "end," "goal," or even "fulfilled purpose." The teleological argument for God's existence has two major parts. The first has to do with *history*; the second with *nature*. As noted above, classical theists sometimes argue that the directing influence of God may be seen in the course of history.

Classical theists who in one way or another subscribe to the teleological argument believe that the hand of God may be seen also in the grand system of nature, in which they see not only orderliness but deliberate design. This they take to be the manifestation of a superior intelligence. One of the most popular biblical texts for subscribers to the teleological argument is Psalms 19:1, "The heavens are telling the glory of God; and the firmament proclaims his handiwork" (RSV).

A great number of classical theists believe that there is widespread orderliness and harmony in the world of nature. Things are regarded as fitting together somewhat like the parts of a watch. Indeed, watchmakers are actually setting their watches by the regular patterns of the heavenly bodies, which are regarded as having been "set" by God.

Before Charles Darwin wrote *On the Origin of Species* in 1859 many scientists seemed to think of the universe or nature as being far less immense in time and space than scientists now believe it to be. They could think of it as something like a grand clock, with countless parts and pieces all working together efficiently and with marvelous precision. But beginning with the middle of the nineteenth century, the steady labors of astronomers, biologists, physicists, and other natural scientists have been producing a much more complex picture of the universe.

The question now is: Is the universe still a perfect harmony even though it is far more complex than people once believed it to be? Or is the universe, because of its great complexity, *not* a perfectly harmonious system? I once owned a watch for twenty years. It was a comparatively simple piece of machinery, with no calendar and no alarm bell. It had few problems. Then I purchased a more complex watch. Within months it partially broke down. The calendar system and the alarm system seemed to interfere with each other. The watch would keep time, but its other functions proved unreliable. So I exchanged it for another, which proved to be no better than the former one. Finally, my money was refunded, and with an additional sum of money I purchased still another watch. For a few months now it has been working smoothly. It keeps time rather well. Its calendar system is perfect. And the alarm bell also works—but not perfectly. It is sometimes off by as much as twelve minutes, although I cannot know when it will be inaccurate and when it will buzz exactly as set.

Some thinkers look upon the universe as a stupendous system of systems—like my multi-functional watch, only infinitely larger and more variegated. But do all the systems of the universe work together in perfect harmony? Do they all do exactly what they are "supposed" to do?

Many classical theists think that the universe is a magnificent and glorious harmony. And they believe that it shows definite signs of a supremely intelligent mind. A perfectly running complex watch indicates that it is the work of a very intelligent human mind. Actually, in Switzerland watches are usually made in factories or shops where a *number* of workers help shape the parts and put them together. No one person makes an entire watch. However, those who accept the teleological argument are not willing to say that nature is the work of many deities forming a holy committee. The Jews and Muslims in particular are strictly opposed to anything like polytheism. Christians, too, insist that they are not polytheists, though some of their critics say that their doctrine of the Trinity is a long step in the direction of polytheism. (According to the doctrine of the Trinity, God is "three persons in one." All three divine persons are supposed to have been involved in creating the world and also in sustaining it at every moment. Some Christians seem to imply that the three divine persons divide their work among them, so that one carries out one task more directly than do the others. Each has his particular speciality, although all three are involved in the total undertaking of the Trinity.)

The existence of a watch is no mere accident. It is not simply the chance accumulation of parts that just happen to fit together with superb precision and design. Similarly, according to the teleological argument, the universe did not just happen. It was created by a purposive, rational, and orderly cosmic inventor—namely, God.

The Orderliness of the Human Body.   "For thou didst form my inward parts, thou didst knit me together in my mother's womb."[1] In these words the psalmist expresses the classical theistic position that even the inner workings of the human organism were designed and created by God. The complexity and general harmony of the members of the body are indeed enough to stagger the mind of any engineer whose envy has not beclouded his mind.

In expressing his admiration of the dynamic harmony among the vital organs of the human body, a contemporary biomedical researcher writes:

Our smooth-muscle cells are born with complete instructions, in need of no help from us, and they work away on their own schedules, modulating the lumen of blood vessels, opening and closing tubules according to the requirements of the entire system. Secretory cells elaborate their products in privacy; the heart contracts and relaxes; hormones are sent off to react silently with cell membranes, switching adenyl cyclase, prostaglandin and other signals on and off; cells communicate with each other simply by touching; organelles send messages to other organelles; all this goes on continually, without ever a personal word from us. The arrangement is that of an ecosystem, with the operation of each part being governed by the state and function of all the other parts.[2]

Jews, Christians, Muslims, and others who hold to classical theism regard the intricate workings of the human organism as clear evidence of the existence and creative activity of the mind of God. A passage from one of the Old Testament psalms expresses these believers' feelings: "I will praise thee; for I am fearfully and wonderfully made: marvelous are thy works; and that my soul knoweth right well."[3]

The Eye As a Marvel of Divine Engineering.   Could the eye have just happened? Those who use the teleological argument to support belief in the existence of God sometimes call attention to the eye as a profound piece of evidence of a superior intelligence at work in nature. Even some writers who are not strictly classical theists are greatly impressed with the intricate detail and refinement of the eye. One of them comments: "It must not be forgotten that all the parts of an organism are necessarily coordinated."[4] How could all the numerous parts of the eye come together with such perfection? Even if the perfect combination had come about once by pure chance, why should we expect this good fortune to be continued and repeated so many times?[5] The theist can only conclude that the good fortune did not arise by pure chance but by the directing power of God. The eye is seen as a marvel of divine engineering.

SOME PROBLEMS FOR THE
TELEOLOGICAL ARGUMENT

A Question of Ends or Purposes. Those who rely upon the teleological argument sometimes confuse two issues. The first has to do with the issue of internal harmony. Given a particular entity (e.g., the eye, the nose, or the solar system), we may ask if the several members composing it do in fact work together harmoniously, with no member upsetting the activity of another. The second issue has to do with what the particular entity is *for*. For example, what is the divine purpose for the nose? Why did God invent it? Why did he include it in his original blueprints, so to speak?

The second question is a much more difficult question to deal with. Perhaps we should say that the nose was designed by God to serve a number of purposes. For example, the deity may have foreseen that someday the eyes of some human beings—marvelous as they are—would not always function perfectly for reading or for seeing at great distances. So perhaps God simply added on a protruding nose in light of his knowledge that eventually some human beings would need something on which to hang their eyeglasses. Furthermore, the need for glasses creates jobs for lens-grinders, oculists, and others. In this way the protruding nose indirectly helps solve the unemployment problem that God undoubtedly knew would eventually come about.

Or perhaps God simply designed the nose to function as a small drainage system. Or, just as the ducts in the attic of a house were designed to carry both cold air in the summer and hot air in the winter, so perhaps God designed the nose to do more than one job. And why not? This would surely make for more compactness. Imagine how awkward we would be if, for every activity and function, we had to have an additional part built into our organism. Instead of a nose to take care of many functions, we would have to have a whole warehouse of parts —a breather, a sneezer, a drainage outlet, a smeller and sniffer, a lump for our glasses to rest on, etc. To be sure, the nose sometimes gets in the way of kissing, but, then, that may be one of God's ways of keeping our passions in check. Ingenious?

We could probably go on showing how the nose is a wondrous instrument for doing many useful things.

Unfortunately, what this seems to boil down to is this: For every way *we* can find to use the nose, the teleological argument tends to assume that *God* had in mind that the nose be put to use in these very same ways. It is, of course, fortunate for *hunters* that the tail of the cottontail rabbit is white, but can we be sure that *God* had it in mind to make the cottontail an easier target for hunters?

Consider the many functions of the human leg. Did God design it for kicking field goals? Did he have in mind karate kicks? Jogging? Trapeze stunts? Dancing? Indeed, how do we discover what exactly God had in mind when he is supposed to have designed the leg? Consider the hand. It is a source of many activities or functions—from washing one's face to holding a pornographic book. Exactly what did God design the hand *for*?

More complicated are entities such as Mars and fleas. Can we say that God had something specifically in mind when he made Mars? If not, then can we say that it serves his purpose? Let us assume that God designed fleas. Why did he? Are they today serving perfectly his goal for them? If we do not know what that goal is, then we cannot determine whether the fleas are doing what was expected of them.

General Ends and Purposes. Understandably, sensitive classical theists are sometimes hesitant to speak of God's specific and exact goals or purposes. In times past, believers were often very sure that they knew what God had in mind for their lives or for the lives of other people. In one Baptist college a few years ago, a young Christian announced to a pretty coed that God had directed him to marry her. Although she was a devout Christian, the young woman insisted that the Heavenly Father had not revealed his divine design to her on this matter. We might suspect that the young man confused his own designs on the woman with God's design for their separate lives.

The point here is that today a large number of Christians are more sensitive to the natural and cultural variables of life than perhaps were some Christians in times past. Rather than the Lord's will, the young man's own id may have moved him, unless the Lord was working "through" the man's id. Christians still believe that God works in mysterious ways, and they are often willing to leave it a mystery.

But this appeal to mystery does a disservice to the teleological argument. For if we cannot know exactly what God's goal or will is, then we cannot honestly conclude that the members and parts of the world are in fact serving the divine purpose or purposes. Much of the teleological argument rests on the claim that the world can be understood as shaping up under the direction of God. But if we do not know what God is about, what his ends and purposes are, then we cannot be sure that the *means* that we observe are in fact serving their ends. It may be that God has failed miserably to carry out his designs. If he designed to "save" everyone, he will apparently not succeed if the doctrine of hell is to be taken seriously at all.

Classical theists seem to be caught in something of a dilemma. If they become too *specific* in naming God's purposes, then they end up in great controversies among themselves in their attempts to say what these divine purposes are. One group of believers claims one thing, a second group claims another, and so on and on, until the teleological argument becomes choked in a cloud of dust.

On the other hand, if the divine purposes are too *general*, then the teleological argument—or at least a great portion of it—never actually says anything that can be nailed down, in which case it is unintelligible at best and verbal trickery at worst. A few years after the Supreme Court had decided against segregation, a clergyman in Chattanooga, Tennessee, stated that while God's purpose was to have integration in heaven, his purpose on earth was to maintain segregation. The noted early-nineteenth-century preacher and college president Lyman Beecher thought it was the will of God to deny to blacks of his time social equality with whites.[6] The art of divining the purposes of God in historical settings seems to vary greatly from one religious group to another. Some Christians and Jews imply that God's will must be defined as whatever is decent and good. This means that the real and difficult task is to try to decide on the decent course of action in a temporal setting and to forget about divining God's intentions and purposes.[7] In order for the teleological argument in support of the existence of God to be an argument at all, it must specify something. It must say what God's goals and designs are and are not. Then it must show that in fact these goals have been considerably approximated. This is a risky argument because it opens the possibility that it might be falsified. That is, the teleological argument could conceivably be used *against* classical theism if it does not work. In a later chapter we will deal more thoroughly with the question of God's putative goals and his success or failure in achieving them. We can now focus on that part of the teleological argument which deals with the harmony of the parts of nature.

THE CHALLENGE OF DISHARMONY IN NATURE

It is unfortunately true that a great number of college students complete their degree without any notion of the revolution that Charles Darwin's research and theorizing produced in the world of ideas. Darwin was perhaps one of the first human beings to grasp in any profound way the enormous amount of time that passed before our arrival on the scene. He also made us aware of the enormous amount of waste that has gone on at the biological level of existence. As a later writer has noted,

Hegner, in his amusing and informing book, *Big Fleas Have Little Fleas*, mentions a protozoon one individual of which is able to have 28,000,000 offspring in a single month—a rate of propagation such that if unchecked, it would fill the physical universe with this species. The struggle for survival entails a death rate among protozoa which causes the figures of the national debt to pale into insignificance. Southerland, in *The Origin and Growth of Moral Instinct*, has calculated that the number of fish that are eating other fish in any given minute is about equal to the number of drops of water going over Niagara Falls in that minute.[8]

The same writer goes on to note the numerous unsuccessful biological experiments, the many species that simply failed in their struggle for survival.[9] Despite romantic notions of nature, the fact seems to be that much of the animal kingdom lives in perpetual fear and at war with other animals. Martin Luther used to think that birds sang to the glory of God, whereas more informed students of bird life have concluded that the bird's song serves largely as a warning to other birds to keep away from his personal territory. The illness, death, aggression, surds, and destructive patterns in nature do not measure up to a notion of harmonious nature.

The Old Testament psalmist may have said that the heavens manifest the glory of God, but the apostle Paul wrote that "the whole creation has been groaning in travail together until now."[10] It is not that the two biblical writers had in mind two worlds of creation. It is simply that the psalmist saw harmony in nature, whereas Paul saw considerable disharmony. Perhaps one reason that these two very diverse interpretations can exist in the same Bible is that the universe seems to have both a measure of order and a measure of chaos. Indeed, if the picture of the world that science has thus far made possible comes anywhere near to the truth, then we must say that most regions of the vast universe "are filled by chaotic radiation."[11]

The teleological argument seems to select the harmony while ignoring the great amount of disharmony and conflict in the cosmos. Old-time theologians used to put forth the argument that the disharmony in nature really serves God's purpose, too. For example, they supposed a tornado to be God's judgment on the very wicked. Unfortunately, in the spring of 1974 a tornado swept through the campus of the Southern Baptist Seminary in Louisville, Kentucky, and created considerable damage, uprooting many great and beautiful trees. Less than fifteen years before, another Southern Baptist school—Baylor University, a thousand miles away in Texas—had been affected by a tornado, and a philosophy teacher there had been killed. The teacher hired to replace the dead professor was an atheist; but while the atheist remained on campus, the Baptist college was not threatened by another tornado.

If tornadoes are not a part of the harmony of nature, but rather are God's special instruments of punishment, then must we conclude that the Lord of the universe has it in for Southern Baptists? The prostitution and gambling in Las Vegas have not been hit by a tornado. So is God more set against Southern Baptists than against Las Vegas? These may seem silly questions to today's Christians, Muslims, and Jews, but the questions come from the same line of thought that many of these classical theists have embraced in past generations.

As philosophers such as Immanuel Kant, John Stuart Mill, and perhaps David Hume have suggested, the argument based on order and harmony in the universe will not support the conclusion that there is a good deity whose knowledge and power are unlimited. The teleological argument might, however, support the hypothesis of a deity who, though good, is limited in his power to keep nature under perfect control. In short, the case for classical theism cannot count on the teleological argument to help it, for the argument better supports the hypothesis of either no God at all or a limited God.[12]

Classical theists usually concede that the teleological argument is not a compelling argument for their God, but they think that it is a supportive argument. That is, this argument from design is taken to be a part of a cluster of reasons which, when combined together, support belief in classical religious theism.[13] One leg will not hold up a table, but when combined with three other legs, it will do the job.

Opponents of this argument reply that the arguments for classical theism are more like links in a chain than table legs. If one of the links is weak—as the teleological argument is—then the entire chain is thereby just as weak. Furthermore, say these opponents, the evidence that the argument from design relies upon may better be used in support of at least two views other than classical theism. That is, (1) either God's power, though great, is less than what classical theism requires, or (2) there is no God at all. The theory of evolution seems to be more compatible with either of these two views than it is with classical theism.

EVOLUTION: A RIVAL HYPOTHESIS

No "Pure Chance."   The theory of evolution might fit either with the view of a benevolent and creative God whose power is limited or with the view that nature alone is the whole of reality: Before looking briefly at the theory of evolution as it relates to the question of God's existence, a misleading argument needs to be disposed of.

Some classical theists—not all—make the argument that the eye and other genuinely marvelous things of nature could not have happened "merely by pure chance." It is difficult to determine who this theistic argument is directed against. Certainly those who accept a present-day version of Darwinian evolution do not think that the eye developed by "pure chance" (whatever that would be). The whole point of the theory of evolution is to show how the eye did in fact develop by natural selection rather than by either "pure chance" or "supernatural miracle." We will soon come back to this controversy about socalled "pure chance."

When classical Christian theists say that God made the eyes of all animals and insects, they presumably do not mean to say that once upon a time there was no eye on the face of the earth and then the next minute—presto!—a fully developed eye simply popped into existence out of nowhere, as if by magic. To be sure, there doubtless are a number of theists who have a kind of magical view of God's involvement in the world. But we must give our attention to the more critical-minded theists. There are some theists who hold that the theory of evolution and some theory of God are compatible views. Whether evolution and *classical* theism can be blended is doubtful, but there are other versions of theism that might be more compatible with evolution.

For the moment, let us consider the theory of evolution. One of its major theses is that species tend to die off if they happen not to develop means for coping with their environment. The dinosaur survived quite well for many years until his environment changed. Lacking the organs to meet the new conditions, the huge animal simply perished. Certain species survive not because of their outstanding organs but because they propagate rapidly and numerously.

Another major theme of evolution is that the members of any given species are not all precisely alike. There are certain *variations* that come about. The important thing is that even though these numerous variations were not designed by cosmic intelligence, nevertheless some of them proved very useful in helping individuals, or at least the species, to survive in a changing environment. Of course, most variations do not have much survival value, but that is what might be expected of a process that develops without any overall cosmic designer.

Implicit here is the view that nature is not simply a closed geometric scheme. Rather, the evolutionist regards it as having some temporal flow; that is simply the way nature is. Of course, the classical theist might ask *why* nature should be as it is. And the evolutionist might, in turn, ask a similar question with regard to God. Usually the theist's answer is that God is just the way he is; that is how he happens to be. This is not to say that God is what he is by "pure chance"; it means, rather, that God is the stopping point for explaining things.

But, similarly, the evolutionist might say that it is not by "pure chance" that nature is what it is; rather, nature is the ultimate stopping point for all explanations. There is no outside reason why nature as a whole should even exist, any more than, for a theist, there should be any outside reason why God as a whole should exist. The theist says God just exists, and that is that; and the evolutionist replies that nature exists, and that is that.

However, the evolutionist believes that it is possible to explain in varying degrees how things develop *within* nature. The theory of evolution is concerned with tracing the gradual development of nature's organs and organisms.

The Evolution of the Eye.   Keep in mind that Darwin came up with considerable evidence to support his conjecture that numerous species have been developing for many more generations than was previously imagined by most scientists of his day. Darwin's conjecture was subjected to serious crossfire and testing, but it has held up powerfully well and is more thoroughly supported by evidence today than it was in Darwin's own time.

Bats are blind. But they do have an organ that keeps them from crashing into trees and hillsides. Those bats *without* this added sensitivity, or something comparable, would predictably not survive as well as their more fortunate relatives. According to the evolutionist, the ancient forerunner of the eye was not designed or planned by divine intelligence, but rather occurred as simply one among numerous variations that happened to members of species. This proto-eye, let us call it, was simply a new kind of sensitivity to objects in the environment. In its early forms it was merely a light-sensitive spot on the organism. It happened to be useful to animals in seeking food and in avoiding harmful conditions in the environment.[14]

This proto-eye would normally have the side-effect of increasing the chances of an animal's survival. By contrast, those organisms without a similar sensitive organ would be doomed to destruction within certain kinds of environments. (To be sure, *inside* an organism are smaller organisms that in some respects are both parts of the larger organism and parasites upon it. The skin of the larger organism shields the smaller organisms against an environment that the larger organism usually copes with successfully.)

The point here is that at least some aspects of nature are more like a great battleground than like the neat watch-like systems imagined by some classical theists. There is an enormous amount of destruction and disharmony in nature. And yet there are also areas of cooperation. The human body, for example, is only one among countless organisms that may be regarded as a harmonious system of smaller organisms. Hence, nature has not only great disharmony, chaos, and destruction, but also countless systems of harmony and creative thrust. In that sense, nature seems to be the only example of perpetual motion, which is comparable to what in theology is God's self-creating power. Most evolutionists regard nature to be without any clear overriding goal, but nevertheless enormously variegated, rich, strewn with possibilities, and forever unfinished. In other words, there are more things in nature (past, present, and future) than are dreamed of in your theology!

The Omega Point.   Despite the fact that the universe does not seem clearly to be going toward any ultimate or omega point, classical theists nevertheless claim that because God transcends the universe, he will eventually bring it to its ultimate destiny. Critics of classical theism regard this boast to be hardly more than mere talk. The notion of an *ultimate* destiny for *living* beings may even be self-contradictory. Death is an ultimate end, but classical theists insist that a living *ultimate* end is somehow possible. Apparently the problem in this controversy is not so much to determine whether there is an ultimate end, as to determine whether the notion of a living ultimate destiny or end is intelligible.

Multiple Functions of an Organ.   Many evolutionists believe that, without making reference to any detailed designs of God for the world, they can go a long way toward accounting for the fact that one organ may serve more than one end or goal. Instead of saying that God designed the nose to hang glasses on, the evolutionists need only say that changing conditions made the nose useful in serving some of the interests of the organism that previously it had not served. *Having* an organ that serves the organism in one way is one thing; but it is another thing for this same organ (e.g., the thumb) to become *used* in new ways. The evolutionists believe that they do not have the embarrassment that classical theists have in trying to determine whether or not the new ways of using an organ are what the Lord God of the universe *intended* for it.

Some classical theists reply that God, in effect, gave people some *general* features and organs, and then he gave them the free will to use the organs in whatever way they pleased, hopefully within moral limits. Sometimes this so-called "gift of free will" is regarded as a sort of invisible adaptable organ itself, not quite in nature but nevertheless having reality as a moral and spiritual entity. Unfortunately, this conjecture must be disqualified if it insists on exempting itself from ever being tested. At its best, it is a fruitful myth that eventually may yield well-formulated procedures for testing its claims. Whether the claims will hold is a question that must be pursued in another chapter.

THE DEVIL HYPOTHESIS

Some classical theists think that a cosmic being other than God must be responsible for the destruction in the world. This other being must be more powerful than human beings but less powerful than God. Earlier in this chapter, mention was made of tornadoes that adversely affected the interests of Baptists in Louisville, Kentucky, and Waco, Texas. In Louisville, the same previously mentioned tornado destroyed the home of a Baptist minister. Another Baptist minister decided to remain in his church during the storm in order to continue midweek prayer services. Instead of being restrained, the storm destroyed the church and killed the praying minister.[15]

Oral Roberts has been saying for years that God is responsible for his school's remarkable growth and development. On June 8, 1974, however, a tornado hit the campus in Tulsa, Oklahoma, and destroyed the Oral Roberts Association Headquarters Building and inflicted heavy damage on the University Aerobics Gymnasium. When destructive forces seem to go especially against Christian enterprises and interests, a shift in thinking is likely to come about in trying to explain the misfortune. Instead of saying that God caused the destruction of these Christian endeavors, many Christians feel it necessary to fall back on the Devil hypothesis. The Devil, enraged at the conspicuous numerical success of both the Southern Baptists and Oral Roberts' ministry, set out to destroy what he could of them.

The famous Protestant reformer Martin Luther believed that storms were caused by the Devil and his associates. In his earlier years, Luther was himself struck by lightning, and this experience greatly impressed itself upon his memory. Like many Catholics of his day, he believed that storms were in actuality the chaotic activity of reckless demons. One apostle spoke of Satan as the "prince of the power of the air." A Catholic priest, Locatelli, wrote a book with the following interesting title: *Exorcisms Most Powerful and Efficacious for the Dispelling of Aërial Tempests, Whether Raised by Demons at Their Own Instance or at the Beck of Some Servant of the Devil.*[16]

Considerable ambivalence exists among orthodox Christians as to whether God or Satan causes violent storms, tornadoes, and the like. A kind of shaky compromise between these two views contends that Satan does the destructive work but only within the limits that God establishes for him. This naturally raises the question as to why God should yield *any* ground to Satan. Some Christians go so far as to imply that when God wants to punish or to destroy, he delegates Satan to do the foul work on God's behalf.

Other Christians seem to think that God will go to great lengths to protect Satan's "freedom of choice." In other words, one of the presumed purposes of God is to give human beings and Satan freedom of choice, even if it means Satan's disrupting the harmony of nature and destroying numerous values. Critics of this viewpoint point out that according to the admission of orthodox Christianity, Satan is *not* free to choose a better life for himself: he is not going to be reformed or redeemed. Most Christians do not pray for Satan's salvation. Hence, when God presumably preserves Satan's freedom of choice, he seems to have restricted Satan's *range* of choices to only foul deeds and destructiveness. Satan is not free to do anything decent. Thus, such a limited horizon of freedom seems certainly of less value than the things that Satan is permitted or directed to destroy.

If Satan were a kind of cosmic garbage collector eliminating the evils of the world, then the use of his services would reflect the wisdom and goodness of God. But the destruction and agony that Satan presumably brings about is more like the creation of destruction and waste than the elimination of it. It is not surprising, therefore, that even among Christians who believe that Satan does exist, there is a growing reluctance to designate exactly where Satan's hand is seen at work. When a child dies, some Christians say it is the will of God. Others say it is the work of Satan. Some say it is both. And, of course, there are other explanations which find no place for the Satan hypothesis at all. However, great evils and disharmony do still exist in the universe, and they must somehow be explained if the teleological argument for classical theism is to command respect. In Chapter VI this question of evil in the world will be more thoroughly examined.

THE WIDER TELEOLOGICAL ARGUMENT

Beyond the Traditional Version of the Argument.   The wider or broader teleological argument is a significant modification of the traditional teleological argument. This new version does not stress the overall purpose of creation. Rather it stresses the existence of *conditions* that make possible numerous finite harmonies and purposes within creation. Or to state this point in another way, the overall goal of the universe is to make it possible for a vast array of finite forms of life to have their own interests and goals. God is conceived of as good and powerful if his world of nature provides the natural conditions for these creatures—including human beings—to satisfy as many of their desires and interests as possible. This viewpoint needs further elaboration.

Thought and Thing Correspond Practically.   First, the world might have been an unintelligible whirl of chaos negating all possibility of knowledge and communication. Fortunately, however, there is considerable correspondence between intelligence and the world of things. If this were not so, you and I could neither find our way about nor make practical categories and generalizations that serve us in satisfying many of our aspirations.[17]

Evidence from Life.   In the second place, the wider teleological argument uses evolution as evidence *for* the existence of God. Darwin spoke of chance variations. But where do these variations come from? The most original proponent of this wider argument, Frederick R. Tennant, points out that the Darwinian notion of the "*survival* of the fittest" already presupposes "the *arrival* of the fit." Without the vital push toward further evolving, nature as a whole would decline into sterility and death. Is it not therefore possible that some external Being is the source of this push?[18]

The Inorganic Environment.   Professor Tennant is quite aware that his attempt to utilize the theory of evolution extracts a price. Unlike traditional teleologists, he can no longer speak of the special design of *each and every* product of evolution. Rather, the emphasis falls on general directivity in the process. This implies that there is a certain amount of free play in the universe, and that is where both the risk of danger and the possibility of freedom enter in. Nevertheless, a certain amount of harmony pervades the process of evolution. In fact, says Tennant, the unique assemblages of unique properties produce a vast and complex environment of the inorganic which the organic needs for its survival. Tennant is struck by the fact that this inorganic world seems itself in some ways to resemble an organism.[19] He thinks that there is reason to suspect that the inorganic world is not the accumulation of blind rolls of the dice. Rather, he suspects "the dice to have been loaded."[20]

Aesthetic Experience.   The coming together of intelligence and the organic realm not only makes practical knowledge possible, but also produces beauty. The world contains appreciation and aesthetic values as well as knowledge. It is as if the emergence of the human mind brings out the best in nature, as if mind were nature's true fulfillment. Tennant might have noted that the aesthetic experience even exists for the "lower" species on the ladder of evolution. He is eager to argue that "Nature is meaningless and valueless without God behind it and man in front."[21] What this means is that nature contains the objective factor making the experience of beauty possible, and the presence of the human species brings this possibility into realization. Nature, then, gives birth to the creature—man —that can more fully appreciate her. But nature if it were blind, says Tennant, could not have brought about a creature with such capacity for appreciation of beauty.[22]

Moral Values.   According to Tennant, morality is something that must be *won*; it is not simply bestowed upon human beings. Morality thus has its roots in nature. This is Tennant's way of saying that nature, rather than being blindly run, would seem to be the manifestation of a superior intelligence who designs to bring about the moral experience among human beings.[23]

One of Tennant's students, Peter A. Bertocci, adds that sometimes hardship and evil are disciplinary.[24] The thought here is that moral values often cannot develop except through discipline, which itself comes in response to the hard conditions of life. Hence, just because there is hardship in the world does not entail that it is all contrary to the designs of a good God. The hardships often serve in generating moral values.

But this raises a question about God's moral values. Many

classical theists think that God enjoys great moral values even though he does not suffer temptations, hardship, and evil. So why should his human creatures be forced to endure such great hardships in order to enjoy moral values? Does God lack the power to create a finite person both free and morally developed?

IMPLICATIONS OF THE WIDER
TELEOLOGICAL ARGUMENT

Bertocci develops Tennant's leads with clarity and thoroughness. But unlike Tennant, Professor Bertocci concludes that the teleological argument cannot support belief in classical theism. Very frankly he notes that sometimes hardships are *not* disciplinary. Indeed, they may beat a person down to the point where he is far from the vibrant moral and aesthetic human being spoken of by Tennant.[25] Through a number of chapters Bertocci builds a case for the hypothesis of a God who is morally good but admittedly less than all-powerful and omniscient. Classical theism is thus judged to be indefensible. In a later chapter we will deal with the issue of evil in a world that is said to have been created by God.

NOTES

1. Psalms 139:13 (RSV).
2. Lewis Thomas, "Notes of a Biology Watcher: Autonomy," *New England Journal of Medicine* 287, no. 2 (1972): 90–91. This article appears in Thomas' book, *Lives of a Cell: Notes of a Biology Watcher* (New York: Viking, 1974).
3. Psalms 139:14 (KJV). I am aware that this translation is probably far from being a reliable representation of the original Hebrew. But ever since early in the seventeenth century, when the King James version of the Bible came out, this translation has been influential among Christians in English-speaking countries.
4. Henri Bergson, *Creative Evolution,* trans. Arthur Mitchell (London: Macmillan, 1911), p. 67.
5. Ibid., pp. 68–71.
6. See J. Earl Thompson, Jr., "The Reform of Racist Religion," in *The Religion of the Republic*, ed. Elwyn Smith (Philadelphia: Fortress Press, 1971), pp. 282 f.
7. Before Darwin, one of the most noted defenders of the teleological argument was William Paley. He wrote: "God Almighty

wills and wishes the happiness of his creatures; and, consequently, that those actions, which promote that will and wish, must be agreeable to him; and the contrary" ("Principles of Moral and Political Philosophy," in *British Moralists*, ed. D. D. Raphael [Oxford: Clarendon Press, 1969], p. 261).

8. E. S. Brightman, *A Philosophy of Religion* (Englewood Cliffs, N.J.: Prentice-Hall, 1940), pp. 315 f.

9. Ibid., p. 316.

10. Romans 8:22 (RSV).

11. Karl Popper, *Objective Knowledge: An Evolutionary Approach* (New York: Oxford University Press, 1973), p. 204.

12. On the question of divine control, see Peter H. Hare and Edward H. Madden, "Evil and Persuasive Power," *Process Studies* 2, no. 1 (Spring 1972): 44–48; J. E. Barnhart, "Persuasive and Coercive Power in Process Metaphysics," *Process Studies* 3, no. 3 (Fall 1973): 153–157.

13. See R. G. Swinburne, "The Argument from Design: A Defense," *Religious Studies* 8, no. 3 (September 1972): 204.

14. On the evolution of the eye see Popper, *Objective Knowledge*, chap. 7.

15. See *Baptist and Reflector* 140, no. 16 (18 April 1974): 10. In the summer of 1974 the Milner Baptist Church of Milner, Georgia, was struck by lightning and burned to the ground (see *Baptist and Reflector* 140 [1 August 1974]: 7). Lightning destroyed some of the First Baptist Church of Ridgely, Tennessee, on August 26, 1974 (see *Baptist and Reflector* 140 [19 September 1974]: 4).

16. See A. D. White, *A History of the Warfare of Science with Theology in Christendom*, 2 vols. (1896; reprint ed., New York: Dover, 1960), 1:336–345.

17. See Frederick R. Tennant, *Philosophical Theology*, 2 vols. (Cambridge: Cambridge University Press, 1930), 2:82. This work is one of the foremost defenses of the broader teleological argument.

18. See ibid., p. 85.

19. See ibid., p. 86.

20. Ibid., p. 87.

21. Ibid., p. 90.

22. See ibid., p. 93.

23. See ibid., pp. 101–103.

24. See Peter A. Bertocci, *Introduction to the Philosophy of Religion* (Englewood Cliffs, N.J.: Prentice-Hall, 1951), p. 395.

25. See ibid., pp. 397–399.

CHAPTER IV

Classical Theism and the Cosmological Argument

DOES THE UNIVERSE NEED A CAUSE?

A Dependent World and an Independent Creator. The Greek word for "universe" is *kosmos*. The *cosmo*logical argument for the existence of God asserts that the cosmos or universe needed a creator. Suppose you ask: Where did the universe come from? How did it all get started? The answer provided by the cosmological argument is that the creator made it from nothing (*ex nihilo*). The universe is assumed to be a dependent being. The special term used to express this dependency is *contingency*. If the cosmos is wholly contingent, it needs something that is not contingent or dependent. That is, it must depend on something that is completely and absolutely independent. The special term used to express this absolute independence is *necessity* or *necessary being*. Those who employ the cosmological argument say that the creator alone is necessary being, whereas the universe (world, nature, cosmos) is wholly contingent or dependent. (Sometimes the cosmological argument is called the *causal* argument because it emphasizes the belief that the creator *causes* the world to exist.)

Could the Universe Be without Beginning or End? Strictly speaking, the cosmological argument allows for the possibility that the world might be everlasting: that is, without either beginning or termination. But in order for that to be possible, the creator must also be everlasting. At least that is what the cosmological argument contends. To say that the universe might be everlasting is not, however, to deny that it goes through numerous changes and processes. Indeed, some believers in the cosmological argument claim that the changes within the universe are examples (or at least symptoms) of the fact that the universe is contingent rather than necessary. The creator, on the other hand, never changes; he is immutable.

Many Jews, Christians, and Muslims hold that in fact the universe is not everlasting, although it might have been had the creator desired to have a universe with him throughout all eternity. Indeed, many believers say that although the universe has not always existed, God will nevertheless see to it that some aspects of it (e.g., at least some of the people in it) will never perish. However, these believers hold that the world once did not exist. Or at least if it did, it existed only as a possibility in the creator's mind.

Change and Motion.   There are various versions of the cosmological argument, but I am offering you the standard version. The name of Thomas Aquinas is most readily associated with this argument. As a Christian theologian, Thomas has enjoyed considerable influence on the thinking of classical theists in the Western world.

According to Thomas, we know that the universe is contingent or dependent on something beyond itself, because around us everywhere we observe that the members of the universe are moving and changing. Today we know even better than did Thomas that, say, a huge rock is changing according to its own time schedule. A large boulder in Colorado is an entire city of atoms moving and whirling about. Futhermore, the wind and rain are slowly but surely changing the face of proud and sturdy boulders. In short, the whole world seems to be perpetually in motion, each part changing at its own particular rate.

Now, says Thomas, if you observe carefully, you will see that nothing moves itself. Before the pages of this book turned, *you* turned them. Or if not you, then someone else, or perhaps the wind turned them. In any case, whatever moves is moved by something else, which Thomas calls the 'instrument'. You are the instrument for turning the pages of your book. But before that, some other instrument moved you to turn the pages, and so on and on.

But how far is on and on? Here is where some classical theists step in with their causal argument for God's existence. They argue that it is absurd to believe that all this moving could be traced back infinitely into the past. Somewhere along the way there had to be something or someone who is not moved. This being must exist, not as a part of the series of movements, but as the *originator* of the series. Why is this so?

The answer of some classical theists is that if the first mover is itself moving, then it is not really the first mover after all. It is only an instrument. So we must keep pushing back until we finally do come to the real and true First Mover. Inasmuch as it is not itself moved, it may be called the Unmoved Mover. Thus, the First or Prime Mover and the Unmoved Mover turn out to be one and the same eternal reality that never changes.

First Cause Is Necessary Cause.   However, Thomas Aquinas sets for himself an even more difficult task, for he is not denying the possibility of an *everlasting world or series of motions and changes going back through an infinity of time*. In other words, he realizes that the idea of an everlasting world, without beginning or end, is not absurd. But he thinks it *is* absurd to think that an everlasting world or universe could run by its own power. What Thomas is concerned to show is that motion or change itself—even within an everlasting universe— is a sign of *contingency*. That is, wherever there is change, there is dependency. So, even if there were an infinite series of changes running forever into the remote past, nevertheless this *infinite series* would itself require something unchanging and independent to maintain it.[1] Hence, for Thomas, the First Cause must not be understood to be merely the first in a long series of causes. Rather, it is the Ultimate Cause or Necessary Cause. It is the necessary cause in the sense that, without it, the universe as a system of motions and changes would never have come into existence in the first place.

To throw light on Thomas' point, an illustration may be taken from a person's footprints in the sand. The prints could not make themselves. The person making them is their cause. Of course, it is conceivable that an infinity of footprints might exist. But if so, then there must be also an everlasting person making them for infinity. If the world is everlasting, it must be perpetually caused by the everlasting creator. Without the creator, the world could no more exist than could footprints without someone to make them.

Might the Universe Never Have Been?   According to the cosmological argument, there is not one thing in the entire universe that just had to be. This is a way of saying that things might never have come into existence at all. So, why did *anything* come into existence? Why did the *whole universe* come into existence? Why should there be something rather than nothing?

The cosmological argument maintains that there is no way to answer this question without admitting the existence of a Necessary Being. It is a Necessary Being for two reasons. First, it exists necessarily in that it could not do other than continue to exist. Second, its existence is *absolutely necessary* for the existence of everything else. All other beings are contingent. They depend on one another; they all depend on the Necessary Being.

Therefore, according to the cosmological argument, this self-contained Being is the ultimate answer to the question, "Why should there be something rather than nothing?" We are told that the universe exists because the Necessary Being or God wanted it and created it.

Implicit in this answer, of course, is the assumption that this God enjoyed the *power* to do what he wanted. But how can we be sure that this is precisely the world he wanted? After all, he might have wanted a better universe but simply lacked the power to create it. This is another issue, which we will have to postpone until a later chapter.

Does Necessary Being Depend on Contingent Being? The cosmological argument says that we come to the view of Necessary Being as we come to realize that our world is thoroughly contingent. Inasmuch as our world obviously does exist, there must be some Being that is not dependent, and upon which the world absolutely depends for its existence.[2]

But let us speculate a bit on this issue. Suppose there were no universe or world at all. Then would there be a God or Necessary Being? Thomas' answer is that God would still exist as he had always existed. If Thomas did not accept this conclusion, he would have to say that God's existence depends upon the world's existence. Thomas thinks that he has already shown that the world might not have existed. But he is not prepared to say that if there had been no world, then God also might never have existed. So, for Thomas, God exists whether or not the world exists. In no way is God dependent on anything.

But let us just suppose for the moment that God *is* dependent on something for his existence. What then? Well, if that thing had never come into existence, then God would never have existed. Or if that thing on which God depends should suddenly cease to exist, then God, too, would cease to exist.

Of course, if the believers in the cosmological argument are correct, then the thing on which God depends would certainly never have existed in the first place. Why? Because in order for it to exist, it must draw its existence from some being that does not depend on anything for its own existence. And that being would be God, the only true Necessary Being. Thomas' point is that if there were no Necessary Being or God, there would today be absolutely nothing, no world at all. But inasmuch as it is obvious to any sane person that something does in fact exist today, we must conclude that there exists a Necessary Being who is absolutely independent.

An Infinite Time Ago and an Infinite Time in the Future. Followers of Thomas Aquinas offer the following very interesting and curious argument. They say, in effect, that the universe would have used itself up by now had it not been constantly replenished by the Necessary Being.[3] In responding to this, one critic of the Thomists claims that the universe may eventually perish. But he sees no reason to insist that it must have *already* perished.[4]

However, this point of disagreement between Thomists and their critics illustrates just how very complicated is the notion of infinite time. A proponent of the cosmological argument might possibly argue that we have *already* gone through an infinity of time. In which case, the world would have already ceased to exist—*unless* there were an infinite God to replenish it. Let me spell out this argument. If a universe (without God) really does go *back* infinitely into time and is without any beginning point whatsoever, then has it not *already been continuing infinitely*? Imagine the universe at a point a trillion years ago. At that point it will have already been in existence for an infinite amount of time. In fact, at any point in the dim, remote past you could say the universe will already have been infinitely old. To be sure, various forms of the universe have come and gone, but as a whole it has been going on forever, and hence it has already passed through an infinity of time.

Now, this argument seems to imply that it is impossible for the universe to have an infinite time in the *past* without having also an infinite time in the *future*. If the universe had no beginning, neither can it have an ending.

Only if something has a *beginning* can it have an *ending*. This implies further that if we had sufficient evidence to say that the universe will eventually perish totally, then we could conclude that it must have had a beginning and hence does not reach back infinitely into the past. Unfortunately, it is a matter of honest debate as to whether we can say that the world either will *end* in the future or once *began* at some time in the past. To be sure, there are various *forms* of the universe that have come into being and passed away. But that is different from the universe in its entirety.

There is something curious about the argumentation as to whether the universe is or is not infinite in time. If the universe does go back infinitely in time, and hence forward infinitely into the future, then it would seem to be dependent on nothing outside itself. Hence, it would itself be the Necessary Being! It would need nothing other than itself.

On the other hand, if the universe did begin, then it would seem to have either come from nothing or to have been created by God. Classical theists are forced to assert the curious doctrine that God made the world *out of nothing*. They have to assert this in order to avoid admitting that God found it necessary to make use of some everlasting raw material or energy that he did not create. Plato could believe that a boundless supply of raw material has existed forever along with God, and that God shapes the world out of this endless reservoir of energy. But classical theists insist that God was not dependent on either this or anything else. Hence, if he is the creator, he must create from nothing.

SOME PROBLEMS FOR THE COSMOLOGICAL ARGUMENT

Does God Change? Is He Moved?   One of the favorite biblical passages among those who emphasize the cosmological argument is Malachi 3:6: *"For I the Lord do not change."*[5] There are many other passages indicating the changelessness of God. Among Christians, Jesus Christ is regarded as a member of the Godhead. Hence, when a New Testament writer says that "Jesus Christ is the same yesterday and today and for ever," Christians often assume that this is a reference to God's changelessness.[6]

On the other hand, the Bible is filled with passages indicating that God does change in at least some respects. Amos 7:3; Jonah 4:2; Exodus 32:12 and 14; 1 Samuel 15:35; and 2 Samuel 24:16 are some of the passages asserting that God sometimes *repented*. Attempting to qualify such passages so that God is not made to appear to have done something very evil for which he had to repent, theologians sometimes explain that the word 'repent' really means *change*. That is, God repented in the sense that he changed his mind, intention, action, or attitude.

It is extremely difficult to sweep under the rug all the passages in the Bible that portray God as being moved by such things as prayers, the sins of people, and their afflictions. The natural way of understanding these passages that portray God as a personal being is to suppose that the writers felt that something *caused* God to do one thing rather than another. In short, God, like things of the universe, changes whenever certain conditions come into play.

Throughout the Bible it is assumed that God *responds* to human beings. Indeed, when saying that God exemplifies loving kindness, believers regard it to be his very nature to respond in some ways rather than other ways. People effect in him certain changes and responses. If *they* change in certain ways, *he* will change in certain ways. "Draw near to God and he will draw near to you."[7] Most of the biblical writers seem to take for granted contingent and conditional dimensions in the life of the deity. God is regarded as *moved* by the sufferings of people.[8] The Greek philosopher Aristotle felt it is necessary to conclude that his God did not so much as know that human beings or the world even existed. Why? Because to know something outside oneself—even God's own self—is to *be affected and influenced by what one knows*. Hence, Aristotle's Unmoved Mover could know only his own thoughts in one eternal moment: absolutely nothing could touch or move him.

But the Hebrews and Christians could not easily think of their God in this way. To them, God is involved, active, alive, dynamic, personal; and therefore *he moves and is moved*. For example, according to Judges 2:18 (RSV), God saved bands of Hebrews from their enemies. Why? Because "the Lord was moved to pity by their groanings because of those who afflicted and oppressed them." Unlike Aristotle, the early Hebrews could not conceive of a God who would not *react* to the misery of his people.

To be sure, there are a number of passages in the Bible that assert that God does not change or repent. But a careful reading of the contexts reveals that Thomas Aquinas' doctrine of God's absolute changelessness is not affirmed in most of these passages. Rather, the passages generally emphasize God's steadfastness in love, or his reliability in keeping promises, or simply his own everlasting life. The idea of a changeless being may perhaps be implicit in some of these passages. But this is a question for serious debate.

Theologians have worried themselves greatly about the thought of God's changelessness. One of the early Christian churchmen, Cyprian, ridiculed one group of Christians by giving them the nickname "Patripassians." In essence, he was rebuking them for saying that God the Father suffered and was moved. It was conceded that this could be said of God the *Son*. But Christians were divided as to whether this could be said also of the Heavenly Father.[9] The parable of the prodigal son suggests that at least Jesus thought of the Heavenly Father as being greatly moved by the sinner's repentance.

Metaphysics and Metaphor.   One approach used by theologians who hold to the notion that God cannot really change is to say that all the passages referring to God as changing must be read as *metaphors*. Then the passages that emphasize God as *un*changing must be read as fundamentally metaphysical or *literal characterizations of God*.

Unfortunately, such a device not only does great violence to the Bible, but invites everyone to turn into a metaphor any passage of the Bible that happens not to fit with his pet theory. It would seem to be more forthright simply to disagree with some of the biblical writers than to force them to submit to a theory foreign to them.

The Dilemma of the Cosmological Argument.   The dilemma of those asserting the absolute changelessness of God is this: Either (1) affirm that God is changeless or (2) give up the assertion that he is at least personal, active, and dynamic. If the second part of the dilemma is accepted, then what remains is a flat, changeless something that hardly qualifies as a living God.

But what would follow if theists should conclude that change and motion are a part of the makeup of God? Well, *if* the cosmological argument is right, then God would have to be regarded as a *contingent* being in need of some more fundamental Necessary Being to keep him from falling into nothingness. In other words, the cosmological argument for a changeless Necessary Being is not an argument for a living God.

But Can There Be a Totally Unchanging Being?   Perhaps the reason the biblical writers could not help portraying God as changing and being moved is that change and movement are a necessary part of a living being. Aristotle's concept of God seems hardly to be that of a living being; he is portrayed as little more than an abstract intellect. Some Christians have wanted to think of God as a pure intellect without feelings and embodiment. But this will not do, for even the *life* of the intellect is filled with change. The thinking mind is alert to new evidence, is sensitive, passionate to learn, open to change, and moved by evidence and logic. Aristotle's God knows nothing about life as it is lived. He enjoys no surprises, no novel experiences. He has just one eternal day. He is not so much a mind or intellect, as a gallery of ideas and thoughts. The living mind, on the other hand, is stimulated, stirred, excited, thwarted and inspired, challenged and agitated. These are all action words involving change, movement, and a measure of contingency.

Some Christian theologians have wanted to make the Bible's versions of God more sedate and passionless, more like Aristotle's impersonal, abstract, Unmoved Mover. The cosmological argument, for example, postulates an intellectual monstrosity—the Unmoved Mover—which not only is different from most of the biblical views of God, but downright incompatible with them. The God of the cosmological argument is not at all like the God of Abraham (who bargained with God) or of Jacob (who wrestled with him or one of his theophanies). Moses is said to have talked with God as a friend and to have even worked a deal with God to see at least his divine back.[10] This God is hardly the unmoved, changeless Necessary Being that Thomas' cosmological argument projects.

Can Perfection Change and Still Be Perfect?   It is necessary to consider again why Thomas and many other classical theists consider change in God to be such an abhorrent notion. This dread of change has a long and understandable history. For one thing, change and time eventually bring death to every human being. So, if God could somehow be exempted from all change, then he might escape death altogether. This way of thinking has very primitive roots. It starts with an active divine agent who works wonders and exerts considerable influence. Change is good because it manifests his power and life. But such a deity ought to live forever. Therefore, he comes to be regarded as not subject to the ravages of time. Eventually God is simply taken out of time altogether, as if believers fear that if he were touched by the finger of time, then even God would be unable to overcome its touch of death.

Early concepts of God—even in the Old Testament—do not always picture him as Perfect Being in Thomas' sense of perfection. A careful reading of early Old Testament passages show God to be quite imperfect. He is sometimes cruel, hot-headed, short-sighted, and forgetful of who he is or of the deals he has made. As the idea of God becomes more or less refined in the thinking of various Hebrews, the idea of a Perfect Being comes to the forefront. And such a lofty idea tends to remove God from all settings and contexts. He is eventually removed from the entire universe.

The idea of change became a terrible threat to the idea of Perfect Being. Consider the following dilemma: If God changes, he must change either for the worse or for the better. (1) If he changes for the *worse*, he ceases to be a Perfect Being. (2) But if he changes for the *better*, then he must not have been perfect in the first place!

In the latter alternative, the fear of change is implicit. To change is to admit the *need* for change. And to admit need is to admit that one is not wholly complete as he *is*. To say that someone needs something is to say that in some sense he is *dependent* on it. And you recall that the cosmological argument is built on the premise that God as Necessary Being depends on nothing for anything. God is wholly independent.

But perhaps while God needs nothing to sustain his *existence*, he does need something to improve the *quality* of his life. This is a very touchy issue for classical theists. What the cosmological argument ends up with is a God who needs absolutely nothing and consequently *has nothing but bare necessary existence*. This can hardly be called the "living God."

Any attempt to use the cosmological argument for Necessary Being *partially* to support classical theism runs into the possibility of using the same argument in defense of the view of the universe without the God hypothesis.

Back to the Universe.   Hence, we are brought back to the possibility of accepting without contradiction the idea of a universe having change and motion but without a transcendent deity. Apparently it is not possible to talk consistently of a Necessary Being who is somehow exempted from all change. Perhaps the cosmological argument arrived surprisingly and finally at a ghost town because it started on the wrong track. Perhaps it is a great mistake to say that a universe cannot exist on its own if it contains motion and change.

Furthermore, if theists allow that perhaps God, too, enjoys change and motion, they will still have to face the following questions: Why postulate God at all? Why not simply stay with the universe, and let that be the whole of reality? If the theory of God is dropped, we might then seek to understand the things of the universe in terms of their interrelations, laws, patterns, and conditions. The attempt to go outside the universe (whatever that means) for an explanation of what is in it simply adds an extra burden to an already difficult job of understanding the things and relationships of the universe.

Without a Transcendent Deity.   The Hebrews and Christians have always had trouble with the idea of a God who transcends the universe. As one Old Testament scholar writes,

After the destruction of the temple in 587/6 B.C., the idea of God's immanence was dealt a severe blow. More and more God was envisioned as remote and otherworldly. In this excessive stress on transcendence the chasm between God and man became so great that some of the postexilic prophets believed that God communicated his message by means of heavenly messengers. Zechariah, for example, refers constantly to "the messenger [angel] who talked with me" (Zech. 1:1, 13, 14, 19; 2:3, etc.).[11]

In the Middle Ages, God was taken by many to be so remote as to be hardly real. Common people thought of themselves as dealing with Mary and the saints, who presumably had known what it is like to live in a world of change and movement. The Christian doctrine of the Incarnation seems to come from an unconscious drive to give the transcendent God some flesh and blood, to embody him, to get him informed about the real world, to move him.

Christians did not want to believe that God is wholly uninterested in them. They conceived of God as initiating the Incarnation as a plan to put him in *touch* with human life. Christianity demanded a God who is more than pure thoughts or mere word. "And the Word became flesh and dwelt among us."[12] The New Testament writers consciously said that God is revealing himself to the human race. Unconsciously they seemed to be saying also that the revelation is a two-way street, that the transcendent God is also in need of *becoming involved.* He is in need of learning, responding to the needs of mortals and developing new sensitivities. Indeed, this development in their concept of God eventually led to the notion that God is actually more than one person, which is perhaps a way of saying that Christians could not fully harmonize God as changeless being with God as one who suffers and is moved. To be sure, the Old Testament already had these ingredients; but the more refined the God of the Old Testament became, the less a reality he seemed to be. The history of Jewish and Christian thought about God is largely the history of one problem: what to do with God with regard to the world. Will he transcend the world or be in it?

The point here is not that a transcendent Necessary Being must take personal interest in *human* affairs if he is to exist. Rather, the point is that the very idea of a Necessary Being void of change and motion cannot be harmonized with the views in the Bible that portray him as very much moved, active, involved, and changing. Yet to bring change and contingency into the Necessary Being is simply to destroy the cosmological argument for the existence of a God who transcends all contingency.

The dilemma of classical theism resides in its desire to have its cake and eat it, too. The proponents of the argument want, on the one hand, to have an Absolute—the Necessary Being taken to extreme. On the other hand, they want a religion that portrays a vital and moving interrelationship between this Absolute and humanity. The philosopher F. H. Bradley states rather well the persistent illness of classical theism:

A discrepancy worth our notice is the position of God in the universe. We may say that in religion God tends always to pass beyond himself. He is necessarily led to end in the Absolute, which for religion is not God. . . . If you identify the Absolute with God, that is not the God of religion. If again you separate them, God becomes a finite factor in the Whole. And the effort of religion is to put an end to, and break down, this relationship—a relation which, none the less, it essentially presupposes. Hence, short of the Absolute, God cannot rest, he is lost and religion with him. It is this difficulty which appears in the problem of the religious self-consciousness.[13]

Classical theists, insisting on both having their cake and eating it, cannot resolve the dilemma posed by the idea of a changeless Necessary Being. Hence, they must settle for pronouncing what has become a mere verbal ritual—"God not only transcends the world, but is also immanently involved in the world." They have had to let it go at that.

Where Did the World Come From?   Classical theists do not wish to say that God made the universe from some sort of material or energy that he discovered, for that would entail that there already existed a reality that was not dependent on him. Hence, God is said to have created the universe *ex nihilo* —out of nothing. Some classical theists choose to label this as a miracle.

They are not, however, willing to take seriously the hypothesis that *the universe simply came from nothing* without the presence of God on the scene. The notion of a universe just coming from nothing does indeed disturb our expectations. But classical theism taxes us doubly. It not only asks us to believe in creation out of nothing, but asks us to accept an Unmoved Necessary Being who was nevertheless moved to create a world. The first alternative (i.e., the universe came from nothing) is at least as easy to accept as the second alternative (i.e., the universe was created out of nothing, and in addition a creator exists). If we are going to have a miracle, why insist on *two*—the universe plus a God? Why not just one miracle—a universe? It is mere habit of mind to suppose that a miracle must have a miracle worker. (In a later chapter the issue of miracles will be explored.)

There is perhaps another answer to the question regarding the origin of the universe. Some theists believe that it is possible to hold that God has both an unchanging side and a changing side to his nature. Some of these theists do not worry themselves with the question as to whether God might never have existed. They concede that God *might* not have existed at all. They profess to see no necessary reason (i.e., no causal ground or logical ground) for either God's existence or his nonexistence. But, according to these theists, God simply does exist, and that is a fortunate thing for us, for without him we would not exist.[14]

These theists take a rather straightforward approach. Since God happens to exist, he is the reason why the universe now exists. Hence, at least half of the argument of Necessary Being still remains. That is, God is seen as the *necessary condition or cause* of the universe. Without him, the universe would not be.

The other half of the doctrine of Necessary Being is left

hanging, for these theists have not fully come to terms with the question as to *whether God could eventually pass out of existence (and the universe perish along with him)*. Classical theists have always been concerned to come up with some guarantee that God would never perish. But the cosmological argument can show no more than that the survival of the universe depends upon the survival of God. Even this conclusion is questionable. But in any case, the cosmological argument cannot show that God will not eventually perish and the world along with him.

Philosophers have wrestled for centuries with the question of the existence of tomorrow. Can we prove that the whole of reality will not simply disappear tomorrow? Philosophers have called this "the problem of induction."[15] The *ontological* argument for God's existence is an attempt to deal with this problem. But we must wait until the next chapter in order to get into this fascinating argument.

Opponents of theism conclude that there is no point in postulating a God who transcends the universe. If God could just happen to exist as a brute fact, then the universe could just happen to exist as a brute fact. So why bring up the hypothesis of a God with all its thorny intellectual difficulties?

Theists who argue that the universe might just perish must face the possibility that a transcendent God might also perish. It is perhaps possible that if there is a God he will live forever. And it is perhaps possible that the universe will continue forever in one form or another. In fact, if the theists claim that God can undergo certain changes and still be the Necessary Being, then their opponents could claim that the universe can undergo certain changes and still be the Necessary Being.

Must the Universe Have a Beginning? There is the hypothesis that the universe had no beginning at all. To be sure, it has undergone various changes and qualifications. But even the Big Bang theory of the universe's origin presupposes that there was already something in existence that exploded. For all we know, the "structure" of the universe as we think of it today is just one of an infinite series of "forms" that the universe takes.

Opponents of theism insist that it makes sense to say that the universe happens to explode into, or to develop, new forms (or that it happens to exist at all). At least it makes as much sense to say this as to say that God happens to exist and happens to want to create a world. Even if we say that God was moved to create it, we could still ask why he happened to be moved. What was it that moved him? Was it something inside or outside him? If inside, then what moved it—and so on and on. Hence, even within God's own life the problem of *an infinite series of motions* breaks out with such a vengeance that Thomas could not face the problem squarely. At best, he spoke mildly and confusedly of a "process" or "procession" in God. But the discussion fades out without his having come to terms with the threatening conclusion that if motion and change within the universe demand something beyond the universe, then motion and change within God demand something beyond God. Unfortunately, no matter how transcendent a hypothesis we produce, the nagging question remains: Is it the living God, or is it a mere lifeless, unmoved abstraction?

Of course, there is still the possibility of thinking of the universe and God as being the *same* reality. In that sense, God or the universe might be called the only Necessary Being in the sense of depending on nothing for his or its existence. Defenders of the cosmological argument have rejected this blending of God and the universe, but some of the proponents of the *ontological* argument have boldly asserted it and argued for it.

NOTES

1. See Thomas Aquinas, *Summa Theologica*, in *Basic Writings of Saint Thomas Aquinas*, 2 vols., ed. Anton C. Pegis (New York: Random House, 1945), vol. 1; pt. 1, quest. 2, art 3. Cf. L. G. Levy, *Maimonides*, 2d ed. (Paris: Alcan, 1932), p. 125. Thomas makes frequent use of the writings of Aristotle. Cf. Aristotle, *Metaphysics*, bk. 12, chap. 7.
2. See Peter Geach, "Commentary on Aquinas," in *The Cosmological Argument*, ed. Donald Burrill (Garden City, N.Y.: Doubleday, 1967), p. 58; Patterson Brown, "St. Thomas on Necessary Being," *Philosophical Review* 73 (1964): 76–90.
3. See Etienne Gilson, *The Christian Philosophy of St. Thomas Aquinas* (New York: Random House, 1965), pp. 61 f.
4. See Donald Wells, *God, Man, and the Thinker* (New York: Random House, 1962), p. 102.
5. RSV. Italics added.
6. Hebrews 13:8 (RSV).
7. James 4:8 (RSV).

8. See Hebrews 4:15.
9. See Williston Walker, *A History of the Christian Church* (Edinburgh: T. & T. Clark, 1953), p. 73.
10. See Exodus 33.
11. Dewey M. Beegle, *Scripture, Tradition, and Infallibility* (Grand Rapids: Eerdmans, 1973), p. 29. The bracketed word "angel" is supplied by Beegle.
12. John 1:14 (RSV).
13. F. H. Bradley, *Appearance and Reality,* 2d ed. (London: Oxford University Press, 1930), pp. 395 f.
14. This version seems to be defended by Cleanthes in David Hume, *Dialogues concerning Natural Religion,* ed. with intro. by Henry D. Aiken (New York: Hafner Publishing Co., 1951). There are also other good editions of this book.
15. One of the best discussions of it may be found in Karl R. Popper, *Objective Knowledge: An Evolutionary Approach* (New York: Oxford University Press, 1973), chap. 1.

CHAPTER V

Classical Theism and the Ontological Argument

THE CONTEMPORARY STATUS
OF THE ONTOLOGICAL ARGUMENT

No argument for the existence of God has fascinated philosophers and theologians more than the ontological argument. In 1960 a noted philosopher published an article in a professional journal in which he defended this ancient argument.[1] On the surface, the article was just another scholarly piece of work making its usual contribution to the advance of human understanding. But it generated a powerful controversy that is still raging. Suddenly the time was ripe for a thoroughgoing debate of the issue. Today, one of the most influential philosophers in theological circles is Charles Hartshorne. More than any other philosopher, he has explored the heights and depths of the ontological argument.[2] He defends a revised and up-to-date version of the argument and regards the universe as "God's body."

Another important contemporary philosopher, J. N. Findlay, had previously argued that the ontological argument proves that there *could not possibly be a God*.[3] Findlay and Hartshorne eventually became for a while members of the same faculty at the University of Texas, where they were able together to examine some of their points of difference and agreement.

The development of debate over the ontological argument has allowed us to shake off some of the poor arguments advanced in the past. To be sure, we cannot predict the future course of a debate over a significant issue. But we may expect that new insights will emerge along the way. Sometimes the unintended insights are of value equal to the major conclusions reached.

This is especially true of the debate regarding the ontological argument. For example, Professor Hartshorne argues force-fully that God as Necessary Being not only can enjoy change, but must do it. This is a long way from Aristotle's Unmoved Mover. Another example of the significant side-effects of the debate regarding the ontological argument is this: the whole concept of *eternity* has been taken out of the bag, so to speak, and spread out on the table so that philosophers, theologians, astronomers, and others may examine it.

WHAT DOES "ONTOLOGICAL" MEAN?

The word 'ontological' is based on the Greek word *ontos*, which means "being." But the ontological argument is con-cerned with *Perfect* Being. This argument often refers to God as G.C.B.—the Greatest Conceivable Being. It is assumed that such a secure Being would not be greatly upset if only his initials were used! Indeed, if there is such a Perfect Being, then anything said of him is likely to be an abbreviation.

While the ontological argument and the cosmological argu-ment overlap in some of their territory, there is one major difference between them. The cosmological argument concedes that it is logically possible that absolutely nothing might have existed. Even God might never have existed. But the ontologi-cal argument refuses to make this concession. Instead, it says that there is one Being whose existence is absolutely guaran-teed.[4] As was just hinted in the previous chapter, this whole question of *whether God might never have existed at all* is a very thorny one. But in this chapter, I hope to pull out some of the thorns so that you may look inside the argument and dis-cover why it has fascinated so many profound minds.

ANSELM'S PROOF

Think of the Greatest. Anselm, appointed Archbishop of Canterbury in 1093, developed what he regarded to be a logi-cal proof for the existence of God. First, think of just any finite reality or being: your father, yourself, or the state of Califor-nia. Second, think of an even greater being: for example, the United States. To be sure, when thinking of the United States, you will not expect to be able to think of every detail of such a great reality. But still you can think of the United States as being great and complex, certainly greater and more complex than either you or I. Keep on thinking until you simply come to the point where you have to say, "Okay, there is a reality that is the greatest of all. It is the greatest that anyone could possibly conceive of. It isn't Texas, California, or the United States. It isn't even the entire globe with all the nations combined as one humanity. I don't know what to call it, but surely there's something that is the greatest reality."

This is the direction that Anselm's mind took. He refers to this greatest reality as simply that reality or being beyond which nothing greater could be conceived. It is the absolute limit to be conceived. It is the greatest conceivable being. Hence, it is perfect because nothing else surpasses it.

How do we know that nothing surpasses it? Anselm's answer is ingenious. He dares us to go ahead and think of some being or reality that surpasses it. And if we come up with something, then we ought to call *it* the greatest conceivable being. In other words, Anselm says that we should not give the title "Perfect Being" to anything that falls short of what can be thought of as the absolutely greatest and unsurpassed.

The Greatest Being Would Certainly Exist.   Anselm says, in effect, when you conceive of the Greatest Conceivable Being, do not be conservative. Do not leave anything out. This Perfect Being must not be lacking in anything. If you knowingly leave something out, then Anselm thinks you really are not yet thinking of the Greatest Conceivable Being; you do not yet have the right idea or concept.

Now here comes Anselm's logical bomb: He asks, in effect, the following question: Would it not be ridiculous to conceive of this Perfect Being and then leave out one of the most important qualities of all? And, what is that important quality? Anselm's answer is *existence*! Imagine a Perfect Being with everything except existence. How absurd!

Well, if you agree with Anselm, then you have, he believes, just admitted that God exists. For 'God' is simply one of the words given to that being beyond which nothing greater is conceivable.[5]

If It Exists in Your Mind, It Exists in Reality.   Anselm knew full well that just because you have in your mind the idea of a million dollars, you do not necessarily have a million dollars in a bank account. A monk challenged Anselm to think of a Perfect Island. I do not know what a perfect island would be to a monk, but his point was this: just because the Perfect

Island exists in the mind, that does not mean that it exists off the coast of Spain or anywhere else outside the imagination.[6]

The monk's point is very simple. Just because you can *think* of a Perfect Being—including his existence—does not mean that he therefore exists. In Anselm's time people believed in a lot of things that today are regarded by many as existing only in the imagination. (Even Thomas, over a century after Anselm, offered numerous arguments supporting belief in angels.) In effect, the monk opposing Anselm said, "Thinking does not make it so."

But Anselm's reply is relentless. He believes that *everything*, except Perfect Being, might never have existed or might cease to exist at any moment. Hence, to have imperfect beings such as angels or islands in your mind does not mean that they *necessarily* exist. Anselm might have been thinking at the moment of going with his beautiful, charming wife to the monk's Perfect Island. But Anselm would have known that this was all mere imagination. The island did not really exist, and, besides, Anselm had no wife. Many a young man in the throes of romantic passion has exclaimed, "My woman has *everything*!" But in a calm moment he would be able to concede that she does not *really* have everything. She is not, after all, Perfect Being—that Being beyond which nothing greater can be conceived. Sad as it may be, the woman lacks all sorts of qualities.

Anselm's point is that there is one and only one reality whose nature of necessity is to exist. And that is the Perfect Being. Everything else may be conceived of as eventually perishing, or even never having come into existence at all. But Perfect Being *must* have existence—otherwise there could not even be the *idea* of a Perfect Being. Anselm believes that the monk already concedes that he has an idea of Perfect Being. The monk even says as much. Thus, Anselm concludes, the very idea of Perfect Being includes the *existence* of that Being. So, the protesting monk must either give up the idea of Perfect Being (and thus become an atheist) or admit that the possession of the idea *proves the existence of* the Perfect Being.

Anselm's Framework.   Those who place Anselm's argument under the microscope, so to speak, sometimes forget that his thinking was greatly shaped by Plato and St. Augustine. Plato and Augustine held that thoughts are somehow "participating" in objective reality. Himself greatly influenced by the

Platonic tradition, Augustine insisted that whenever the mind apprehends truth, it is already apprehending God to some degree, for God is truth.

For Augustine, when the mind knows truths, it knows eternal realities. All knowledge is regarded as in some sense acquaintance with the eternal mind of God. So whether entertaining mathematical ideas or principles of logic, Augustine was, he thought, participating somehow in the mind of God. It is not surprising, therefore, that as a staunch Augustinian, Anselm would assume that in entertaining in our mind the idea of *Perfect* Being, we would be "participating" in the mind of God. The idea of Perfect Being more than any other idea would presumably put us in contact with the reality of God's eternal existence.

I will not dwell on Anselm's Augustinian framework because the ontological argument is thought by many to be an important argument on its own grounds.[7]

God Had to Exist.   When studying the cosmological argument, you saw that God was regarded as infinite, indestructible, and unchanging. However, those embracing the cosmological argument admit that the nonexistence of God is conceivable. They argue only that *if* God exists, then his existence had no beginning and will have no end. The cosmological argument is supposed to show that *in fact* God does exist, not that he *must* exist. The cosmological argument concedes that "it is *logically* possible (i.e., conceivable) that nothing exists or ever has existed, including God."[8]

By contrast, the *ontological* argument asserts that it is inconceivable that God might never have existed. When defenders of this argument say that God is a Necessary Being, they mean that his existence is absolutely necessary. God had to exist because it is the very nature of a Perfect Being to exist. Existence is regarded as just as much a quality of God as is his love or power. To say that God might not have existed is like saying that he might have lacked love, mercy, power, knowledge, or justice.

When we ask, "Why should there be something rather than nothing?", the defenders of the ontological argument believe that the cosmological argument cannot handle this question. True, the cosmological argument says that the world exists because God exists. But this does not answer the question as to why *God* should exist. The ontological argument, on the other hand, answers by saying that it is the very nature of Perfect Being to exist.

Logical Necessity and Factual Necessity.   The cosmological argument says that if we keep asking why something exists, we finally come to God. There the question stops, for God is the ultimate answer as to why anything is caused to be what it is. But suppose we say that the universe is simply the brute ultimate fact which, while it might not have been, nevertheless happens to be? Well, the cosmological argument will not permit this, because it says that only God can be the brute ultimate fact that cannot be explained but nevertheless exists.

According to this cosmological argument, God enjoys *factual necessity*. This raises the question: Necessity for *what*? The cosmological argument answers that God is absolutely necessary to the world's existence. Furthermore, to speak of the factual necessity of God is, in addition, to call attention to the fact that his existence depends on nothing outside himself.

But the *ontological* argument presses even further the issue of necessity. Those adhering to this argument are disturbed by the thought that God might never have been. They receive no comfort in the reply that nothing else would have existed if God had not existed. Hence, the ontological argument contends that God has not only factual necessity, but *logical* necessity. To say that he exists of logical necessity is to deny that God might never have existed. The *logical* necessity of God entails that the thought of his nonexistence is a contradiction. The cosmological argument is criticized for having fallen into self-contradiction.

You might feel like asking, "Why does the defender of the ontological argument keep pressing his point? Why cannot he simply accept God's existence and let it go at that?"

Well, something in the back of his mind keeps disturbing him. What worries him is the chilling thought that God exists as a matter of *pure chance or accident*![9] You recall that classical theists find it to be a terrible thought that the *universe* might simply be here as an accident. And those who embrace the ontological argument are not about to allow that *God* might simply be here as a matter of pure chance or accident. Why, if this were so, then what is to prevent another accident —the utter disappearance of God and the whole of reality!

There is only one way out. Declare the existence of God to be a logical necessity. Only then can believers be assured that God's existence will not accidentally fall into the abyss of nothingness.

PROBLEMS FOR THE ONTOLOGICAL ARGUMENT

The Problem of Logical Necessity.   It will be useful to look more critically at the ontological argument. Any sensitive person can understand the human anxiety motivating this ancient argument, for most of us wish for deep and abiding security. We do not wish to bring "The eternal note of sadness in."[10]

The ontological argument is, however, misguided in thinking that "logical necessity" really means something in the indefinite context in which it is used. What the argument is designed to do is to make an absolute distinction between God's *necessary* existence and his *possible* existence. But it fails to make clear that "necessity" and "possibility" do not mean *anything* without a definite context or setting. You cannot tell whether something follows necessarily unless you know what its setting permits. The number 4 follows necessarily from 2 times 2. The reason is that the mathematical context in which this formula is set will not permit another answer.

On the other hand, it is only *possibly*, not necessarily, true that the trees I planted yesterday will be alive at this date next year. Why is this so? Because the empirical setting in which I planted the trees will not allow anything other than the possibility that they will grow. To be sure, I might be able to increase the odds in my favor by doing some things that the empirical context will permit. But if asked "Will your trees be alive next year?" I cannot say with *logical* necessity that they will.

Now let us look back to the ontological argument. The point to be made is that the question, "Is it necessary that God should exist?" is not a genuine question. Like a mirage, it looks real, but it is not. Why? Because it presupposes something that it cannot presuppose, which is to fall into self-contradiction.

The illicit presupposition, very simply, is the presupposition of a *context or setting for God*. Classical theism will not allow an eternal context for God. Without realizing what they are doing, the ontological argument defenders are really asking the following question: "What will God's setting or context permit? Will it not permit a logically necessary being, namely, God?"

No one can answer this question because classical theism rejects any established context for God. And even if there were such a context or setting, the whole problem would spill out again. For we could then ask about this wider setting or context. Is *its* existence logically necessary? Unfortunately, in order to answer this question we would have to look for still another setting: the setting of the setting, and so on throughout infinity.[11]

It is therefore misleading to speak of God's existence as either *logically necessary* or *accidental*. Neither of these words has any meaning apart from a setting. When the cosmological and ontological arguments are advanced, their defenders certainly do not *intend* to take for granted any setting at all for their God. If they did take one for granted, then they would be talking not about an independent Being but rather about a dependent being. A dependent being must have a setting and conditions. These determine what is necessary in order for the dependent being to exist.

Now if there is a Being who is absolutely independent, then there can be no *reason* for his existence. There can be no reason for some actual being or quality until there is already a setting of at least one other actual being with qualities. This is not to say that if there is a totally independent Being, then his existence is *unreasonable*. No, it would be neither reasonable nor unreasonable. It might be called nonrational—which is to say that its existence would be neither rational nor irrational. God's existence would be just an ultimate brute fact.

Or if there were no God, then the *universe* would be just an ultimate fact. Such a universe requires no God. To ask for its origin as a whole would be to presuppose that it needs an origin or that it needs a context. Nontheistic naturalism is the view that nature or the universe exists as ultimate reality and that the idea of a creator of the universe is an unnecessary piece of mythology. To ask for the origin of the universe as a whole is like asking for the sex of the universe. Of course, Jews, Christians, and Muslims have often thought of God as male. But inasmuch as "he" seems now to have no distinguishing parts or qualities that are conspicuously male, the tendency to regard God as male has been repressed and treated as an early expression of Hebrew male chauvinism flowing from the vain imagination of patriarchs. In the nineteenth century, the pope increased the status of the Virgin Mary, which appears to many people to be a humorously tokenist ploy. It would seem that nature is less sexist than some of the male theologians and cardinals would have their God to be.

What Is Perfect Being?   You perhaps recall from earlier in this chapter the steps we took in trying to think of Perfect Being. You knew that neither you nor your father, neither the United States nor the whole globe, could be designated as the Perfect Being. Yet there is a very serious question as to whether it even makes sense to talk of a perfect *Being* at all. We can speak of a perfect high jump at the track meet, or a perfect day for a picnic. But perfect *Being* seems to be too all-inclusive to be meaningful.

Only within a given context or setting may something be called perfect. Also it must measure up to certain standards or expectations. But asking for a Perfect Being without any limit or setting is like asking for a perfect perfect. Or a perfect perfect perfect—and so on. A perfect adjective is one that more exactly fits the expectations of a given sentence than does any other. A perfect day depends on what we want or need. For a farmer, a perfect day might be one of steady rain because his crops need the water. His children might think the perfect day is a hot sunny day for going swimming. If you want to go fishing, then a perfect day will be moderately warm and still, whereas if you want to fly a kite you will think that the perfect day should be windy.

Anselm says that God is the greatest conceivable *being*. To be the greatest living swimmer is to be able to swim farther than any other living person and to perform in an unsurpassed way other feats to be listed under the heading of swimming. The greatest home-run hitter is the one who hits the most home runs under proper and official conditions. But what does one do in order to be the all-time greatest *being*? What activities count as "being" activities? Obviously Anselm's God is not the greatest basketball player, safecracker, dentist, Russian diplomat, house painter, or catfish. Unless God is everything (pantheism), then God is not the greatest rose or Iowa hog. (If God were everything, he would also be the worst rose.)

The point is that there does not seem to be universal perfection or greatness. But that is what the desire for Perfect Being seems to demand. Unfortunately, there is no clear standard for determining when a *being* is perfect.[12] However, it is very likely that religion begins, not with a desire for something as vague as Perfect Being, but with much more definite needs and desires.

In his own defense of the ontological argument, Professor Norman Malcolm thinks that the sense of guilt and the desire for forgiveness are some of the psychological roots of the ontological argument for God.[13] Feeling themselves to be guilty beyond all measure, people have sometimes longed for a Being whose power and willingness to forgive is beyond all measure. Hence the longing for the perfect forgiver.

Buddha and countless other people have seen how impermanent things are all about them. What Buddha sought was perfect serenity in the face of impermanence. He wanted a Nirvana of perfect bliss. Some Christians have characterized the life of God as perfect bliss.[14]

Versions of Perfection.   Classical theism has its roots in at least three versions of what perfection is. Unfortunately, these versions often stand in contradiction to one another.

(1) For some of the ancient Greek philosophers, perfection is understood to be an *intelligible and limited form*. Perfection in this sense is order and structure in contrast to limitless chaos and anarchy. If perfection were incomplete and limitless, then it would presumably not be intelligible and comprehensible to the mind. For Plato and others like him, perfection is the very opposite of unstructured and limitless being. Perfection is not the whole of reality but is to be distinguished from the mass of chaotic motions.[15]

(2) On the other hand, the Neo-Platonic tradition sees perfection as the *all-encompassing reality* which is somehow drawn together *into one total and simple unity*. Unlike Plato's perfection, however, the Neo-Platonic perfection is not comprehensible. It transcends the powers of human intelligence.[16]

(3) There is still a third version of perfection. It stresses the *realm of limitless possibilities that can be actualized*. This realm may be seen as an infinity of possible worlds in the divine mind. According to this version of perfection, God contains an endless supply of resources and possibilities. He is adequate because he is an infinity.[17]

Without going into great detail on points of conflict among these three versions of perfection, I wish merely to note that the first one stresses order, form, and limits, whereas the last one stresses limitlessness. Now clearly, a Being who has no limits as to what he will actualize cannot be regarded as supremely good, for he will make no value judgments. To have an infinity of possibilities is possibly to be a greatly evil being, depending on what possibilities are actualized. But to actualize only *some* potentialities is to suppress or limit certain others. Moral and aesthetic perfection must be discriminating and evaluative—hence placing *limits* on the infinite realm of possibilities.

As for the Neo-Platonic unity, there is no essential reason why unity must be superior to plurality. It all depends upon the needs, interests, and purposes to be served. For some purposes, unity in a certain area is to be preferred, whereas other needs and desires require plurality and diversity. Total unity per se has been designated as "perfection," but there is no convincing reason for accepting this designation.

If we take perfection to mean total, all-inclusive unity, then the God of classical theism must be judged as imperfect. This is because the universe is regarded as outside God's own being and is not a part of his unity. Classical theism regards God to be a unity, but not an all-inclusive unity. If God creates a world outside himself, he is limited in the sense that he does not include it in his own being. On the other hand, if an all-inclusive Being cannot create a world outside of himself, he is limited in *power*. Hence, God may be regarded as either perfect or imperfect, depending on what version of perfection we use as the standard of judgment.[18]

It might be argued that God must reveal to us which version of perfection is to be used as the general standard. The trouble with this argument is that we would need to know whether this alleged God is really God. Even assuming for the sake of argument that a very powerful Being could reveal to us some version of perfection, how could we know that this powerful Being is God? He might be simply a powerful almighty Being, but he could not be God unless he were perfect—at least according to those who profess classical theism. It is possible that an all-powerful Being might wish to offer *his own* version of perfection. But why should we accept it? If we accept it *because* he is all-powerful, then we have unwittingly subscribed to the version of perfection that simply defines *'perfection'* as *unsurpassed might or absolute power!* This is indeed another version of perfection. But there is no convincing reason for accepting it, although there may be some threatening reasons. That is, if we do not accept it, we might suffer some of the ill effects that the most powerful Being might inflict upon us. Those people who worship power per se would be impressed with this display of force, but the morally sensitive would abhor it.

Change and Perfect Being.   Anselm takes for granted that any change in God would render him less than Perfect Being.[19] In the previous chapter, I tried to show that it is self-contradictory to think of God as both a living personal Being and a changeless Being. Perfect Being as conceived of by Anselm is sometimes regarded as static. But for Charles Hartshorne, God is dipolar. That is, while changeless in some respects, in other respects he undergoes change and is the most dynamic and changing being of all.

Anselm wrote his famous *Proslogion* in 1078. Since that time the ontological argument has taken many turns and received various amendments and qualifications. Perhaps the most noteworthy qualification is the one made by Charles Hartshorne. Like Anselm, he argues that God's existence is logically necessary (although sometimes Hartshorne is not consistent on this point). He parts company with Anselm on the matter of God's qualities. Hartshorne contends that while God necessarily exists, nevertheless *not everything* about God is necessary. In other words, some of God's life is *contingent*. That is, it might have been otherwise had God so chosen or had other aspects of his own life been different.[20] This suggests that God has an internal environment that influences the quality of his life.

Indeed, Hartshorne postulates that certain aspects of God's being will forever be changing. But this is not regarded as a threat to divine perfection, for no one surpasses God. If he surpasses himself, he is still the most perfect being. Here is another example of the many ways the words 'perfect' or 'perfection' may be used. For Hartshorne, a Perfect Being must be capable of growth and development. If God is indeed personal, then he must be responsive, sensitive, and therefore capable of gaining in new experiences. But there are many classical theists who cannot use the word 'perfect' to describe such a self-surpassing being. For these theists, perfection demands absolutely no change at all.

Unfortunately, there is no way to "prove" that one version or vision of perfection is the true one, whereas the others are fakes or frauds. We can only point out the great difficulty that emerges whenever people try to say what Perfect Being "really" is.

Indeed, the ontological argument seems to be an excellent example of how language is sometimes pushed up to the edge. Anselm himself confesses that Perfect Being is beyond our comprehension.[21] Two decades ago a large convention of Buddhists described Nirvana as that state of neither existence nor nonexistence. Like Anselm in his ontological argument, these Buddhists were walking at the edge of language.

Anselm fails to prove the existence of the God of classical theism, and Hartshorne fails to prove that this God of neoclassical theism exists of *logical* necessity. What has been shown is that poets, lovers, and certain kinds of religious believers are willing to say that their highest visions, dreams, and expectations will not be disappointed–that if they throw their rope across the chasm, it will somehow take hold on the other side.

As Anselm made quite clear, the ontological argument is motivated by the heart's longings. It is the expression of a faith born of desperation and swelling with hope and expectation. Sometimes increased expectations will bring into existence certain relationships and experiences that would not have existed before. The believer in classical theism holds that faith creates the possibility of "experiencing God."

But there are many others who hold that no amount of mere finite human faith and hope can conjure up or create a God who simply does not exist. What faith and hope can sometimes do, however, is open human beings up to new experiences, relationships, and dimensions of living and knowing that previously were beyond their ability to conceive.

The theist contends that there are more riches and wonders in God than are dreamt of in philosophy. The nontheistic naturalist replies that there are more riches and wonders in the universe than are dreamt of in theology. The theist rejoins that the universe would not be here had not God created it. The naturalist answers that the concept of God is itself a product of the imagination of human beings, who in turn are a product of the universe. In either view—theism or naturalism—the human creature stands in a context that he merely receives and did not invent, but to which he may add some human element. The fundamental question, then, has to do with how the finite creature is to relate to this vast and wondrous context in which he lives and moves and has his being.[22]

NOTES

1. Norman Malcolm, "Anselm's Ontological Argument," *Philosophical Review* 69 (1960): 41–62.
2. See Charles Hartshorne, *The Logic of Perfection and Other Essays in Neoclassical Metaphysics* (LaSalle, Ill.: Open Court, 1962).
3. J. N. Findlay, "Can God's Existence Be Disproved?" in *The Ontological Argument,* ed. Alvin Plantinga (Garden City, N.Y.: Doubleday, Anchor Books, 1965), pp. 111–122. This article first appeared in *Mind* 57 (April 1948): 176–186.
4. See Norman Geisler, "The Missing Premise in the Ontological Argument," *Religious Studies* 9, no. 3 (September 1973): 294.
5. See Anselm, *Proslogion,* trans. Sidney Morton Deane (LaSalle, Ill.: Open Court, 1961). The second edition of Deane's translation of *Anselm's Basic Writings* (Open Court, 1962) has an introduction by Charles Hartshorne.
6. The monk's name is Guanilo. His response to Anselm's ontological argument, entitled *In Behalf of the Fool,* appears in Deane's book *Anselm's Basic Writings.*
7. For a discussion of the Augustinian and Platonic setting of Anselm's ontological argument, see M. J. A. O'Connor, "New Aspects of Omnipotence and Necessity in Anselm," *Religious Studies* 4, no. 1 (October 1968): 134, 136–138, 140–143; Paul M. van Buren, "Anselm's Formula and the Logic of God," *Religious Studies* 9, no. 3 (September 1973): 281.
8. Geisler, *Religious Studies* 9: 293.
9. See Adel Daher, "God and Factual Necessity," *Religious Studies* 6, no. 1 (March 1970): 30.
10. Matthew Arnold, "Dover Beach."
11. Charles Hartshorne *seems* to give up the ontological argument when he speaks of God's being as "an *absolutely* inexplicable brute fact" (Hartshorne, *Anselm's Discovery* [LaSalle, Ill.: Open Court, 1965], p. 10).
12. See David A. Pailin, "Hartshorne's Presentation of the Ontological Argument," *Religious Studies* 4, no. 1 (October 1968): 117.
13. See Norman Malcolm, "Anselm's Ontological Arguments," in *Knowledge and Certainty: Essays and Lectures* (Englewood Cliffs, N.J.: Prentice-Hall, 1963), pp. 160–161.
14. See Ninian Smart, *World Religions: A Dialogue* (Baltimore: Penguin Books, 1966; S. C. M. Press, 1960), p. 61.

15. See Leroy T. Howe, "Existence as a Perfection," *Religious Studies* 4, no. 1 (October 1968): 92.
16. See ibid.
17. See ibid., pp. 92, 94.
18. See Thomas W. Settle, "A Prolegomenon to Intellectually Honest Theology," *Philosophical Forum* 1, no. 2 (new series) (Winter 1968): 146–170. Perfect all-inclusive unity is a unity of *being*, in which case God is everything. But a perfect unity of *purpose* might exist between God and other beings. Unity of *purpose* does not necessarily entail unity of *being*.
19. Anselm, *Proslogion*, pp. 167 f.
20. See ibid., p. 131.
21. See ibid., chap. 14.
22. See Michael Scriven, "The Age of the Universe," *British Journal for the Philosophy of Science* 5 (1954–55): 181–190; idem, *Primary Philosophy* (New York: McGraw-Hill, 1966), pp. 113–126; Ronald W. Hepburn, s.v. "Creation, Religious Doctrine of," in *Encyclopedia of Philosophy*, ed. Paul Edwards (New York: Macmillan, The Free Press, 1967); A. C. Ewing, "Two 'Proofs' of God's Existence," *Religious Studies* 5, no. 1 (October 1969): 35–41.

CHAPTER VI

God, Evil, and Suffering:
Two Versions of Classical Theism

CALVINISM AND ISLAM

The Sovereignty of God.   Among Christians, Calvinism is one of the major traditions. It receives its name from the sixteenth-century Prorestant reformer and theologian, John Calvin. His most famous writing, *Institutes of the Christian Religion*, stands as one of the monumental works in Christianity.[1] There are many threads woven into Calvin's theological system, but one thing stands out: his stress on God's sovereignty and omnipotence.

This same emphasis is found in the theology of Islam, which was initiated when Muhammad came to regard himself as the special prophet of Allah. 'Islam' means "submission"—to the will of Allah. Adherents of Islam or the Muslim faith believe that their faith is the further development of what began in the Old Testament and the New Testament. However, Jews and Christians do not regard Islam to be superior to their own faith. They deny that the Qur'an is the infallible word of God.

Calvin and Muhammad speak often of the mercy, graciousness, and goodness of God. As classical theists, they hold that God is good, omnipotent, omniscient, and omnipresent. Differing sharply on their view of Jesus, Calvin and Muhammad nevertheless stress the view that God accomplishes his will (or gets his way) because he is the Lord and sovereign of the universe. Indeed, both Calvinism and Islam embrace enthusiastically the doctrine of divine *predestination*, which says that God has decreed and planned every detail of his creation, including the details of your life and mine.[2] He has arranged all things and knows precisely all that will ever come about. God is absolutely all-knowing and all-powerful.[3]

Predestination and Freedom.   The doctrine of predestination asserts that God causes all things. Nothing escapes his directing power. This naturally raises questions about human freedom, and I will try now to explain how predestination is held to harmonize with the freedom of God's creatures. The reason it is important for both Calvinism and Islam effectively to harmonize predestination with creaturely freedom is very simple. Both faiths believe that the evils and sufferings of the world are mostly (perhaps wholly) the result of human free choice and action.

Suppose that during a windstorm a tree falls against the side of a house and does damage. If we say that the cause of the damage was the tree, we would be accurate. If we say also that the cause of the damage was the unusually high wind, we would again be accurate. Had the wind not come up, the tree would not have fallen—at least not at that time.

Now, the tree may be compared to human choice, whereas the wind may be compared to God's power or will. Hence, if one person stabs another, it is the power or will of God bringing about the act of violence. However, God is not to be blamed; it was the human agent who was directly involved in the killing. True, God caused the individual agent to do this foul deed, but God did not do the deed himself. He had it done by another.

Let us look again at the tree lying against the damaged house. We might observe that termites in the roots of the tree had weakened its foundation, thus making it more likely to fall during a storm. Of course, for Calvinism and Islam, God caused the wind, the tree, and the termites to do what they did. Everything is the product of his power or will. Hence, returning to the murderer, we might at first glance be able to say that he did his foul deed because he was weak of character. Like the tree infested with termites, the killer was weak "inside."

However, Calvinism and Islam do not fail to assert that just as God caused the termites to eat the tree, so God caused certain things to destroy the inner character of the would-be killer. Hence, under certain conditions, the killer would commit his evil deed, just as under certain windy conditions the tree would eventually fall on the house.

Is Every Human Action a Free Choice?   It might look as if Calvinism and Islam interpret every human action and response, no matter what it may be, as a free choice. But this view is too extreme. One of the most gifted thinkers among Calvinists, Jonathan Edwards, wrote an outstanding treatise entitled *Freedom of the Will*. In it, he tries to distinguish acts of freedom from other acts. Very simply, a free act or deed must meet two tests. First, it must be one that you want to do. Second, you must not be hindered in satisfying the wish to do it.[4] If you went to the supermarket because you wanted to, then your arrival there was a free act. But if you were prevented from carrying out your want, then your freedom was thwarted to that degree. Of if you were forced to go to the supermarket even though you did not *want* to, then your freedom was at that point frustrated.[5]

Those classical theists who hold to strict predestination do not deny that people often do things that they want or choose to do, including some very wicked things. Indeed, if people want to do evil deeds and then carry them out, then they are to be classified as sinners. In fact, they are often regarded as sinners even when merely *wanting* to do evil. For example, Calvin, like Jesus, thinks it is sinful just to *want* to commit adultery.

Calvinism and Islam seek to harmonize predestination and human freedom in the following way: First, people are free when *they want to do something and carry out that want*. Second, *God causes* them to have the wants that they have. He brings about these wants either directly or through other instruments. (Theologians differ on this technical point.) In any case, human wants are brought about through the deliberate directing power of God.

Anyone who believes in the strict predestination of either Calvin or Muhammad cannot fall back on the doctrine of God's "permissive will." According to this view, God merely *permits* people to do things; he does not *cause* them to do things. But an orthodox Calvinist or Muslim regards this doctrine to be a surrender of God's sovereignty and omnipotence. After all, God cannot direct the course of events exactly as he pleases unless he has complete control of every single event.

In order to stress their point that God predestines or foreordains the wants or choices of people, as well as their accomplished deeds, one consistent Calvinist theologian presents the matter in the following graphic way:

Are there factors or powers which determine a person's choices . . . ? Could Judas have chosen otherwise? [The question is] not, could he have *done* otherwise, had he chosen. . . . [Rather, the question is,] could he have *chosen* in opposition to God's foreordination? Acts 4:28 indicates that he could not.[6]

Does God Foreordain Immoral Acts?   In the words of the orthodox Calvinist, "It may seem strange at first that God would decree an immoral act, but the Bible shows that he did."[7] The Lord put a lying spirit in the mouths of prophets and made them to lie.[8] This view follows from the predestination theory that

every detail of history was eternally in [God's] plan before the world began; and he willed that it should all come to pass. . . . God determined that Christ should die; he determined that Judas should betray him.[9]

Calvinists, like the Muslims, are convinced that God directs every event, including every *evil* event. Again, an orthodox Calvinist states this point bluntly:

I wish very frankly and pointedly to assert that if a man gets drunk and shoots his family, it was the will of God that he should do so. The Scriptures leave no room for doubt . . . that it was God's will for Herod, Pilate, and the Jews to crucify Christ. In Ephesians 1:11 Paul tells us that God works all things, not just some things only, after the counsel of his own will.[10]

This may appear to you to be a theology of macabre and gruesome depths, but it appears to follow consistently from the premise that God is in complete control of history and all the minute details thereof. Calvinists and Muslims take seriously the theory of classical theism that God is all-powerful.

In the fields of theology and the philosophy of religion, one of the most persistent problems is that of explaining the existence of evil. By "evil" is meant both immoral behavior and natural conflict. In the case of natural conflict, for example, some parts of nature seem to thwart other parts. Earthquakes and tornadoes destroy, insects bite animals, animals prey on one another, cancer cells grow at the expense of the host organism, etc. The word 'theodicy' is often used to refer to the intellectual problem of trying to explain how these evils could exist in a world created and governed by a good God. The problem is especially acute if this God is taken to be not only good, but also all-powerful. Calvinism does not play down the omnipotence of God. It boldly insists that God causes evil in the world by causing human beings and others to harbor immoral motives and to execute immoral acts.

Classical Theism Demands Divine Providence. Other leading Christians in addition to Calvin have insisted that no action of any creature can be other than what God predestined that it should be. If free will is understood to mean some act or choice that is somehow exempted from God's full and complete control, then numerous influential Christians have not believed in free will. In his book *The Bondage of the Will* the famous Protestant leader Martin Luther writes: "For if we believe it to be true that God foreknows and foreordains all things, . . . then there can be no free will in man, in angel, or in any creature."[11]

Thomas Aquinas, who has profoundly influenced the Catholic version of Christianity, writes: "God alone can move the [human] will, as an agent, without doing violence to it."[12] Thomas is careful to argue that the "will" and "choice" of human beings are very special, and that therefore human beings must be moved in ways in which other entities are not moved. But the point is that everything about human life is caused, with absolutely no exceptions. Nothing escapes the net. In fact, Thomas vigorously opposes the view that God simply created people with a neutral will. He insists that God causes people to will *this or that in particular*. Furthermore, "God is the cause not only of our wills but also of our willing." "He is the cause of the movements of the will." Thomas claims to be following Aristotle's principle that "anything new must have a cause."[13]

Thomas proceeds even further to reject the view that God moves merely the body but not the intellectual aspects of human beings. He rejects this view because he says that to embrace it would be to conclude that "there will be no providence at all." In fact, because God loves human beings so much, he does not use *instruments* to move their will and choice. Rather, says Thomas, "acts of choice and movements of will are under the *immediate* governance of God."[14]

Neither Calvin, Muhammad, Thomas Aquinas, nor Luther denies that human beings make choices, exert their wills, and desire this and that. But the point here is that these religious leaders and theologians all realize what the doctrine of divine providence and omnipotence entails. It entails that in one way or another human willing, desiring, choosing, and acting must be *caused and controlled* by God. To deny this is to deny the divine Lordship. Classical theists are convinced that God is going to get his way, for he causes and controls what is going on in the universe. This is the classical theists' doctrine of divine providence. To the degree that this doctrine is modified, then to that degree the hypothesis of classical theism is modified.

Thomas makes it quite clear that God works not only on things "external" to the human individual, but on such alleged inner phenomena as choice, will, desire, and willing. Nothing is left to chance.[15] There is, then, only one way to deny that God causes people to do evil, and that is to deny that God is in control of things. Giving up their doctrine of divine providence is a price that consistent classical theists are not prepared to pay.

But What of Hell?   When contemplating what to him was the fact that so few people would go to heaven while so many would be damned to hell, Martin Luther became greatly disturbed. But he was not disturbed enough to give up his doctrine of divine providence and predestination. About all he could recommend was an increase in faith. Hence he says,

This is the highest degree of faith, to believe [God] merciful when he saves so few and damns so many . . . so that he seems, according to Erasmus, to delight in the torments of the wretched and to be worthy of hatred rather than love. If, then, I could by any means comprehend how this God can be merciful and just who displays so much wrath and iniquity, there would be no need of faith.[16]

What puzzles Luther so much is the question of why God does not change the *wills* of those who choose hell instead of heaven. After all, you recall, the human will is not something neutral that dangles in suspension. It, too, is supposed to be controlled by God's providence. So, if God could shape the wills of a *minority* of people to go to heaven, why could he not shape the wills of the *majority* to go there! Indeed why deliberately foreordain even *one* person to go to hell?[17]

Luther concludes that he is unable to explain even to his own satisfaction how God could, on the one hand, be merciful and omnipotent, while, on the other hand, send masses of people to hell. But instead of yielding on at least one point of this dilemma, Luther responds that it is all a great mystery. The practical upshot of this attitude is found in Luther's warning against trying to understand this mystery. He describes as "perverse" anyone who prys into what he calls God's "secret will."[18]

Jesus is reported to have offered the following warning:

Enter by the narrow gate; for the gate is wide and the way is easy, that leads to destruction, and those who enter it are many. For the gate is narrow and the way is hard, that leads to life, and those who find it are few.[19]

Christians have generally taken this passage to mean that more people will go to hell than to heaven, although some Christians interpret Jesus' reference to "destruction" to mean something other than hell. Writing in the *New Bible Commentary*, one orthodox Protestant acknowledges that he does not understand why "Only a minority has found salvation." Like Luther, he calls it "one of the mysteries of God's providence." He goes on to note that "each succeeding generation is a testimony to Jesus' claim that only a few will receive salvation."[20]

The Two Wills of God. Many Calvinists and other classical theists sometimes wish to distinguish God's "secret will" from his "revealed will."[21] This distinction is a device for escaping the charge that God seems to be working at cross-purposes.[22] Many classical theists take the "secret will" of God to be his more fundamental aim or plan. Knowledge of this "secret will" would presumably put our human minds at ease. Why? Because if we possessed this knowledge, we would see that all the sufferings, miseries, and destructive conflicts of both this world and hell are really a part of God's encompassing strategy. Of course, Napoleon believed that the agonies and torments brought on by his wars were simply a part of his overall strategy, but this did not morally justify his strategy. Once it was made known, many people judged Napoleon all the more to be an immoral lunatic.

To be sure, if there is a God and if he has a *"secret* will," then we cannot know whether his *"revealed* will" contradicts it. Why? Very simply, we do not know what the secret will is.

However, many classical theists seem to harbor in their own minds a secret *wish* that God will in the end look better morally than his alleged revealed will or wills have managed to make him look. The secret wish of these individuals seems to be a major source of their faith in God's ultimate goodness. They insist that somehow God's goodness will reveal itself to be so wonderful as to make even the torments of hell fade into insignificance. But this could be interpreted as a wish to *forget or ignore* this life's miseries as well as the miseries of people in hell. Ironically, in order to forget those who are tormented forever in hell, the believers in heaven would have to become much more morally hardened and callous than they are on earth. Thomas Aquinas assured Christians that in heaven they will not feel compassion for the damned.[23] As you know, compassion can be painful until you do something to help those in great need.

The Answer of Omnipotence.   The postulate of the "two wills of God" appears to be a device for patching up the heavy damage that morally sensitive questions have inflicted on classical theism. If the "revealed will" of God cannot hold up under attack, then the "secret will" is brought in to save the cause. On moral grounds, a number of Christians have felt it necessary to conclude that Jesus himself would not really have believed in hell. It is thought that if theism could at least throw overboard the doctrine of hell, then God would at least not have *that* to justify morally.

However, even without this doctrine of hell, Christianity and Islam are still in trouble, for much evil and suffering remain in the world. Calvin and most of his professed followers do not even attempt to throw out the doctrine of hell, for they think they already have a sufficient answer to the problem of evil and suffering in the world. The answer, very simply is this: regardless of what God's short-term and long-term purposes are, the truth remains that he can do what he will or wants because he is the *Supreme Power*.

A Split in Classical Theism.   At this crucial point, various classical theists begin to part company with one another. Two major views dominate the field. One school says, in effect, that the Supreme Power must measure up to certain standards of goodness if it is to be counted as good—especially as the *supremely* good Being. But the other school says, in effect, that God's *supreme might or power* is sufficient to justify whatever he does. It seems that most Christians prefer the first school to the second. But the first is in such severe trouble that it is forced either to resort to blind faith in a mystery or to turn finally to the second school.[24]

This second school solves the problem very simply by, in effect, giving up the moral defense of God. In short, Calvinism and Islam lead eventually to a position of *supreme might makes right*! One Calvinist states this position crisply and crudely:

God . . . cannot be responsible for the plain reason that there is no power superior to him: no greater being can hold him accountable; no one can punish him; there is no one to whom God is responsible; there are no laws which he could disobey.[25]

Another Calvinist writes, "What [God] does is good just because he does it."[26] The same writer goes so far as to conclude that if God had chosen to send the *entire* human population to hell, he would have been perfectly good and just in doing so.[27] This conclusion follows from the Calvinistic doctrine that "The good is what God does."[28] Clearly, on this view, the one who has the greatest might is above any and all standards of morality and goodness. That is what the Calvinist means when he says, "By definition God cannot sin."[29]

Calvinists and the like agree that if any human or archangel assumes to be above all moral standards, he must be condemned as wicked and evil or else as morally underdeveloped. But this is not admitted to be the case with the Supreme Power. According to Calvin, "the will of God is the highest rule of justice; so that what he wills must be considered just." Why must it? Calvin answers quickly: "for this very reason, because he wills it."[30] Again, the ultimate appeal is to superior power, not in the service of morality, but as the *ultimate standard of* morality and value. Whenever the strict Calvinist says "Whatever God does is just,"[31] he is saying nothing less than this: *No matter what* God does, he will be called good and just simply because he does it.

In attempting to work loose from such an abhorrent conclusion, one uncomfortable Calvinist says, in effect, that once the Christian has had "fellowship" with God, then he will learn thereafter to trust God to use his omnipotence in a moral way.[32] Unfortunately, this answer does not face up to the question as to whether a Being is to be called "God" simply because it is the Supreme Force and Power. Presumably an omnipotent Satan would not be God just because of his supreme power. What the uncomfortable and wavering Calvinist fails to realize is that in speaking of "fellowship" with God, he is smuggling in a distinct moral standard and attributing it to the Supreme Might. This is perhaps commendable, for strict Calvinism is a ruthless doctrine unless it is supplemented with standards beyond itself.

The point here, however, is that the wavering Calvinist already and unwittingly *presupposes* that the Supreme Might is also supremely good on some ground other than his power alone. Without this presupposition, the wavering Calvinist could not greatly value his alleged "fellowship" with the Supreme Power—unless, of course, power were his ultimate value. But far from being a defense of Calvinism, this appeal to fellowship with God merely shows that Calvinism must reach beyond itself if it is to enjoy the right to refer to its Supreme Might as "God." The assumption here in this critique of Calvinism is that no Being deserves the title of "God" unless it is greatly moral as well as powerful.

The strict Calvinist, however, realizes that any appeal to a moral or value standard other than Supreme Might alone will in effect break apart the distinctive Calvinist structure.[33] Strict Calvinism's perpetual temptation is to solve the ancient "problem of evil" by capitulating to, and worshiping, raw power. Most modern Calvinists seem inclined toward believing that God's power is somehow checked by other facets of his own being. But they do not see clearly that this is inconsistent with their own doctrine of God's complete providence and predestination.[34]

ARMINIANISM

The Doubts of Arminius.   Arminianism is an attempt to free God from the blame of sending great numbers of people to hell and of creating an enormous amount of suffering and evil in the world. It arose around 1600 with Jacobus Arminius, who, although trained as a Calvinist, eventually began having serious doubts about the Calvinist version of predestination and providence. Eventually he advanced a protest against Calvinism's doctrine of predestination. The influence of Arminius spread quickly and widely; eventually it helped to shape the Wesleyan branch of the Methodist movement in the eighteenth century, as well as many other Christian bodies thereafter.

In order to shift all blame from God, Calvinists had not hesitated to place all the blame for the world's trouble onto his creatures. But the Calvinist method of doing this seemed to Arminius and subsequent Arminians to be unconvincing. After all, the Calvinist arguments that were used to defend the view that God is in perfect control of things were the very same arguments that seemed to make him responsible for all the evil and sufferings of life. Arminius thought that he himself had hit upon a better way to recognize God as both in control and wholly blameless.

The first thing that Arminius did was to completely rework the doctrine of predestination. His ingenious revision retains the ancient Christian doctrine that God created the world from nothing—*ex nihilo*. Siding with traditional Christianity, Arminius agreed that God was not forced to create with some primordial energy or stuff. But Arminius was eager to stress the position that God did start with *information*.

Calvinism had talked a lot about "the counsels of God." In these "divine counsels" the plans of the universe were supposed to have been originated. But Calvinists did not like to probe the inner chambers of God's thinking. These were, after all, secret—strictly for the three persons of the Godhead. Indeed, Calvinists felt that even the phrase "the counsels of God" was only a metaphor pointing to a greater mystery; and Calvin warned against looking behind the metaphor.

But Arminius, like Moses standing before the burning bush, felt that he might be able to move in closer. Arminius seemed to have asked himself what might have been thought in the divine counsels. It seemed quite logical to believe that God would not create blindly. God would create with maximum knowledge at his disposal. Here the doctrine of omniscience comes to the forefront. After all, without full knowledge, power could become an irrational burst of energy flying off aimlessly. Hence, God's omnipotence needs his omniscience to steer it. Such was one of Arminius' major conclusions.

Omniscience and Predestination. Arminianism says that, before creation, God could not have possessed information of what already existed, because nothing yet existed. Yet God could have possessed total information regarding what surely would be if only he should decide to create it. In other words,

Arminians say that God looked ahead (in an eternal sort of way) and foresaw all the future choices and acts of those individuals who would exist *if* he should give them existence. This is what the doctrine of foreknowledge means.

However, Arminians insist further that even though God *foreknew* everything that you would do, he did not thereby *predetermine* any of your choices and decisions. Presumably the only thing he absolutely determined was that you should exist. But he did not arrange what you would *choose and do* once you came into existence.

As a matter of fact, say the Arminians, God knew that you and everyone else would invariably fall into sin. He foresaw exactly how things would develop, including how Adam would sin. He foreknew how this first man's sin would pollute the whole of earthly creation so that each and every subsequent human being would without exception fall into sin naturally and of his own choice.[35] In other words, instead of God receiving the blame for releasing the forces that would cause the whole human population to fall into sin and suffering, Adam is blamed for doing it. True, God brought Adam into existence, but thereafter Adam made his own choices.

Why Did God Initiate Such a Poor Plan?   Of course, a philosopher might ask, "Why did God start with Adam if he foreknew infallibly that the fellow would bring about a colossal disaster?" Arminians seem to want to close up the counsels of God at this point. But the philosopher presses further. He continues by asking whether in his infinite imagination God had other human experiments in mind. Or was Adam the only one available? Was God's inner counsel so lean and meager as to have no option better than an Adam who would eventually choose sin? Was there no other individual in God's mind who, if created, would have *freely resisted* all temptation? If not, then does this not suggest that *God's resources were limited*?

Suppose that from his infinite resources God had at least one other individual in mind who would freely choose never to sin. God, you recall, would have known in advance who would resist temptation and who would not. So, if God had selected a man or woman who would always choose righteousness and happiness, then presumably this person would have released forces that would make it very likely that all subsequent humanity would freely choose righteousness and happiness.

Or, still another alternative is perhaps better than the old

Adam option. It would seem that on Arminius' own assumptions a good God ought to have selected with much greater compassion and care. If he knew well in advance that certain human beings (at least) would go to everlasting hell, then why did he not exercise moral responsibility by restraining the urge to create them? You recall that, as the omnipotent one, God was not *compelled* to create them. Self-restraint on God's part in this case would not have caused any suffering or deprivation of freedom in any individual not created. After all, no individual can suffer the feeling of rejection if he has never come into existence in the first place.

As the most responsible and benevolent of all beings, God might have selected to create *only* those intelligent creatures who would *freely choose* a life of bliss and righteousness without sin and suffering. It will do no good to say that God could not have done this without denying the freedom of choice of those not created. The freedom of nonexisting individuals can no more be violated than the petals of a nonexisting flower can be removed. To be sure, *imaginary* petals may be imaginarily removed from an imaginary flower, just as imaginary freedom may be imaginarily removed from imaginary individuals. But only by confusing the fictional world with the actual world can Arminians claim that freedom is denied someone who does not even exist.

The Alternate Plan. Consider more carefully the alternate plan that the Arminian God might have enacted. God would create only those who choose everlasting happiness rather than misery in hell. Note again that the Arminian concern for freedom of choice is not violated by this plan. God does not control the lives of those whom he creates so that they are *compelled* to accept everlasting happiness. Rather he foresees that, if created, some people will *freely choose* everlasting happiness. Hence, upon the basis of this prior information, he brings into existence *only those* who will *freely choose* everlasting happiness.

So, before creation was even begun, why could not the God of Arminius have selected only *some* possible persons to exist and others not to exist? Indeed, there is nothing in Christian theology that says he did not do this anyhow. The point here is that a moral God would have selected with greater care by bringing into existence *only* those who would freely choose everlasting happiness.

Imagine that you have the power to bring into being any of ten children whom you please. No restrictions are placed on you except your own moral standards. Now imagine further that you have the unusual power to foreknow precisely which of your possible children will live happy lives forever, and which ones will live utterly miserable lives forever. To be sure, the latter group might enjoy at least a few decades of happiness, but thereafter they would suffer one agony after another, relentlessly and without relief forever. The question is, Which of these children would you bring into existence, and which would you refrain from bringing into existence?

The Arminians seem to think that prior to creation God was in a somewhat similar position. He foreknew that some of his potential or possible children would end in eternal misery if he should create them. Yet, say the orthodox Arminians, God proceeded deliberately to bring them into being. Furthermore, once they were brought into being, they *had to* live forever. If in hell they wish to end their lives, the God of Arminius will not give them this option. They *must* suffer endlessly.

Do People Knowingly Choose Everlasting Torment?   Some Arminians insist that the human population is literally filled with members who, knowing full well that there is a hell of infinite horror, nevertheless choose to go there. Now, this is an unusual claim, to say the least. What it lacks is evidence to support it. Or, more precisely, it is stated in such a way as to make itself untestable.[36]

For example, suppose that you ask great numbers of non-Christians whether they are choosing to suffer infinite horror in hell as some Arminians say they are. It is very likely that these people will respond that they definitely do *not* have it in mind to choose such everlasting horror and agony. So what will the Arminian say in reply? Will he insist that these people are all lying? The Arminian cannot maintain his original thesis if he shifts his ground by claiming that these people are nevertheless choosing hell even though they do not know it.

There is a great difference between knowingly driving your car into a cow on the road and doing so unknowingly. It is stretching the word "choose" to say that you "chose" to drive into the cow if you did not even know that there was a cow there. Similarly, if there were a hell, a person might conceivably go there accidentally; but this is quite different from *choosing* to go there. Indeed, few Arminians will agree that they themselves choose *heaven accidentally*. Rather, they will insist that they knowingly choose heaven. In other words, they distinguish in their own lives between doing something *accidentally* or unknowingly and doing it by choice. Hence, if they can accept this distinction in their own lives, they would seem to be under obligation to accept it in the lives of people who reject Christianity.

What some Arminians seem to be doing is this: they are claiming that anyone who rejects Christianity will go to hell. Then they are in their own minds treating this rejection of Christianity as if it were the individual's own *choice* to go to *hell*. This, of course, denies the individual the opportunity to give his own testimony. What he may claim is that he chose specifically to reject Christianity; he did *not* choose to go to hell. In fact, he may sincerely believe that there is no eternal hell at all, or that an honest rejection of Christian belief will not send him to hell. Hence, he cannot be said to be choosing hell.

On the other hand, if there is a hell and a God concerned to send certain non-Christians there, then it may be said that *God chooses* to send them there. Arminians, of course, have traditionally wished to relieve their God of this heavy choice and responsibility, but it cannot be said that they have found a legitimate way of doing so.

Lack of Sensitivity. It may be that what the Arminian case for hell reveals is a certain insensitivity on the part of some Christians. That is, they cannot understand people who do not accept their faith. Such Christians seem genuinely unable to think it possible that people who reject Christianity would even *want* to be happy and moral. While being able to imagine Christians enjoying themselves (in heaven) without involvement with "unbelievers," some Christians seem unable to imagine non-Christians enjoying themselves without being involved with Christian notions of God, salvation, etc. Apparently these Christians simply cannot imagine that people greatly different from themselves theologically are capable of even wanting a peaceful, creative, and enjoyable existence. Such Christians have become convinced that unbelievers are more selfish, wicked, and vile than Christians. Hence, unbelievers are portrayed as destined always to choose hell wherever they are.

However, it may be that Christians have created hell for

those whom they cannot convert. In criticizing some of his fellow Christians for believing in a doctrine of eternal torment, one philosopher charges that the doctrine is the product of a "sinful imagination."[37] Perhaps a hypothesis worth looking into is that the belief in eternal torment is the expression of the burning inner rage of those who are frustrated in their ambitions to convert the world to their faith. Hell is human resentment against those who have rejected what has been graciously offered as the only worthwhile way of living. A fruitful comparison may be made with the lover who, on the one hand, would give his very life for the object of his love, and on the other hand, would take revenge on the very same person if she rejected his offer of marriage. Indeed, orthodox Christians portray Christ in this very light. He gives his life, and to hell with whoever rejects it!

Some believers are convinced that only evil motives could cause a person to reject Christianity. They cannot accept gracefully the thought of a universe in which people, on the one hand, differ with Christianity on some important theological matters, and, on the other hand, desire to lead reasonably happy and moral lives. These believers seem unable to wish happiness for unbelievers; and there are, in turn, unbelievers who seem equally unable to wish happiness for believers.

Most Christians seem to be much more hospitable and sensitive to unbelievers than their God is often thought to be. It appears that their deity has a certain trait—sometimes called "holiness"—that prevents him from wishing lasting happiness for those who do not accept his theology-laden "gift of salvation."

Whether this "holiness" is indeed a divine moral standard is a matter of debate. It often appears as pathological aggression toward outsiders. And far from being a divine trait, this amity-enmity complex seems to be quite human (and even animal) in origin. It has roots in love for insiders and hostility toward outsiders. Orthodox Christians believe in hell, and are very eager to take in outsiders to make them into insiders. But this is different from the toleration of, or respect for, the outsiders' desire to follow their own lights without the threat of punishment and everlasting torment.

It is conceivable that the doctrine of hell is a mythologized projection of the worst side of human beings, of human beings in their most vindictive and intolerant depths. Telling us nothing about a supernatural Being, the doctrine of hell perhaps reveals the most imperfect side of the human species. It is the ontological argument of Perfection turned upside down.

Must People Sin in order to Appreciate Everlasting Happiness? Some Christians insist that God could not have created a better world than what exists now. This is not because he is lacking in power, but because his creatures simply could not yet appreciate a better world. Hence the miseries of sin and suffering are, unfortunately, required to help people appreciate everlasting life. To fully enjoy life at its best, they must first fall into sin and misery and afterward be redeemed. Only then will they be prepared to enjoy the bliss of everlasting life.[38]

Now, there seem to be some problems with this view. First, we might note in passing that God is regarded by Muslims and Christians as exceptionally happy even though he has never been threatened with the terrors of sin and hell. Second, what about those who never make it to heaven? Did they simply not learn enough to appreciate heaven? If not, then orthodox Christianity offers them no other alternative but to suffer endless torment.

Another Proposal. Let us assume for the moment that everlasting life becomes more meaningful to human beings only if they have sinned and subsequently are redeemed. On this assumption, in the long run it would be better that human beings fall into sin. That is why God, let us say, proceeded to create people who would sin. He foresaw that they would first become wicked and then later become redeemed.

Unfortunately, this hypothesis runs into a very serious snag, so serious that it may unravel the entire hypothesis. The snag comes in the admission on the part of orthodox Arminians that in fact great throngs of people will not become redeemed at all. Hence, they will lose out on the goal to which falling into sin was supposed to be a means in the first place.

But perhaps there is a way out of this admittedly sad state of affairs. Arminius' omniscient God would surely have known in advance all who would *both* fall into sin and *accept redemption*. Furthermore, this God would have known those who would both fall into sin and *remain unredeemed*. So, even if it were true that falling into sin and misery is necessary for bringing people to appreciate everlasting life, there still was no moral reason for Arminius' God to create those who would remain unredeemed. A fully knowledgeable and good God would have brought into existence *only those* who, after falling, would also accept redemption. There would have been no more reason for creating those who would end their lives in eternal misery.

The Dilemma of Orthodox Arminians.　　Unfortunately, orthodox Arminians are unable to accept the above alternative because they simply have a commitment to believe in hell. They think that God has revealed in Scripture that there is a real and endless hell for the damned. As orthodox Arminian Christians, they hold that they have no other alternative but to accept this doctrine. It might seem that a modern Arminian such as Alvin Plantinga would welcome the alternative of believing in a God who creates only those individuals who would accept redemption. However, in order for this alternative to be accepted, the hypothesis of an infallible Bible would have to be given up.

Plantinga cannot give up belief in an infallible Bible, and there exists no strong empirical evidence to support a belief in blissful life after death for everyone. Hence, Professor Plantinga seems to be left with the notion of a God who either (1) *wants* a world that contains eternal torment for some of his creatures or (2) is *eternally frustrated* because he lacks the power to prevent himself from sustaining hell forever.

If Plantinga's God could restrain himself from supporting hell but does not choose to do so, then he would seem to be more perverse and vindictive than any human sadist.[39] Collect together all the horrors and terrors that the Stalins and Hitlers of the world have inflicted on their fellow human beings, and then compare these savage accounts with the torments that Plantinga's God sustains unendingly in hell for great masses of humankind. The conclusion is clear: Plantinga's God is incomparably more cruel and vindictive than all the combined Hitlers and Stalins of the world.

It will not work for orthodox Arminians to argue that God has nothing to do with hell because it is totally self-supporting without him. This argument will not work because, you recall, a central doctrine of all classical theists is that absolutely nothing can survive for a second without God's causing it to survive. Hell, therefore, is perpetually sustained and maintained by the power of God. Remove that power, and hell would immediately vanish. Such a conclusion follows strictly from the

Christian doctrines of God's providence, omnipotence, and omnipresence.

CLASSICAL THEISM IN REVISION

Christianity without Hell.   It is not surprising that a number of Christian thinkers and laymen have given up belief in everlasting torment. Even when such torment is popularly called "separation from God," the doctrine of divine providence reminds the orthodox that nothing can exist wholly in separation from God. The reason that many Christians give up belief in hell is that such a belief is too much to deal with both morally and intellectually.[40] God cannot be made to appear victorious and good if the doctrine of hell is to be attributed to him. Either he takes on the appearance of a cosmic sadist whose goals are morally inferior, or he is a bungler of the worst sort.

Perhaps what has become clear is this: So long as Christians held to a doctrine of everlasting hell, they were very hard put to claim that God is greatly moral. Even the argument that "the ends justify the means" cannot work, for hell turns out to be not simply a means, but an end itself that is nothing less than the worst of all known atrocities.

To say that God's holiness demands the perpetuation of such an atrocity does more to cast doubt on the meaning of "holiness" than it does to justify hell as serving a moral end. Holiness takes on the appearance of pathology.

Will Theological Pruning Improve the Case for Classical Theism?   If Christians, Muslims, and other classical theists give up the doctrine of everlasting and hopeless torment, will they be in a better position to defend the view that there is a God who is *both* omnipotent and good? In responding to this, one might say, first, that the existence of a hell would pretty much guarantee that God is not moral.

Second, a classical theism that eliminates hell may be compared to a rapidly sinking ship that has an elephant on board. If the elephant is pushed overboard, the ship will probably sink anyhow. With the elephant aboard, it will surely sink.

Whether in the form of Christianity or in some other form, classical theism has often embraced the view that sin and suffering in this present life are a means to something wonderful that only God can fully envision. Cancer, war, disease, death, tragic accidents—these have always been most difficult to explain. The notion of hell can be more easily dropped because, after all, it is not something that can be observed to exist. But such phenomena as cancer, accidents, and the like cannot be so easily disposed of. They strike down theologians and deacons as well as unbelievers. So, leaving behind us the discussions of hell, we must now confront such obvious evils in our world as sickness, suffering, death, alienation, hatred, and fruitless conflict.

Two Major Trends.   Among classical theists who reject everlasting hell, two major trends have developed. The first plays up the element of mystery. That is, God's aim is not questioned in terms of its being good. Rather, doubts exist regarding the *content* of God's good aim or purpose. And this is understandable. For no known aim or goal seems to satisfy as a justifying goal. That is, theists look at the projected goal; then they look at the various means in the form of great suffering and evil in the world. And they conclude that the means seem to be excessive and even irrelevant to the goal.

The second trend seems to be that of scaling down the claims of God's omnipotence. At times even Calvinists talk, somewhat vaguely, of harmonizing God's power and will with the rest of the divine nature. This trend has ventured a long way into theological forests, and many theologians and philosophers have set up camp at various places along the way. Some of them contend that God's own nature has rational and moral elements that give direction to his power. But this only increases the problem of explaining the vast amount of evil in the world.

However, the trend toward more forthrightly qualifying the omnipotence of God has sometimes gone to the extent of advancing the hypothesis that God's power to do good is conditioned—conditioned by a nonrational dimension of his own nature. On this view, God's power or energy is not completely and totally integrated. God is seen as not only creative and powerful, but as also struggling, suffering, and undergoing certain partial defeats and new victories.

But once this degree of qualification of divine omnipotence is made, classical theism has been forsaken. Indeed, an increasing number of theists seem very eager to set themselves apart from *classical* theism, which they regard as intellectually and morally indefensible, and therefore emotionally meaningless to them. In recent years a *revised* theism has been rigorously defended and debated. Its proponents stress that any religion worthy of commitment must measure up morally, intellectually, and emotionally.

But can a person be profoundly religious if he believes in a God greatly different from the God of classical theism? In the next two chapters you will encounter some views of God that may be new to you. After those chapters, you will find two chapters on naturalism, which denies the existence of any God. One of the most fruitful exchanges in the philosophy of religion is the interchange between naturalism and views of God other than classical theism.

NOTES

1. See John Calvin, *Institutes of the Christian Religion*, 2 vols., trans. John Allen (Philadelphia: Presbyterian Board of Christian Education, 1936).

2. See B. A. Warfield, "Predestination," in *Biblical and Theological Studies*, ed. Samuel G. Craig (Philadelphia: Presbyterian & Reformed Publishing Co., 1952), pp. 280–285.

3. See *The Koran Interpreted*, trans. A. J. Arberry (New York: Macmillan, 1970), XLII, 1–13.

4. See Jonathan Edwards, *The Freedom of the Will*, ed. Paul Ramsey (New Haven: Yale University Press, 1957), p. 164.

5. Some Calvinists prefer to use the word 'choice' instead of 'want'. 'Choice' is defined as "a mental act that consciously initiates and determines a further action" (Gordon H. Clark, *Religion, Reason, and Revelation* [Philadelphia: Presbyterian & Reformed Publishing Co., 1961], p. 228). Of course, a strict predestinationist holds that the choice is caused. "A choice," says Clark, "is still a deliberate volition *even if it could not have been different*" (ibid.; italics added).

6. Ibid., p. 227. Italics added.

7. Ibid., p. 222.

8. See 2 Chronicles 18:20–22.

9. Clark, *Religion, Reason, and Revelation*, p. 238. See Psalms 136:6; Daniel 4:35; Isaiah 45:7; Proverbs 16:4; Romans 9:19–20, 11:22. See also *Koran*, VXXV, 52–62, XXVII, 65, XLII, 12–15, 45–46.

10. Clark, *Religion, Reason, and Revelation*, p. 221.

11. Martin Luther, *The Bondage of the Will*, trans. J. I. Packer and O. R. Johnston (London: J. Clarke, 1957).

12. *Summa contra Gentiles*, in *Basic Writings of Saint Thomas*

Aquinas, 2 vols., ed. Anton C. Pegis (New York: Random House, 1945), vol. 2; bk. 3, chap. 88.

13. Ibid., vol. 1; bk. 3, chap. 89.

14. Ibid., vol. 1; bk. 3, chaps. 89–91 Italics added.

15. See ibid, vol. 1; bk. 3, chaps. 89–90.

16. Luther, *Bondage of the Will*, trans. Philip Watson, in Philip Watson and Gordon Rupp, *Luther and Erasmus: Free Will and Salvation* (Philadelphia: Westminster Press, 1969), p. 138.

17. In an article entitled "Are There Few That Be Saved?" one Calvinist theologian attempts to improve God's image by portraying him as foreordaining the minority, rather than the majority, of human beings to hell (B. B. Warfield, in *Biblical and Theological Studies*, ed. Samuel G. Craig [Philadelphia: Presbyterian & Reformed Publishing Co., 1952], pp. 334–350). Presumably God is regarded as not immoral if he discriminates against the minority instead of the majority. When Warfield's article was written in 1911, it was generally believed by Christians that their religion would steadily increase its influence and convert the masses of the world, thus ushering in the Kingdom of God. This optimism has generally been given up, although today some Christians still expect a sudden and sensational worldwide revival to break out soon, a revival that would end in wholesale conversion to Christianity. The thought of the majority of humanity going to hell is not easy to swallow, and it understandably triggers off the desire for a mass conversion.

18. See Luther, *Bondage of the Will*, in *Luther and Erasmus*, pp. 206–207.

19. Matthew 7:13–14 (RSV).

20. Basil F. C. Atkinson commenting on Matthew 7:13–14 in *New Bible Commentary*, ed. F. Davidson (Grand Rapids: Eerdmans, 1966), p. 782.

21. See Clark, *Religion, Reason and Revelation*, p. 222.

22. The conflict within God is inadvertently brought out in Holmes Robertson III, *John Calvin Versus the Westminster Confession* (Atlanta: John Knox Press, 1972), chap. 2.

23. See *Summa Theologica*, 22 vols., trans. Fathers of the English Dominican Province (London: Burns, Oates & Washbourne, 1922), vol. 21; pt. 3 (supp.), quest. 94, art. 2.

24. See Pattison Brown, "God and the Good," *Religious Studies* 2, no. 2 (April 1967): 275.

25. Clark, *Religion, Reason, and Revelation*, p. 241.

26. Edward John Carnell, "How Every Christian Can Defend His Faith" (pt. 3 of "The Providence of God"), *Moody Monthly* 2 (March 1950): 507.

27. Carnell, *An Introduction to Christian Apologetics* (Grand Rapids: Eerdmans, 1948), p. 343.

28. Ibid., p. 298, n. 11.

29. Clark, *Religion, Reason and Revelation*, p. 239.

30. Calvin, *Institutes of the Christian Religion*, bk. 3, chap. 23, par. 2.

31. Clark, *Religion, Reason, and Revelation*, p. 233.

32. See Edward John Carnell, *A Philosophy of the Christian Religion* (Grand Rapids: Eerdmans, 1960), pp. 314–317; idem, *Christian Commitment* (New York: Macmillan, 1957), pp. 69, 83, 85–87, 91, 101.

33. See Gordon H. Clark, "Apologetics," in *Contemporary Evangelical Thought*, ed. Carl F. H. Henry (Great Neck, N.Y.: Channel Press, 1957); idem, *Religion, Reason, and Revelation*, pp. 190 f.

34. See G. C. Berkouwer, *The Triumph of Grace in the Theology of Karl Barth* (Grand Rapids: Eerdmans, 1956), pp. 310 f. Cf. J. E. Barnhart, "An Ontology of Inevitable Moral Evil," *Personalist* 47 , no. 1 (Winter 1966): 102–111. This article discusses the topic of God's taking a risk. One of the most noted proponents of divine sovereignty, Karl Barth, says that God experienced *real* risk in creating human beings.

35. Orthodox Christians have held that Jesus did not sin and hence was an exception to the Fall. However, his birth was thought to have been quite unnatural because his mother was a virgin. Some Christians seem to make a connection between Jesus' virgin birth and his sinlessness.

36. See E. Y. Mullins, *The Christian Religion in its Doctrinal Expression* (Philadelphia: Judson Press, 1917), pp. 502–503.

37. See John Hick, *Evil and the God of Love* (New York: Harper & Row, 1966), p. 184.

38. This appears to be the point of the orthodox Christian and Arminian, Alvin Plantinga, in his book *God and Other Minds: A Study of Rational Justification of Belief in God* (Ithaca, N.Y.: Cornell University Press, 1967), pp. 152–155. Plantinga's first-draft style of writing sometimes generates unnecessary controversy as to what exactly he is saying.

39. For a strong critique of Plantinga's article "The Free Will Defense," see Anthony Flew, "Compatibilism, Free Will and God," *Philosophy* 48 (July 1973): 231–244. Plantinga's "The Free Will Defense" is chap. 6 of his book *God and Other Minds*.

40. Ian Ramsey, a leading spokesman for the Church of England, offers some telling arguments against the doctrine of hell and tries his hand at a demythologized interpretation of hell in his article "Hell," in *Talk of God: Royal Institute of Philosophy Lectures, Vol. 2, 1967–68* (New York: St. Martin's Press, 1969). This volume has excellent articles by twelve philosophers.

CHAPTER VII

God, the Absolute, and the Process

AN ANTHROPOMORPHIC GOD

Selecting a World from Chance, or for a Reason.   According to classical theism, if he had wanted to, God could have created some world other than the one he did. This raises the interesting question of whether God could have *wanted* to create another world. Or we might ask, "What caused God to want to create this particular world? What *stimulated* him to create *when* he did rather than earlier or later?" The answer of classical theism is that God was not caused or stimulated by anything *external* to himself.

Does this mean that something *internal* to him caused him to create this world? This is a sticky question. One traditional answer is that God decided to create this world rather than another simply because his *wisdom* led him to decide in this way. Another traditional answer is that God decided on this world simply because he *willed* to do so.

Let us look at each of these answers. If God had just willed the world, then he would have done so without any particular reason. To will something is, presumably, to do so either for a reason or for no reason. If God created for a reason, then we cannot say that he *just* willed it. We cannot let God's will be the final explanation. We must explain *why* God willed one world rather than another.

Let us assume that in his mind God had a number—perhaps an infinite number—of possible worlds from which to choose to bring something into existence. Let us also assume that he did not simply select a world by chance—from a hat, so to speak. He did not, let us say, leave his choice to mere random selection in the way that gamblers at the wheel are said to do. Hence, God must have had already *in himself a preference* for a certain kind of world rather than another. And presumably with an infinite selection of possible worlds to choose from, he must have chosen the one that fitted with his preference. He selected it for a reason.

If this account is more or less what classical theism holds to, then we would have to say that the world now existing had certain qualities that recommended it to God. That is, God with his omniscience could foresee every detail of this world. And what he foresaw, he liked enough to select to be transformed from a mere idea into a reality.

Anthropomorphic Language. Now, the above account will appear to be too *anthropomorphic* to some classical theists. To speak in anthropomorphic terms is to give human attributes to whatever we are speaking of. In the case of God, we would be clearly anthropomorphic if we said that he has a big toe. When most people speak of the hand of God, they do not mean to be taken literally, for that would be anthropomorphic. God, they assure us, does not really have knuckles and fingernails. It would be considered silly if some believers were to get into a debate as to whether God always has clean fingernails.

It is said, however, to be appropriate to speak of God's mind. This is considered to be either quite appropriate anthropomorphic language or not anthropomorphic at all. In any case, classical theists regard it as legitimate to speak of God's mind. As for divine passions or desires—well, that is something that is still debated among theologians.

So, let us speak of the divine mind. What is on God's mind? In some respects, everything is on his mind, especially if he is omniscient. But not everything is on his mind in the same way. For example, he thinks about certain things, but he may not approve of them. He knew when King David slept with Uriah's wife, Bathsheba. But presumably God did not prefer this to happen. To be sure, before creating the world, he knew that if he should choose this world, then David and Bathsheba would make their arrangements and that David as the king would have Uriah sent to the front line of battle where he would be killed.

The Divine Mind Considers the Consequences. It is important for you to see what is entailed in the notion of the divine mind. If God knows everything, then he knows every joke that will ever be told. It is supposed that he could not laugh at the shady jokes, for he is just not that kind of divine person. But could he laugh at good clean jokes? In other words, does God have a healthy sense of humor? Some people have thought that our whole universe is one grand joke that God is playing on everybody. Some of the theologians of India have spoken of the universe not as God's joke but as divine play. Christians having an emphasis upon work tend to look upon creation as the "work" of God. In any case, almost all classical theists wish to say that in creating the world, God was not simply amusing himself. Rather he was quite serious in the sense that he anticipated the *consequences* and presumably weighed out the advantages over the disadvantages.

Does God Take Time to Think?   Most classical theists say that it is misleading to imagine that God had to take time to figure out the consequences. However, if they could allow that God had to take time to deliberate his decision before making it, then they could better answer the question as to why God waited so long before creating the world. Also they could answer the question as to what God was doing before creation. Their answer could be that he was carefully surveying all the possible worlds to see what was involved in each one. You recall that God had an infinite number of alternative worlds to evaluate before creating, for the divine imagination that produces all these imaginary worlds is thought of as unlimited. Hence, it would have taken an incredibly long time for God to imagine each world and then examine it thoroughly to see if it measured up to what he wanted.

SPINOZA'S ATTEMPT TO ELIMINATE ANTHROPOMORPHIC TALK OF GOD

God As a Logical System.   If the above view of God seems to be more anthropomorphic than you think justified, then you have the problem of where exactly to cut off the anthropomorphic language. The famous seventeenth-century philosopher Baruch (or Benedict) Spinoza, growing increasingly wary of so many anthropomorphic references to God, tried to speak of the deity with as few anthropomorphic terms as possible.

For example, it seemed inconceivable to him that the eternal God would have to *spend time* reviewing plans of the world in the way that, say, a husband and wife might study a number of house plans before selecting the one that would satisfy their demands. Hence Spinoza conceives of God as moving immediately to create the world. But even this must not be understood as a kind of instinctive skill on God's part. After all, it still takes *time* to move instinctively. Furthermore, even the ordinary notion of creation leads us to expect the created objects to be different from their creator. For reasons that you will see shortly, Spinoza does not want to make a separation between God and creation. Spinoza's thinking is more on the order of geometry or mathematics. For example, if you know two of the angles of a triangle, then you can *deduce* the third angle. Similarly, Spinoza is trying to say that God's creation is a product of God only in the sense that it can be deduced from God. If you know something about God, then you could know *logically* that he would have a world. A creator without a world is not actually a creator. So it is of necessity that God has a world, just as the world must of necessity have God. It is not that God *desires* a world, for that is too anthropomorphic. Rather, God of the necessity of his own nature produces a world. The world is indeed the necessary product in much the same way that 10 is the product of 2 times 5.

In fact, 2 times 5 may be regarded as another way of saying 10. They mean the same thing. Similarly, Spinoza wants to say that *God and nature are really the same reality*. They are identical realities talked about in different ways. Of course, we might say that a number of expressions are identical with 10. For example, 5 plus 5, 4 plus 6, 3 plus 7, etc. Spinoza seems to be saying that God, like the number 10, has many manifestations. In fact, if God is Perfect Being, then he must have an *infinity* of manifestations. This is precisely what Spinoza concludes: namely, that God has an infinity of eternal manifestations or attributes.

Unfortunately, because you and I are only finite modes of God, we cannot have any concrete acquaintance with an infinity of God's attributes. We can know only two of them— Thought and Extension. As thinking beings, you and I are finite modes of Thought; as material bodies, we are finite modes of Extension. What you and I call the world of nature is simply nature as known through either of these two attributes. So-called physical nature is Nature or God as we know him through such physical sciences as astronomy, optics, and the like. But Nature can also be known through the thought world of ideas and concepts. No matter which route of knowledge we take, we can know that all reality is one, that it is God, and that Nature is not something different from God but rather is identical with him.[1]

God without Purpose or Goal. With a view of God as subject to neither time nor the process of thinking and making up his mind, Spinoza is bound to conclude that God would have no purposes and goals. A goal is something you aim at and hope eventually to attain or at least to approximate. To speak in this way is to open the door to such words as "perhaps," "maybe," and even the question, "What if?" Spinoza thinks it inconceivable that such contingency could exist in God. The deity does not calculate as to what are the odds of his world turning out according to his preference. Rather the world is deduced from God—of the necessity of his own changeless nature.

This way of thinking is, Spinoza believes, implicit in traditional classical theism. Spinoza believes himself to be *explicating* what these theists had left only implicit. One modern orthodox Calvinist, Gordon H. Clark, feeling the force of Spinoza's arguments, concedes that our world is "the only possible world." Clark calls this "a Calvinistic twist to a Spinozistic phrase." But it looks more like a Spinozistic explication of what Calvin was reluctant to bring out in the open. Indeed, Clark himself concludes that God could not have thought differently from the way he did.[2]

This raises again the question that was asked in the first paragraph of this chapter: Could God have *wanted* to create another world instead of this one? Clark's answer seems to be that God could not have even *wanted* another world. This simply leads to Spinoza's twofold position: (1) Nothing in God's life could have been different from what it is. Everything about God is logically sealed. There is no "free play" or contingency in God. (2) Nothing that God does or creates could have been other than what it was and is.

God's Control Is a Logical Control. The Christian Puritans used to say that God's decree is simply his decreeing. Spinoza agrees with this and spells it out further than the Puritan theologians did. The picture here is of a God who is "immutable" (unmoved and unchangeable). The world is under the strict control of God because it logically flows from God's own necessary being. God is in control of the world, but not in the sense that a dog trainer is in control of dogs on a leash. Rather,

God controls the world in the way that the properties of a triangle are controlled by the definition of the triangle. That is, the properties are contained in the triangle, and all the parts of the world are contained within God.[3]

If there is neither chance nor randomness in God, then how could there be such in his creation unless he should somehow give it contingency? However, if he should allow real chance to enter into his creation, then God's knowledge of the world would no longer be absolute and infallible.

God Permits No Contingency.   Why would God's fore-knowledge become fallible if his creatures could have done other than what they did in fact do? Spinoza, like the Calvinists, could understand that if God does know (without possibility of error) precisely what you are going to do ten years from now, then it is a contradiction to say that you *might not* do it.[4] You do not have the option to do anything other than what God knows you will do. If you did have, then there would be a real chance that you might just take this option. And if in only one case throughout all your life you should take this option, then we could no longer say that God's foreknowledge was in your case one hundred percent correct. We would have to say that he honestly *thought* that at a certain time you would do something that in fact you did not do but rather did something very much different. If God really does know infallibly everything in the future, then he can never know surprise. You could never choose an option that he had not predicted that you would choose. To say otherwise would be to imply that God's foreknowledge is probabilistic rather than absolutely certain and infallible.

When writing about God's foreknowledge, John Calvin says that the future for God is no future at all. It is simply *present* to him.[5] This seems very close to the view that Spinoza developed a century after Calvin, and half a century after Arminius. By eliminating time from God's own experience, Spinoza makes God's mind a kind of geometric or mathematical system in which everything exists necessarily where it does in the scheme of things. You might *think* you could have done other than what you did yesterday or on any day in the past. But Spinoza says that God knew what you would do and hence you could not have done other than what you did. "Things could not have been brought into being by God in any manner or in any order different from that which has in fact obtained."[6]

To be sure, you might have acted differently yesterday had your circumstances been different. But each set of circumstances depends on other circumstances. So not even a set of circumstances can change unless its own special circumstances permit the change. In any case, God would have known that entire train of circumstances and your actions coming from them.

Only God Is Free.   Spinoza defines freedom as that which exists and acts by its own nature alone and without any cause outside itself. But what being in all of nature is exempted from the influence of everything outside itself? The answer is that there is none. Hence, nothing in nature is free. Everything is what it is because of its conditions. If the conditions were other than what they are, then everything related to these conditions would be different in varying degrees. For Spinoza, the conditions cannot be other than what they are because they are modes of God's own internal nature. They exist as they are, and behave as they do, because they are determined by the necessity of God's eternal nature. They are not contingent in the sense that they might have been different from what they are. But Spinoza has a second meaning of 'contingent'— namely, *dependent*. In this sense of contingency everything in nature (and nature includes everything) is dependent upon God.

But although nothing within nature is free, nevertheless nature itself is free. This is because nature and God are the same reality. And, you recall, Spinoza regards as free that which exists and acts by its own essence and without any external cause. Inasmuch as nothing exists outside nature (or God), then nature (or God) cannot be dependent in any way on anything. Hence, God or nature must be perfectly free.

You can see how Spinoza arrived at his definition of freedom in terms of total independence. In ordinary parlance we regard ourselves as enjoying a measure of freedom when our wants and desires are satisfied. Often, certain dependent relationships prevent us from gaining this satisfaction. Hence, we may seek more independence from whatever frustrates our desires and wants. So it is rather understandable that Spinoza should think of an *absolutely independent* being as possessing total freedom.

Unfortunately, Spinoza deprives God of something essential to the existence of freedom. He does not permit God to have wants and desires. Without them, there can be no satisfaction or freedom. To be sure, people have wants that they cannot satisfy because there are other wants that compete with the original wants. People sometimes wish to be rid of these other wants and desires so that they may better satisfy their original wants. But Spinoza seems to have gone to the extreme of eliminating *all* wants and desires from God.

In doing this he renders God neither free, nor purposive, nor personal. All emotions are considered to be unworthy of the Perfect Being. Doubtless even the emotion of joy is ruled out because it depends somewhat on conditions and circumstances. As we have seen, Spinoza regards the Perfect Being to be the Necessary Being depending on nothing for either his existence or the quality of his existence. "God is without passions, nor is he affected by any emotion of pain or pleasure."[7]

In many respects, Spinoza is much closer to naturalism (which denies the existence of God) than to theism. Yet in other respects he follows to its conclusion the premise of God as a changeless, immutable being. Most recent versions of naturalism reject Spinoza's view that nature or the universe unfolds like geometric or logical implications. Spinoza tends to regard time, process, and novelty in the world as somehow less than real.

We turn now to a view which, like Spinoza, asserts that the highest degree of reality is the Absolute. Unlike Spinoza's God, the God that F. H. Bradley speaks of is not regarded as the Absolute. He is rather an *appearance* of the Absolute. The philosophy of F. H. Bradley does to God what Spinoza does to every finite reality.

F. H. BRADLEY'S ANALYSIS
OF RELATIONSHIPS

Whatever Is in Relationship with Something Else Is Not Reality. The English philosopher F. H. Bradley offers perhaps the most sustained attack on pluralism that has existed, at least in the Occident. By 'pluralism' is meant the view that reality is *many* rather than one only. Spinoza and Bradley are monists because they say that reality is one only. Many thinkers believe that Spinoza's philosophy exposes fatal weaknesses in classical theism. Taking seriously the view of God as perfect, changeless being, Spinoza drives it to the point where the pluralism of classical theism must either yield to Spinoza's monism or give up its particular version of God.

The major premise of Bradley's criticism of pluralism (a criticism that includes every form of theism) is that *whatever stands in relationship to something else is not fully real*. Why is this so? Because, says Bradley, wherever there is a relationship between two or more things, then self-contradiction will break out in any attempt to speak of it. In his remarkable book *Appearance and Reality* Bradley makes it clear that only the Absolute is truly real. Everything else—you, trees, time, space, and even God—are all mere appearances.[8] In saying this, Bradley is very close to some of the Hindu philosophers who say that the world of things and people is *maya*, which is sometimes translated "appearance," at other times "illusion." No form of pluralism is spared Bradley's critical analysis. According to classical theism, God and the created world stand *in relationship* to one another. Hence, Bradley regards them as only appearances of a deeper reality, namely, the Absolute.

The Paradox of Relationships.   Bradley has said some very profound things about relationships, and theism as well as naturalism must somehow come to terms with what he has to say.

His central point is that the relationships that a thing, idea, or person has are not incidental to its being what it is. If you change a person's relationships, you change *him*. This means that everything has "a double character."[9] On the one hand, it is what it is as a *consequence* of the relationship. On the other hand, it is a *ground or condition* making the relationship possible. The question is, How can something be both the consequence of the relationship and the ground of the relationship? If we ask how its consequence and ground are *related*, we are in trouble all over again, for our original problem was to explain and try to understand what a relationship is.

The gist of Bradley's point is that a person (or anything) in relationship to something else stands on the verge of breaking out into an *infinity of relationships*. If this is true (as it seems to be), then where does that leave, say, an individual person? He seems to be absolutely nothing without his relationships. Strip him of all his associations, connections, and references: what you have left is no person at all.

People sometimes say that they do not like a certain person as a worker, a citizen, a teacher, a shopper, etc. But neverthe-

less they like him *as a person*. Unfortunately, when you eliminate all relationships, memberships, and references beyond
him, then what remains is no person at all. A person simply
cannot be, except in relationship. With their view of many
Gods, the pagans saw this, and then later the Christians with
their doctrine of God in three persons. Without having some
relationship with the other two members of the Trinity, the
Heavenly Father was on the verge of being no God at all.

The self-made man who boasts of his independence is not
without a navel. Far from being wholly independent, he is
dependent on a host of conditions and variables at every second of his life. The very language he speaks is a gift from his
society, a gift that his partial amnesia has overlooked.

Bradley's Fallacy.   Bradley is entirely correct in arguing
that the relationships (of whatever kind) actually affect the
very being of the thing (or person) itself. But the fallacy of
Bradley lies in supposing that somehow if something is in relationship with something else, then it cannot be real. He is not
justified in declaring as mere appearance everything except the
all-inclusive Absolute. But he is justified in saying that *nothing,
not even God, is wholly self-contained* if it relates to, or is in
any way involved with, anything else. This is true because *the
involvement is a part of the very being* of the individual reality
in question. It is not misleading to say that you *are* your involvements and relationships and your responses to them. So
also with God.

Bradley's View of God.   For Bradley, God cannot be this
self-contained Absolute if he is to be a person in any meaningful sense of the term. For it is the nature of a person to be in
relationship and to be affected by relationships. This leads to
the interesting suggestion that the world to which God relates
will leave its own special impact or have consequences on God.
When people ask you whether you believe in God, you might
respond by asking "Which God?" A God who knows that there
is a hell and that he has the power to eliminate it is not the
same regardless of whether he eliminates hell or declines to do
so. If God is perpetually aware of his choosing not to eliminate
the most excruciating agony conceivable, this awareness will
have an impact on him. In short, it will harden him, that is,
make him morally insensitive. (Some Christians seem unable
to decide whether hell is or is not the worst of agonies. In
warning sinners, they say that it is. But in defending their God

against the charge of cruelty, they tend to make hell less than perpetual torment.)

Overlooking the hypothesis of hell, we still have the question of evil and suffering in the universe. If Bradley's analysis of relationships and involvements is correct, then God is going to reflect in his own being some of the suffering of the world. It will affect him and elicit some sort of response and make some sort of impact. Classical theism sometimes says that God created in order to share his love. This raises the question as to whether, in turn, God shares in the sufferings of his creatures. Bradley was mistaken to pronounce something as unreal if it is *involved* with anything else. But he has shown that to be involved and in relationship is to be no longer exactly what one was before the relationship. This would be true even of God.

A. N. WHITEHEAD'S NEO-PLURALISM

To Be Is to Be in Relationship. A. N. Whitehead stands as one of the most influential philosophers of the twentieth century. In the area of theology and the philosophy of religion, *Process and Reality* stands as his most influential book. You will recall that one of Bradley's books was entitled *Appearance and Reality*. As a process philosopher, Whitehead is concerned to show that change and process are not signs and symptoms of unreality or mere appearance. While greatly influenced by Bradley, Whitehead nevertheless upends Bradley's doctrine of process. You recall that Bradley contends that if something is in relationship with anything else, then it is in process and undergoes some change, whether slight or great. This observation was enough for Bradley to declare it to be unreal. But Whitehead challenges this with the following conclusion: *Nothing is real unless it stands in some relationship to something other than itself.*[10] In other words, changeless being unrelated to anything is a mere abstraction at best. For Whitehead, to be is to be in relationship. Each member of the world, as well as God, must be seen as relative to the other members. "By reason of the relativity of all things, there is a reaction of the world on God."[11]

God's Consequent Nature. In the Middle Ages, some theologians referred to God as "simple," meaning that God is not a derived compound composed of more fundamental ingredients. Unfortunately, this doctrine of divine simplicity was

carried to the extreme of rendering the deity completely unaffected by the environment that he had created.

In Whitehead's thinking, both God and the world are everlasting and influential each upon the other. Whitehead uses the
phrase "the consequent nature of God" to refer to God in his
mode of receiving the impact of the world on himself. This is
God insofar as he is a consequence—that is, a consequence of
the world of actual entities with which he is involved. Later in
this chapter you will see what Whitehead means by the primordial nature and the superject nature of God.

For Whitehead, God is a unity, but not a static unity. Static
oneness lacks concreteness and actual existence. The universe
enriches the unity of God. "In the process God acquires a
consequent multiplicity, which the primordial character of
[God] absorbs into its own unity."[12] Contrary to the Aristotel-
ian and classical theistic bias against feeling, Whitehead conceives of God and the world as a field and hierarchy of categories of feeling.[13] In this sense, God and the world compose a
kind of loose but interacting organism of stimulus and responsive feeling. God in his responding and in his responsive consequent nature is limited, open-ended, incomplete, everlasting,
fully actual, and conscious.[14]

What this means is that the universe is not merely incidental
to God. It is only because the universe in process affects him
that God is conscious. In one form or another, the universe is
everlasting with God. God in his primordial nature is the infinite replenisher of the universe. The universe, in turn, enriches the divine life and keeps it forever conscious and sensitive. This interchange between God and the world is a part of
the ongoing process and reality. It is reality in process, and
process in reality. The interchange is not one of Spinoza's "logical flow." The process is dynamic and real, not illusionary. It is
not outside time but in and through time.

The Totality and Harmony. In direct opposition to Spinoza as well as Bradley and other monists, Whitehead asserts
that there is "no totality which is the harmony of all perfec-
tions."[15] If the process, with its endless novelty, is a reality,
then there can be no perfect harmony. The floor of the totality
is always open for a new presence, so to speak. Hence it is
grossly misleading to suggest that Whitehead believes in a
totality or whole in the sense of an all-inclusive Being. Whitehead holds that if Bradley had kept in touch with immediate

and felt experience, he would not have invented the notion of this Being called the Absolute.[16]

The issue that Bradley forces upon philosophy is this: *Either the Absolute is real or everything is in process.* Whitehead accepts the second horn of this dilemma and turns it upon every form of monism that would render time, process, change transition, purpose, and the like as mere appearances. In Whitehead's words:

If the universe be interpreted in terms of static actuality, then potentiality vanishes. Everything is just what it is. Succession is mere appearance. . . . But if we start with process as fundamental, then the actualities of the present are deriving their characters from the process, and are bestowing their characters upon the future.[17]

God and the world of actual entities are sources of novelty for each other. As each entity of the universe perishes, its impact passes on into God to enrich his consequent nature. In turn, the consequent nature passes out again into the world as God's superject nature.

The Primordial Nature of God.   Whitehead conceives of God as incomplete in one sense, and boundless in another. God is incomplete in the sense that the world composed of countless finite actual entities, coming into being and perishing, is everlasting and hence will forever enrich the consequent nature of God. There will never be a time when God will be finished and closed up for eternity. Always sensitive to the world, God will take in forever new feelings from the world of finite actual entities.

But if finite actual entities of the universe keep perishing, and perish at different times, what is to keep the entire supply of new actual entities from perishing altogether? This is where the notion of God's primordial nature enters the picture.

When conceived of only from the viewpoint of his primordial nature, God is the unconscious and limitless reservoir of potentiality. God's supreme category is creativity, and in his primordial character he exemplifies the creative advance. He is in this respect the everlasting basis of all process in the universe, the infinite "lure for feeling, the eternal urge of desire."[18]

God is unchanging, not throughout every depth of his being, but as the source of replenishment for the universe. But in this primordial mode God does not evaluate. He shows no tendencies except to advance the process from general feeling to greater intensity of feeling. When understood only as the primordial and eternal replenisher, God is indifferent to the variations among particular entities as they emerge out of his general love for creativity. In itself alone, the divine creativity remains uninformed and unaffected by the feedback of the feeling world of actual entities. It remains "without a character of its own."[19]

This primordial nature yearns after "no particular facts, but after *some* actuality."[20] It guarantees a future of some kind, but no particular future. The necessity of God *as primordial being* is that of an undying preference for concrete intensity: that is, for transforming the random yearning for feeling into more intense and definite feelings. But the direction or form of this yearning comes not from the primordial depths, but from the consequent depth of God in perpetual response to the universe of actual entities. These actual entities, beginning only primitively in God, eventually take on a reality of their own as they become more intense and definite in their feeling tone.

Unlimited and devoid of precise evaluation and judgment, the primordial vision of God is untouched by the world and is indifferent to its processes. It excludes no possibility and ranks nothing as more important than another. In itself alone, it is the unlimited, the absolutely tolerant, and the indiscriminate urge to actualize all that can be actualized in concrete multiplicity. God's primordial nature is only an abstraction from his total being, and only in this sense may God be thought of as timeless and neutral (except for his ceaseless urge to create: that is, to move from vague feeling to greater intensity and harmony of feeling).[21]

The Superject Nature of God. To review very briefly, Whitehead conceives of God as a unity of his threefold nature or depths. Without any one of them he would not be the living God. The primordial nature is the dimension of God that is limitless potentiality indiscriminately exemplifying the longing for definite and multiple instances of intense feelings. This is the background of the ceaseless creativity of God.

God has always been creating, and there has always been a world with God. Forever they enrich one another. Each is necessary for the other. Without the world, God would always be unconscious—an aimless craving for intense feeling. But without God, the world or nature would eventually perish altogether. For Whitehead, the world is composed of societies and complexes of actual occasions or entities, which are something like drops of experiences of varying degrees of intensity and duration. Each occasion perishes, but not all of them at once. The most general and perpetual source of all finite actual occasions is God's primordial nature.

Yet God's primordial nature is itself conditioned and "informed" by his consequent nature. As the actual occasions or entities come into being, reach their peak, and perish, they leave their impression on God, who is the everlasting Sensitive One.

The *superject nature* of God is the response that God makes back to the world. It is the actual synthesis of his primordial and consequential depths. The primordial lure for feeling becomes conditioned and made definite and evaluative by the divine consequent nature. The superject nature of God is the surging primordial nature as it becomes sensitized and is made responsive by the divine consequent nature. The superject nature of God is God in the mode of outgoing influence into the world.

The tragedy in the universe is that while God can replenish it with novelty and some control, he can save no actual entity from eventually perishing. He himself alone survives forever because he alone has the primordial depth of infinite potentiality. The world as a whole endures as God's everlasting companion, but no one aspect of the world survives forever. Each perishes and, through God's creative faithfulness, contributes to the phases of worlds to come. God saves of each moment of the world what can be saved, but he cannot stop the process by which each step of the world dies and comes to life in new form.[22] Yet the process continues because God feeds it from himself—from his primordial nature. He guarantees a new supply of feelings and their initial direction into the world that is already in process.

Much of the process philosophy of Whitehead is expressed in technical terms that cannot be introduced in this book. In this section on Whitehead, it is perhaps sufficient to indicate that some forms of process philosophy offer a view of theism that boldly challenges the monism of Spinoza and Bradley as well as the classical theism that has dominated much of theology for so long.

NOTES

1. See Spinoza, *Ethics*, pt. 2, props. 1, 2, in *The Chief Works of Benedict De Spinoza*, 2 vols., trans. R. H. M. Elwes (New York: Dover, 1951), 2:83–84.
2. Gordon H. Clark, *Religion, Reason, and Revelation* (Philadelphia: Presbyterian & Reformed Publishing Co., 1961), p. 189.
3. See *Ethics*, pt. 1, prop. 17, note.
4. See Nelson Pike, "Divine Omniscience and Voluntary Action," in *Philosophy of Religion*, ed. Steven M. Cahn (New York: Harper & Row, 1970), pp. 74–76. This article appeared originally in *Philosophical Review* 74 (1965): 27–46.
5. See Calvin, *Institutes of the Christian Religion*, 2 vols., trans. John Allen (Philadelphia: Presbyterian Board of Christian Education, 1936), bk. 3, chap. 21, par. 5.
6. *Ethics*, pt. 1, prop. 33.
7. *Ethics*, pt. 5, prop. 17.
8. See F. H. Bradley, *Appearance and Reality*, 2d ed. (London: Oxford University Press, 1930), p. 394; idem, *Essays on Truth and Reality* (London: Oxford University Press, 1914), p. 431.
9. Bradley, *Appearance and Reality*, p. 31.
10. I have discussed this in "Bradley's Monism and Whitehead's Neo-Pluralism," *Southern Journal of Philosophy* 7, no. 4 (Winter 1969–70): 395–400. This is a special issue of the journal devoted exclusively to articles on Whitehead.
11. A. N. Whitehead, *Process and Reality* (New York: Social Science Book Store, 1941), p. 523.
12. Ibid., p. 529.
13. Ibid., p. 252.
14. Ibid.
15. A. N. Whitehead, *Adventures of Ideas* (New York: New American Library, 1933), p. 356.
16. See A. N. Whitehead, *Modes of Thought* (1938; reprint ed. New York: Putnam, Capricorn Books, 1958), pp. 70, 111.
17. Ibid., p. 136.
18. Whitehead, *Process and Reality*, p. 522.
19. Ibid., p. 47.
20. Ibid., p. 50.
21. See ibid., p. 524.
22. See ibid., p. 525; idem, *Religion in the Making* (1926; reprint ed. New York: Meridian, Living Age Books, 1960), p. 148.

CHAPTER VIII

Panentheism and Process Philosophy

DOES HISTORY HAVE A MEANING?

You recall that classical theism holds that God is unchanging and yet actively involved in directing the course of history. This providential view of history is challenged by the outstanding modern philosopher Karl R. Popper. He raises the question, "Is there a meaning in history?" and concludes that history has no overall meaning at all.[1]

This is not to deny that you and I can have meaning and purpose in our lives. It is simply to deny that history as a whole has any apparent purpose or goal. The first point that Popper makes is that although the details of history are infinitely rich, the *writing* of history is necessarily *selective*. According to Popper, the actual study called history has been not so much the story of mankind as the history of political power. In biting words he amplifies this point by adding that "the history of power politics is nothing but the history of international crime and mass murder." He criticizes the history taught in schools for doing hardly more than persuading children to believe that the greatest criminals are to be extolled as heroes. What is worse, sometimes the *selected* history of this or that nation or movement is portrayed as the story of God's own purpose. Perhaps this way of teaching history has changed somewhat since Popper first wrote his criticism in 1950, but there is still more truth in what he says than we might wish to admit.

Popper also expresses his contention that the story of humanity does not seem conspicuously to be directed by a loving Heavenly Father. Popper criticizes those who conceive of history as "a kind of lengthy Shakespearian play" directed by the Cosmic Producer. For Popper, this mythical way of thinking is not so much meaningless as false. He believes that there is considerable evidence to refute the hypothesis that somehow a loving Heavenly Father is the writer and director of a grand historical drama. He regards as blasphemy the claim that God is actively guiding history, or is busy getting his way and shaping the course of events to suit himself perfectly. With the noted Protestant theologian Karl Barth, Popper criticizes those who think that they can discern the purpose of God in this or that event or movement. To be sure, leaders of various movements are often quite willing to assert that the Lord God of the universe has placed his stamp of approval on their own particular programs. But Popper is highly skeptical of such assertions, and Barth denounces them as idolatrous boasts.

GOD AS THE GROUND OF POSSIBILITY

In the twentieth century especially, a revised view of theism has slowly been taking shape. Unlike classical theism, it does not attempt to claim that God's will is perfectly accomplished in the world—or even that it eventually will be. This revised theism goes under many names: e.g., panentheism and personalism. It conceives of God as the everlasting ground of possibility for the development of value. But no claim is made that God can guarantee that Christians or any other group will enjoy everlasting personal victory over all suffering and death.

In order to claim that God will indeed see his will completely and perfectly fulfilled in some future day of victory, classical theism was forced to divide the divine will into two, only one of which would become completely satisfied. Unfortunately, this view poses problems for classical theism. It in effect dismantles the celebrated doctrine of God's omnipotence. You recall that this doctrine asserts that God has full power to accomplish his will exactly. But omnipotence seems to presuppose one divine will, not two or more.

Some of those who claim that the will of God will be (or is in process of becoming) perfectly realized fail to show how either the history of mankind or of the rest of the universe is accomplishing God's will. It is, they say, a matter to be taken on faith. But the answer of faith, in this case, is not additional evidence in support of the claim, but rather a statement of the believer's *determination* to believe despite the lack of evidence or logic.

In many cases, the notion of the will of God is so general as to provide no way for us to determine precisely whether God's will is being accomplished. There does, however, seem to be for many theologians a general notion that God's purpose or will includes the happiness and righteousness of all his intelligent creatures. This, then, forces these theologians to renounce the traditional doctrine of hell as more a product of human revenge than a part of the divine plan. Still, with hell out of the picture, classical theism seems unable to show that the divine will is being perfectly attained.

But classical theism is only one view of God. Panentheism is a major alternative to classical theism. But before exploring this alternative, it is important from the start to grasp the difference between panentheism and pantheism.

PANTHEISM AND PANENTHEISM

Pantheism. The term 'pantheism' is based on the two Greek words *pan* (which means "all") and *theos* (which means "God"). For a pantheist, God is the whole of reality. Nothing exists outside his own being, including your experiences and mine. Some versions of pantheism regard finite creatures to be *effects* within God, but not *causes*. Pantheists tend to conceive of God as a changeless unity. The world of countless entities tends to be regarded as somewhat less than fully real, whereas God is regarded to be the only genuine reality.

Panentheism. The term 'panentheism' stresses the point that the world is *in* God as a real and vital part of his being. The world is not thought of as an illusion or a mere appearance of God but as integral to his life. Yet at the same time, God's consciousness is his own and is distinguishable from the world. According to this way of thinking, the world is something analogous to the body of God.

Panentheism emphasizes that the unity of God is not static. Furthermore, the finite creatures within God are not simply the passive effects of God but are also *causes* having an impact on one another and consequently on or in God.

In contrast to some versions of pantheism, the view called panentheism accepts the temporality of God. This fits with the emphasis on divine dynamism. Traditionally, pantheism has not known what to do with the idea of God as experiencing succession. Pantheism cannot recognize time as a part of God's own being. Somehow God is supposed to be timeless in the way that 2 plus 2 equals 4 is a timeless truth. But panentheism boldly asserts that it is self-contradictory to think of God as both alive and changeless. If God is alive, then he must experience some change. And this means that God literally experiences and exemplifies process. That is, he enjoys the experience of before and after. He is everlasting and omnitemporal, but not timeless.

You recall that, according to classical theism, God gives meaning to the universe. But according to panentheism, the *world of finite beings also provides meaning to God's life*. While he does not need you or me or any one particular world of finite realities, God nevertheless needs *some* particular world of finite entities to enrich his everlasting existence and to give it stimulus and meaning, as well as "embodiment."

Full-blown panentheism meets naturalism half-way by acknowledging that the universe (or the various forms of it) is without beginning or end.[2] For panentheism, God and the universe are in some sense identical. This is the view of Charles Hartshorne especially. Many philosophers of religion and theologians accept much of Hartshorne's panentheism even though they reject his ontological argument as both unnecessary and mistaken.

We are now in better positions to examine the panentheism of two twentieth-century philosophers, namely, E. S. Brightman and Charles Hartshorne.

E. S. BRIGHTMAN'S PERSONALISTIC PANENTHEISM

God and Nature.   One of the most fascinating twentieth-century attempts of a panentheist to come to terms with the problems of evil and the experience of time is E. S. Brightman's personalism. It is a *partial* panentheism. The world of nature is within God, or is a part of God's own everlasting being. But Brightman uses the word 'nature' to refer only to the system of energy that is studied primarily by physicists, astronomers, chemists, physiologists, and biologists.

What this means is that the *conscious experiences* of finite selves and persons are *not* a part of nature, although they emerge from nature and are dependent on nature. For example, according to Brightman, your body and brain are a complex interplay of energy centers belonging to the wider energy system of nature. All of physical nature is taken to be God's own "body" system. But in contrast to pantheism, Brightman's personalism asserts that your feelings and experiences are *yours* and not God's. That is, you are composed of your own experiences as well as your body and brain. God, too, has his own unique experiences or consciousness. The primary point of contact between each finite self and God is the body and brain of each self. All finite bodies and brains are a part of nature. And inasmuch as nature is a part of God, then your *body* (*with its brain*) is a part of God's own life.

Human Bodies and Brains Have Meaning for God. If nature is indeed something like God's cosmic body system, then God's own life undergoes everlasting process. The bodily and cerebral activities of all finite creatures have meaning to God because they are a part of his own energy system. When a human body perishes, then God loses a certain activity within himself.

Brightman does not claim to know whether the consciousness of the finite individual perishes along with his finite body and brain. Perhaps in God are other limited energy centers or bodies that the finite consciousness can plug into, as it were. This, for Brightman, is an open question that has not been fully settled.

Nature As God's Public Behavior. Brightman does not exactly say that nature is the public behavior of God, but his thinking leads straight to this conclusion. According to this view, if you want to know what God is like, you must observe and learn from the divine behavior. Astronomers, chemists, and others who systematically explore the patterns and relationships of the vast physical universe are in effect studying the overt activity of God. For Brightman, the Scriptures of the world are various *interpretations*—not infallible revelations— of human encounters with nature and with other finite selves. The physicist as a physicist must study nature without raising the issue of value or of anxiety over human finitude. What physics tells us about nature—or God's public behavior—is an abstract report. That is, it has deliberately and rightly excluded certain human questions in order to focus on certain other questions.

Physics and astronomy in particular study God's behavior as it exists independent of human life and human concerns. Nature preceded the human species. God, in other words, has a dynamic life independent of humans, and it is the role of physicists and astronomers to study the behavior of nature without regard to human concerns.[3]

The Role of Scriptures.   Religious Scriptures, however, emerge with their burning questions about the human situation. What, for example, happens to people when they die? Do they stand in favor or disfavor with God? Will someone eternal save them from their short duration, or their enemies, diseases, poverty, and countless hardships?

The implication of Brightman's approach is that ancient Scriptures, like ancient science, are not the final word about God's relationship to human beings. Rather, these ancient interpretations are conjectures, without which theology and the philosophy of religion might never have begun to develop. Mankind's Scriptures are filled with fruitful suggestions and mythologies. Trouble develops, however, when such imaginative flights are cut loose from the realm of nature altogether. With Freud, Brightman acknowledges that too often religion has allowed its concepts to develop along the line of wishful thinking rather than that of the concern to face reality. Brightman's point is not that imaginative religious speculations are bad, but that they are not infallible. They are to be taken as hypotheses and conjectures to be tested critically.

Poets, farmers, lovers of nature, and the like also respond to nature in terms of nature's potentiality for value-creation. These responses are to be considered by a philosophy interested in understanding nature in its capacity to elicit responses from sentient creatures. For the poet, nature is not colorless, as it is for the physicist. For Brightman, color is the joint product of nature and sensitive consciousness. Beauty lies in neither nature alone nor in the finite mind alone; it is born in the interaction between the two. Beauty is not always order; it is also intensity of positive feeling, which only sentient creatures can enjoy.

Nature, History, and the Problem of Evil.   Classical theism, Brightman holds, has failed to take seriously the presence of suffering, conflict, destruction, and evil in history and nature. Realizing that thinking without theories is impossible, Brightman nevertheless insists that one's theory is not simply to be imposed upon the data. If we adhere to our theories regardless of the data, then we are not so much explaining the data as disregarding them. Brightman insists that empirical evidence gained through experience and observation must have some impact on one's theory of God if the theory is to be taken seriously.

He charges that some versions of pantheism and classical theism have rolled on in their blind way, oblivious to the sufferings and destructions within history and nature, as if these were nothing more than contributory sounds in a spiritual symphony.[4] Brightman regards such a view to be the result of insensitivity to the groans and sorrows of fellow human beings and to the aggressions, fears, and destructions in the world of animals. Classical theism and some forms of pantheism simply *say* that God is both moral and omnipotent, but what we observe in nature and history cries out against such an insensitive theory.

The Nonrational Given.   There is no need here to review the various attempts of classical theism to support its thesis of both perfect divine love and divine omnipotence. Brightman examines these attempts and finds them to be unconvincing. He concludes that nature, which is the public behavior of God, indicates that God is not a perfect harmony. The life of God includes a certain element of genuine chance and disharmony. God did not invent his own nature, rather he is his own nature, although his life, as we will see, is not static. To be sure, there are certain "given" factors composing the divine nature. But part of this givenness is the tendency of God to take on new experiences and to act in new ways.

Perhaps the most creative, as well as the most controversial, notion that Brightman came up with is his hypothesis of the *nonrational Given* as an everlasting factor of God's own given nature. His studies led him to think that the stresses and conflicts in nature enter into the very life of God. The hypothesis of God's nonrational Given is Brightman's way of accounting for much of the fruitless conflict, disvalue, defeat, chance, and novelty in the world. While God's will is declared to be perfectly good, his own nature has a "givenness" that is not wholly rational. That is, God is understood by Brightman to be a conscious system of energy whose fields and directions are not in perfect coordination. Brightman is impressed with the teleological argument for God because it calls attention to the order and structure throughout nature. But he believes the argument ignores the chaos and disorder that also exist throughout nature.

To say that God has a nonrational depth to his life is to say a number of things, two of which can be expressed here. First, God's own everlasting makeup includes time and power. Without the concreteness and dynamism of this nonrational depth, God would not be an actual living being. Pure formal ideals and norms cannot exist on their own. They must be "embodied," and God is their everlasting embodiment. The nonrational depth of God is God in the mode of powerful, surging energy. In itself it is an infinite reservoir of endless activity.

Second, the nonrational Given is not in itself wholly purposive. Or, to say it better, this divine energy is an infinite field of multiple directions without perfect coordination. It is thus a source of frustration as well as power and universal perpetual motion. It is temporal (omnitemporal), processive, potentially destructive, and potentially creative.

The Rational Given of God.   Brightman uses the phrase the *rational Given* to refer to the everlasting control and structure that God manifests. God's everlasting activity is the rational Given to the extent that it is not irrationally destructive but rather is creative, corrective, and purposive. The rational Given is the steady, stable, and orderly control that God has on himself. It is his norms and ideals, and the lawful pattern to which his nonrational Given partially submits.

Clearly, Brightman understands God to be a surging, powerful, and creative Cosmic Person whose very "body" is the entire physical universe. This physical system called "nature" is a dialectic of God's nonrational Given and his rational Given. Nature is pregnant with structure and pattern as well as randomness, change, and chaos. For Brightman, God may be understood as possessing an overall disposition to create maximum possible value. But within God are also countless other subsidiary wills or tendencies that do not hum together, as it were, in one perfect harmony. The doctrine of the nonrational Given is Brightman's way of calling attention to the different levels of structures and constants in the divine nature. Brightman will have none of the theory that pictures the deity as possessing a tight and perfect rein on all subsidiary direction and tendency in his own consciousness. There is enough control and structure so that God is one and the universe is one. But there are also in God perpetual streams of chance, randomness, and novelty. This is the ground for richness and freedom, and also destruction and creativity.[5]

Over the centuries, in one episode of God's everlasting life, numerous earthly species have emerged who, like their creator, manifest at their own minute level the interplay of rational structure and wild energy. In this interplay the possibility of human freedom comes into existence.

The Doctrine of Omnipotence. For Brightman, God as the infinite source of all emerging finite creatures cannot be greatly threatened by these finite creatures; for they, unlike himself, have their day and then perish. This leads Brightman to think that God is enriched by the emergence of new subjects of experience—whether they be amoebas or human beings. The love of God is unlimited in the sense that he will forever create and enrich himself "socially" with responsive creatures enjoying conscious experiences of their own.

For Brightman, the orthodox Christians' penal theory of Christ's atonement is a melodramatic bit of human fantasy, for it is based on the unlikely premise that finite mortals could greatly threaten the everlasting God. Time is always on God's side. Patience alone is his guarantee of victory over any finite threat to overthrow him completely. God cannot simply wipe out his creatures at a stroke.

Some of those who criticize Brightman's doctrine of the non-rational Given rightly see it as a challenge to the classical theistic doctrine of divine omnipotence. They fear that eventually God's nonrational energy might veer off into completely structureless chaos. This is perhaps conceivable, but so is another hypothesis, namely, that God will continue forever to exert considerable, but not absolute, *control* of his own infinite energy with a view toward value-creation. (God has already experienced a continuity that reaches back infinitely into the past.) Brightman can only *hope and trust* that God will continue to be successful in his will-to-value. Of course, the orthodox classical theists have no other alternative than to trust their deity, although they sometimes seem to demand an *absolute guarantee*. Any guarantee will depend always upon God's goodness and power. Orthodox theists question whether Brightman's God will always have the *power* to control all his subsidiary tendencies and aims.

Brightman's answer, very simply, is that those subsidiary

aims and tendencies of God that veer too far out of the divine unity will cut themselves off from the replenishing center. God *changes* here and there, but he cannot be *exchanged.* To be sure, the range of diversity within God as nature is overwhelming. To contemplate this with seriousness approaches having a mystical experience. This range of diversity may be called the tolerance of God for the possibility of finite freedom. But as is always true of freedom, this is a risky business. For Brightman, the risks of God are not the play-acting risks of the orthodox God whose omniscience informs him of the exact and detailed outcome of everything. Unlike this orthodox God, the God of which Brightman speaks is a genuine lover as well as "cross-bearer." He is supremely involved, inasmuch as the personal lives of all creatures—great or small—are at least vicariously a part of his own life. While he does not literally possess their conscious experiences, he does literally share their bodies and thus vicariously enters into their experiences.

Brightman's criticism of classical theism is that while presumably its God has the power to do better, he *will not* do better. Brightman's God, by contrast, *cannot* solve all problems with perfect harmony. But he can sustain conditions whereby relatively independent creatures may work out some of their own solutions. According to this way of thinking, the universe is an infinitely ongoing possibility for value-creation and enjoyment. But it is also a world of genuine chance and risk, where no finite creature is given the absolute guarantee that he will live for eternity. What each person has, for a season, is some chance to live and love. "A temporalist God, then, is a God of many universes and of many evolutions."[6]

CHARLES HARTSHORNE'S TOTAL PANENTHEISM

God Includes Both Finite Bodies and Conscious Experience. Both Brightman and Hartshorne hold that God's own being includes the *physical organisms* or bodies of all finite beings. They enrich God's own life because they *are* a part of the growth of God in that they elicit new experiences and activities for God. Brightman and Hartshorne part company, however, over the question of the *conscious experiences* of finite selves and persons. Unlike Brightman, Hartshorne believes that God literally contains all these finite experiences as a part of his own experience.

Hartshorne's major reason for regarding God as all-inclusive —even of finite conscious experiences—lies in his notion of divine perfection. You recall that Hartshorne believes it is possible to defend the ontological argument for Perfect Being. But as I tried to show in the chapter on the ontological argument, the notion of absolute perfection of so general a reality as Being is empty. Hartshorne elects to *define* perfect being in terms of *all-inclusive* being. But he does not show why anyone should accept this particular definition. There certainly is no empirical evidence to lead anyone to accept this definition, nor is there any logical move that can lead to it.

Why Monism?   Why could not Hartshorne say that God is superior to each finite being in numerous ways even though he is not all-inclusive? The superior racehorse does not have to *be* the other horses in order to be their superior. In fact, he could not be superior if he contained some of the weaknesses of the other horses. Indeed, why does Hartshorne insist that there must be an all-inclusive reality or being? Why demand such a monism? Hartshorne is very much aware of the way Spinoza's monism tends to treat finite realities as somehow unreal. He criticizes Bradley for treating as mere appearances anything short of the all-embracing Absolute.[7]

A considerable amount of Hartshorne's writings is devoted to attacking the static monism of the kind that classical theism would fall into completely if this doctrine were more consistent with some of its own premises. When discussing illness in the world, Hartshorne says that illness "may be caused by all sorts of agents other than God."[8] This suggests that a distinction can be made between God as an agent and other agents, which is the distinction that pluralism would make in contrast to monism. Actually despite his claim that God is the all-inclusive one, Hartshorne's works have a strong tendency toward the recognition of pluralism.

God's Infallible Knowledge.   Hartshorne wants to say that God is infallible in his knowledge of everything that exists or has ever existed. He believes that in order for such knowledge to be possessed, God must *include* in his being everything that is known. And in some ways this argument seems to be correct. Because of the great difficulties in the theory of monism, however, Hartshorne would have done well to give up the notion of divine infallible knowledge. Brightman thinks that infallible knowledge is impossible for anyone, including God.

Indeed, what exactly *is* infallible knowledge? Does it mean that God can *predict* everything that will come to pass? If so, then Hartshorne himself denies that such knowledge is possible, because of the element of chance and novelty present even in God. The future, says Hartshorne, is predictable to some degree only, but in minute specifics it is not always predictable —not even by God.[9]

Classical theism insists that God is omniscient; that is, he knows everything infallibly of the past, present, and future. But Hartshorne's notion of an open-ended future makes it impossible for God to know infallibly all the future, inasmuch as it does not yet exist to be known.[10] Still, Hartshorne wants to argue that God can know fully all that has existed in the past and does exist in the present. And apparently the only way for God to do this is actually to *be* everything in some sense, or for everything to exist in him. That is, to know something completely is to *be* that which is known.

However, even though you *are* in some respects every member of your own body, you nevertheless cannot be said to know all about your body. In other words, if God should somehow contain as his body the whole world that exists, this still would not necessarily entail that he could know the world completely. Perhaps this suggests some ambiguity in the terms 'knowledge' and 'to know.' We might ask in all sincerity, "Does God really know personally what it is like to be out of work and unable to find a job? Does he know the humiliation and terror of such a situation?"

Hartshorne would say that God can know what it is like because he *contains in himself* all the conscious feelings of the finite person who is terrified at not being able to find work. But this answer is a bit too hasty. God presumably knows things in total perspective, whereas the desperate person without a source of income cannot experience life from God's perspective, inasmuch as he is not God. For all his compassion, Hartshorne's God cannot know personally what it feels like for *himself* to face starvation, total elimination of his own consciousness, paralysis, or the loss of most of his own creative power.

Classical theists might argue that God knows personally what it is like to kill someone, but they will not agree that God

knows personally what it is like to commit adultery. The whole
issue of God's omniscience is a thicket of problems. For example, if God does know even all the future, then he cannot
personally know what it is to be surprised, for everything that
happens was already foreseen by him.

Hartshorne, of course, contends that God can experience
and know surprise because the world is not wholly predetermined. There are chance elements that leave some room for
the unforeseen details of the future. This is Hartshorne's way
of taking time and process seriously.[11] But he must also come
to see that as unsurpassed and superior as God's knowledge
might be, it is hardly omniscience or infallible knowledge. In
fact, classical theists have an abstract ideal of what omniscience
must be. For them it entails no surprises for God. But this
leads to the conclusion that the universe of the future is in a
real sense already totally existing. Time, process, change, and
novelty are thus only illusions.

**The Problem of One Experiencer Possessing the Experi-
ences of Another.**   Hartshorne does not claim that God knows
infallibly everything that will come about in the future. In the
above paragraphs I have tried to point out some difficulties
with the belief that God infallibly knows everything even in
the *present*. Even if God should somehow contain all conscious
experiences and bodies of finite beings, he would not necessarily have infallible *knowledge* of and about them. Knowledge is more than possession. To be sure, a wholly disembodied God would seem to be an ethereal nothing. On the
other hand, there are strong reasons to reject the belief that
God can somehow simply "possess" the conscious experiences
of others as his own.

Hence, Brightman's partial panentheism seems to have
fewer problems. Brightman's God is embodied in the physical
world of nature—including human and animal bodies and all
the material in the galaxies. God is thus not disembodied spirit.
At the same time, however, he is not regarded as being able
somehow to possess the experiences of another as his own. God
has his own experiences, not yours and mine.

God Affected by Finite Beings.   Brightman, Whitehead,
and Hartshorne (especially in his later thinking) stress the fact
that God can learn and grow in his own experience and knowledge.[12] The world of finite agents has an impact (through its
bodies at least) upon God. Finite agents "impress" him in

some sense, and, of course, he is always the necessary condition of every finite experience.

Hartshorne stresses over and over the point that God remembers forever the activities of finite mortals because he is sensitive to them and because he is their only undying survivor.

The Freedom of Finite Beings.   Hartshorne, Brightman, and Whitehead do not have a simple notion of what is involved in freedom. Very central to their view, however, is novelty. I think they are saying, in addition, that richness of experience and activity is also central to freedom. Higher freedom seems to be connected with an *interesting* life. Without interest, life would be flat, because wants and desires would hardly come into existence.

Novelty, therefore, is crucial to freedom because it increases the possibility of the emergence of new interests, desires, and wants. This presumably would be true of any dynamic being, including God. We might speculate that an eternal consciousness going through the same routine eon upon eon would eventually experience eternal boredom.

At the same time, a life of uncontrolled surprises and absolute chance would not be a life worth continuing. In fact, the very notion of *continuing* entails some *continuity*. Process philosophers such as Whitehead, Brightman, and Hartshorne regard God's life as a vital balance of continuity and novelty. Freedom lies in this balance. But Brightman and Hartshorne in particular point out that novelty also entails risk. This makes for both joy and tragedy. The tragedy of each finite existence is that it eventually perishes. The tragedy for God is that he cannot prevent death even for his very dearest.

Brightman holds open the possibility that God may rescue from death at least some of his human creatures, but he does not think he has made a very strong case for everlasting human survival. Hartshorne believes that immortality for a finite being is impossible. Indeed, even if we should live forever, we would still always experience death of a sort. The friendship we once had and enjoyed would now reach its peak and begin to die. The joys of our childhood would perish. A father's children would cease to be children in their becoming adults. Our views, which once gave us strength, would now be exposed to the sunlight, so that we would no longer be able to embrace them. Indeed, as the Buddha could see, tragedy exists wherever change exists. Such is the anxiety lying at the door of freedom. What some Buddhists have failed to emphasize is that change also brings the possibility of new joys and commitments. The fact that these, too, will perish (at least in one's own death) does not mean that love is not love, or that beauty is not beauty, or that commitment is unreal.

Why Go On?   Religion has always wrestled with the questions, "Why go on? Why choose? Is it all meaningless?" In another chapter these questions must be faced explicitly. Traditionally, philosophy has dealt not only with the issue of truth, but also with the issue of human meaningfulness. For a few decades of this century, the positivist school of philosophy seemed to belittle the question of "life's meaning." But in recent years, even philosophers of the tough-minded variety have felt the need to speak forth on this issue.

SOME PERSONAL AND PRACTICAL QUESTIONS

In the previous chapters, many twists and turns were made in our attempt to travel on the river of inquiry regarding the existence and nature of God. You are doubtless asking where it leaves you in your practical life as a finite being who thinks, feels, and must act. I want now to attempt a forthright response to this legitimate concern.

First, if the previous chapters about God's nature and existence point in one direction, it is this: We cannot say with certainty that there either is or is not some Cosmic Consciousness who is at least the necessary condition of all finite life. There may very well be an everlasting Cosmic Consciousness of some sort. Second, I am prepared to conclude with much more confidence that two of the views considered in this book have been exposed as not very likely to be true. These two views are (1) classical theism and (2) the doctrine that the Absolute alone is reality, with everything else being mere appearance.

This pretty much leaves the range of options somewhere between the revised theism of Whitehead, Brightman, and Hartshorne, on the one hand, and naturalism, on the other. We will discuss naturalism in the next chapter.

NOTES

1. Karl R. Popper, *The Open Society and Its Enemies* (Princeton, N.J.: Princeton University Press, 1950), chap. 25. The discussion in this chapter of Popper's view of history will be taken primarily from this work. It should be noted that Popper is not to be classified as a logical positivist; he has in fact been one of the most persistent critics of positivism.

2. As you will see in the next chapter, naturalism asserts that the universe or nature is the whole of reality; i.e., nothing exists apart from nature. Naturalism denies the existence of God.

3. See E. S. Brightman, *Person and Reality*, ed. P. A. Bertocci in collaboration with Jannette E. Newhall and R. S. Brightman (New York: Ronald Press, 1958), pp. 243–248.

4. See E. S. Brightman, *The Problem of God* (Nashville: Abingdon Press, 1930), pp. 92–98.

5. See E. S. Brightman, *A Philosophy of Religion* (Englewood Cliffs, N.J.: Prentice-Hall, 1940), pp. 340, 384 f.

6. Brightman, *Person and Reality*, p. 330.

7. See Charles Hartshorne, "The God of Religion and the God of Philosophy," in *Talk of God: Royal Institute of Philosophy Lectures, Vol. 2, 1967–68* (New York: St. Martin's Press, 1969), p. 152.

8. Ibid., p. 160.

9. See Charles Hartshorne, *The Logic of Perfection and Other Essays in Neoclassical Metaphysics* (LaSalle, Ill.: Open Court Publishing Co., 1962), pp. 304 f., 313 f.

10. See Charles Hartshorne, *Divine Relativity: A Social Conception of God* (New Haven: Yale University Press, 1948), pp. 120–134.

11. See Hartshorne, *Logic of Perfection*, pp. 168–174.

12. See Frederic F. Frost, "Relativity Theory and Hartshorne's Dipolar Theism," in *Two Process Philosophers: Hartshorne's Encounter with Whitehead*, ed. Lewis S. Ford (Tallahassee, Fla.: American Academy of Religion, Studies in Religion, 1973), pp. 98 f.

CHAPTER IX

Naturalism As an Alternative to Supernaturalism

NATURALISM AS A METHOD FOR GROWTH OF KNOWLEDGE

A General Statement of Method.   The term 'naturalism' is used in a variety of ways. In this chapter I will begin by using it to refer to the general framework that emphasizes the experimental method, scientific rigor, and antisupernaturalism. Because of its experimental method, this naturalism cannot set forth once and for all a system of statements as to what the universe is like on the whole. There is an open-endedness to naturalism that obligates the seeker of knowledge to revise, or replace, if necessary, even his dearest hypotheses. If you ask, "When is it necessary to begin thinking of revising or giving up one's hypotheses?", the naturalist's answer is, "Whenever they begin breaking down under logical analysis or when they confront strong evidence that runs counter to their claims." There is no great mystery here. Scientific thinking is ordinary thinking made more rigorous, critical, sensitive, and systematic. As Sidney Hook puts it, "The systematization of what is involved in the scientific method of inquiry is what is meant by naturalism."[1]

Tension between Logical Rigor and Experimental Openness.   There is a certain perpetual tension within this naturalistic method of inquiry. At one end of the line of continuum is rigorous analysis, logical testing, and critical scrutiny. At the other end is openness, experimentalism, willingness to learn, imagination, and sensitivity to new experience and new data. The naturalistic method is a commitment to *both* ends of the continuum. A good example of the tension in this commitment is exemplified in the current research and debate having to do with ESP and other paranormal experiences.

Advance in knowledge and understanding in any area is

believed to come about when these two commitments of rigor and openness are kept alive and in communication with one another. If either becomes subservient to the other, the dynamic conditions essential to the growth of knowledge become subverted. Without sensitivity to new observations and data, logical analysis would be reduced to a narrow circle of trivia. But without rigorous empirical testing and logical scrutiny, the life of experimental openness would drown itself in a sea of gullibility and self-deception.

Looked at from a slightly different angle, the naturalistic method stands in tension between (1) the ideal of coherence, in which all propositions fit together harmoniously and consistently, and (2) the ideal of the radical growth of knowledge.[2] The ideal of coherence demands that new claims be cross-examined and made consistent with other claims, whereas the ideal of the radical growth of knowledge forces the established coherent theory to either account for the new observations or step aside for a new theory. The background of a more-or-less established system of knowledge makes it possible for new problems and questions to emerge. Without this background, new questions would be meaningless. At the same time, however, without the challenge from new questions and problems, the established background of knowledge would dwindle into rote memory and a ritual of irrelevant clichés.[3]

An Example of the Naturalistic Method of Inquiry. The charge has often been made that naturalists simply stipulate what the proper method of inquiry should be in the quest for knowledge. Naturalists reply that they are not trying to impose a method, but rather are spelling out more clearly the methodological procedures that even the most outspoken opponents of naturalism are already employing daily.

Take for an example Gordon H. Clark, one of the more extreme critics of the naturalistic method. He has denounced even some of his fellow Calvinists for yielding to the temptation to become empirical-minded, that is, for remaining open to, and observing, new data in the field of religion. According to Clark, all that is needed, in order to obtain the proper knowledge of God, religion, and moral principles, is the Bible together with logic. Protesting against the use of perceptions, observations, sensations, and broadly empirical methods, Clark writes: "If the Biblical doctrines are self-consistent, they have met the only legitimate test of reason."[4]

But the naturalists (and others) point out that "Biblical doctrines" do not simply pop into the mind. It turns out that a person must do a considerable amount of observation and empirical investigation in order to come up with biblical doctrines. Even Clark says that if we want to determine what justice is, we must do so "by *observing* what God actually does."[5] Clark means that an empirical investigation of the Bible is required. In the final analysis, he is forced to yield to the experimental method, which entails observation of new data. His attack against experimentalism is misleading, for he is actually acknowledging that observation is perfectly legitimate—even necessary—*so long as it is restricted to the limits of the Bible.*[6]

Clark seems not to realize that the Bible is hardly a neatly packaged theological treatise. A person must bring *to* the Bible some outside learning, categories, and data if he is to make any sense of it at all. The Bible was not written in cultural isolation, and it cannot be read in cultural isolation. It was not immaculately conceived. To be sure, some biblical scholars used to believe that the languages of the Bible were pristine divine languages, untouched by cultural contingencies. The Greek language of the Bible was regarded to be a very special theological or religious Greek. But in the nineteenth century this thesis was thoroughly discredited by the discovery that most of the Greek language of the New Testament was ordinary marketplace Greek.

Clark's attempt to restrict the realm of religious observation to the Bible alone fails to grasp fully the point that research in archaeology, linguistics, and textual analysis, as well as literary and historical documents, shows that the Bible is not the fenced-in theological range that Clark had imagined. And even for those who desire to roam only within biblical limits, the number of biblical passages to be observed, compared, sifted, etc., is so many as to have kept theologians and biblical scholars in constant debate for centuries.

Clark insists that people must find out what the Bible itself claims regarding its own inspiration. But in order to do this, people must *observe* the texts, *search* the Scriptures, *comb through* passage after passage, and then arrive at some generalization. To be sure, they doubtless will have started their inquiry with some expectation or generalization already in

mind. But if the initial generalization is not what Clark takes
to be the truth, then he invites them to engage in what is in
effect an empirical observation of the biblical texts. Clark is so
convinced that the Bible supports the conclusion he himself
has reached that he is prepared to risk inviting others to engage in an empirical investigation to see whether they, too,
will agree with him. But he appears not to be so confident
regarding many of his other generalizations.

Another Calvinistic and Evangelical critic of the method of
empirical observation charges that Dewey M. Beegle has failed
to conduct an empirical analysis of the teaching of the Bible
regarding the influence of sin on the human mind.[7] Professor
Beegle could reply that his critic may or may not be correct on
this particular point, but at least the critic has admitted the
inescapability of empirical analysis and observation in the pursuit of knowledge of at least what the Bible says.

The naturalist, pointing this out to Clark and to others like
him, asks them to acknowledge that even in their own practices they do not deny empirical observation per se. Rather
they simply wish to fence off the *area* in which theological and
moral investigation can be carried out. Having already dealt
with the hypothesis of the infallible Bible, I will not pursue
this particular point further.

The word 'fact' is used in a number of ways, but this does
not permit the critics of empirical and experimental investigation to conclude that all observation is completely reducible to
theory.[8] Our observations are indeed conditioned by our expectations (or theories). But this is only half the story, for *our
theories are in turn sometimes influenced by our observations.*[9]
Naturally we are made uncomfortable and feel threatened by
observations that seem to go against our dearest theories. But
to declare war on observation and empirical investigation per
se is to mount a crusade against the entire quest for knowledge
and understanding. Naturalists are correct to point out that
often it takes as much courage as brains to grow in knowledge
and understanding, for to risk observational tests is to risk
having one's dearest theories revised or replaced.

Central Principles of One's Frame of Reference.   The complaint that naturalists make against supernaturalists is that
they are arbitrary in their commitment to observational procedures. On the one hand, they appeal to observable phenomena

that tend to support their claims, but on the other hand, they denounce observational procedures that tend to refute and challenge, rather than support, these claims.

It has often been charged, however, that the naturalistic sciences, as much as supernatural religions, also prejudice their observational procedures. How? By observing only what the fundamental framework permits, and nothing more.[10] Despite its reckless excess, this charge may serve as still another voice advising us to be more critical of scientific claims. It should not, however, be used to give anyone—naturalist or supernaturalist—the license to stamp as "truth" any new and strange interpretation because it presents itself dramatically as a message or visit from what Bishop Pike called "the other side."

The line between science and philosophy, on the one hand, and gullibility, on the other, is not always easy to draw. Science and philosophy must be not only rigorous, but adventurous, open, experimental, and willing to take in new data. Hence there is always the risk of becoming misled, duped, and deceived. But in order to be true to their own principles, science and philosophy must sometimes take this risk. Reservation in making judgments is one thing; but reservation *in pursuit of data* is an altogether different thing. This latter reservation is *not* a part of rational inquiry. It does not belong to the naturalistic method. Caution in drawing conclusions is not to be confused with the irrational refusal to venture out in search of new data and challenging observations.[11]

Doubtless every fundamental framework (world-view, "blick," or whatever we may call it) contains certain central principles, categories, and concepts.[12] Then there are principles and the like that are not so central. To understand this is to realize that we are usually (but not always) less willing to have our central principles challenged and more willing to have our peripheral concepts challenged.

But this is not to say that people can *never* successfully challenge one another's core principles and categories. Rather, it is to say that the challenge is *difficult.* Also, we do not *refute* any framework by pointing out merely that its central principles and categories are indeed central. After all, the person pointing this out will have his own framework, with its central principles. Does that, then, refute (literally refute) the questioner's framework? If so, will he assume another framework, with its central principles?

The Naturalistic Commitments.   The naturalist contends that in many areas of their lives even the severest critics of naturalism are already committed to the central principles of naturalism. The job of the naturalist in debate is to challenge his critics either to forsake these principles altogether and thus see where this action leads, or to apply the commitment more vigorously and forthrightly. To do the latter would be to become more openly a naturalist in method.

THE NATURAL AND THE SUPERNATURAL

Atheism and the Supernatural.   Atheism is the view that belief in God or Gods is mistaken or illusory. However, there are many views of God, and hence many versions of atheism. Some views are called atheistic even when they have what would appear to be something like a providential God in them. Not every frame of reference that is atheistic is compatible with the naturalistic method. For example, the Nazi movement, while opposed to Christian and Jewish classical theism, nevertheless held to all sorts of supernaturalistic beliefs. Furthermore, there are some versions of revised theism that may be greatly compatible with the naturalistic method.

However, supernaturalism is generally regarded as clearly incompatible with naturalism. Even here, there is some confusion because the word 'supernatural' is often used in more than one way. Let us suppose for the moment that we know that there are in fact ghosts. Are these ghosts supernatural beings or natural beings? Well, the naturalist would have to say that they are natural. Why? Because if we genuinely know that there are ghosts, then they would have had to meet the tests of the naturalistic method. That is, some sort of systematic observation of ghost data would have been recorded and checked out.

Putting the Hypothesis to the Test.   What does this mean? It means that in the case of ghosts, their existence cannot be established upon the random claims of individuals or groups of individuals. If there are ghosts, then we cannot know about them unless they appear or give signs and indications of their existence. Furthermore, these appearances or signs must meet certain tests. But what are the tests? That is not an easy question to answer without prejudicing the case. Still, unless some sort of observational tests are set forth, the naturalists must declare that the vague experiments with ghosts, while very fascinating, are at best inconclusive because they lack thoroughness and follow-up.

One place to start in setting up tests is to let the believers themselves suggest tests. For example, are there any *appropriate conditions* under which ghosts appear or show signs of their alleged presence? Can these conditions be made definite? If they cannot, then the believer may have to admit that he has really not told us what the appropriate conditions are. Has he, instead, engaged in trickery, perhaps tricking himself more than anyone else?

In scientific laboratories, individuals sometimes either fake their data or mislead others about the conditions under which certain observable data came about. It is the job of the scientific community to expose these deceptions. Whether the research scientists *intend* to deceive is only a secondary question in science. The primary scientific question is this: If the specified conditions are met, will the predicted observable results come about? If not, then has the scientist really been definite and precise as to what the conditions are? If not, let him strive to improve.

Finally, if the conditions are precisely met, but the observable results are *not* forthcoming, then a crisis has developed. The scientist is going to have either to revise his conditions or to declare at least some of his promises to be unjustified. It is not scientific to presuppose that there cannot be ghosts. Nor is it scientific to presuppose that there are ghosts. It is very likely that different scientists (or others concerned to put the ghost hypothesis to the test) will have varying initial expectations (i.e., theories and hypotheses) as to what will be observed. But it is not important as to which expectations they *start* with. What is important, however, is the *commitment to make their expectation or hypothesis responsive to what is observed.*

The trouble with claims about alleged supernatural phenomena is that too little careful and systematic inquiry has been made of either the claims or their alleged supportive data. This is no more the fault of believers than of unbelievers. Instead of complaining about the skeptical attitude of scientists, believers would do well to set forth their own testing procedures and to find ways for making it convenient for people to scrutinize these tests. By the same token, instead of complaining about those who fail to test their hypotheses about supernatural beings and events, scientists would do well to move into the area of the putative supernatural phenomena in order to begin observing, trying out new hypotheses, and subjecting each promising hypothesis to observational tests.

The Refusal to Be Put to the Test.   Naturalism's major complaint about supernaturalism is the latter's lack of nerve in following through with the developed tests. There are many supernaturalists who claim that ghosts (or God or whatever) will not manifest themselves except under conditions of human *faith*. On the surface, this would seem to be just a way of saying that the supernatural being in question can be manifested only under the proper conditions. No naturalist could find fault with that. However, what the naturalist does find fault with is the supernaturalist's unwillingness to be forthright in indicating just what the *faith conditions and procedures are.*

In fact, the demand for faith as a necessary condition for receiving the manifestations or data often turns out to be a very excessive demand. It stipulates that before anyone can receive manifestations, he must first believe that the manifestations could not possibly be explained by any interpretation other than a certain version of supernaturalism. What that version of supernaturalism is will vary from one believing group to another. Each group will be convinced that it is immoral to entertain any view other than its own. In fact, many supernaturalists teach their followers to treat as sinful any doubt regarding the truth of their particular doctrine of supernaturalism. For some of these believers, the source of doubt is a kind of evil supernatural agent, such as Satan, or some wicked spirit, witch, etc.

Some supernaturalists demand that when their predicted observable phenomena fail to appear, this failure must in no way count against the truth-claims of their supernaturalistic theory. In other words, they are saying that the alleged observations or manifestations will not appear unless you are already convinced that the supernatural being exists *irrespective* of whether there are or are not corroborating manifestations or evidences.

But that is not all. To have faith in the supernatural often means to refuse to allow any experience or any kind of evidence to count *against* the hypothesis. This is a call for faith regardless of what happens. Nothing relevant could falsify the faith-claim. It is this meaning of 'faith' that naturalism declares to be destructive of any inquiry leading to the growth of knowledge.

The Attack on Causal Conditions Per Se.   Some supernaturalists make a wholesale attack on the very notion of *conditions*. They charge that it is only a prejudice to require everything to happen in connection with observable conditions. Sometimes, they say, things just happen without causes and conditions, and sometimes supernatural beings just appear without any why or wherefore.[13]

But the naturalist is not impressed with this argument because he sees that no one is thoroughly committed to it. Why? Because it is factually impossible to be so committed to it. Hence, a kind of standoff between the naturalist and the supernaturalist develops. The supernaturalist says that of course he takes seriously such principles as causality and specifying conditions—but only in *ordinary* life. In his extraordinary life, however, it is a different matter. There the spirit (or spirits) blows where it will without natural causes or conditions.

The naturalist, on the other hand, believes that he observes the tendency of supernaturalists themselves to talk of natural (i.e., testable) conditions by which the putative supernatural happenings come about. For example, one of the conditions might be that the extraordinary event or visit (or whatever) comes primarily, if not exclusively, to *certain kinds of people*. But to say even this is to begin selecting a certain set of appropriate conditions. The supernaturalists make claims that the extraordinary event comes when people believe certain things or do certain things. But these, too, are all statements of *conditions and causal variables* making more likely the appearance of the extraordinary event.

Well, if this naturalistic argument is sound, then have not the supernaturalists pleased the naturalists? What are the naturalists complaining about? The naturalists turn the argument back on the supernaturalists and ask them what they are complaining about. After all, supernaturalists are themselves great doubters and skeptics as well as great believers. They do not believe the statements of many others claiming supernatural visits or whatever. What this boils down to is that one group of supernaturalists contends that others either have not met the *right conditions* or have not produced the *observable phenom-*

ena that they promised to produce. Naturalists simply take the supernaturalists' own arguments against one another and use some of them against supernaturalism per se.

Oral Roberts believes in supernatural events brought about in the name of Jesus Christ, which is Roberts' *condition* for a supernatural event. The supernatural event is understood to be, not the work of some finite spirit or ghost, but of Jesus Christ himself. For the same event, a supernaturalist in the Orient might insist on his own set of *conditions* and his own *interpretation* as its source; but Oral Roberts would be *skeptical* about this Oriental's claims.

The naturalist believes that all who put forth statements of supernaturalism need to be more definite in what their required conditions are and are not. They also must be more accurate in specifying what was predicted and what was observed to happen.

It is sometimes charged that the naturalist is begging the question by demanding that the supernatural be reduced to the naturalistic view of the world.[14] But this fails to see that naturalism is not a static metaphysical view. The naturalism referred to in this chapter is not primarily a set of fixed conclusions as to what the world is, but a demand for both rigor and openness in investigative procedures. The above charge against naturalism forgets that the naturalist may, upon studying claims of extraordinary phenomena, come to see that they are indeed extraordinary. But he may also discover what the conditions are by which these phenomena occur. Furthermore, he may have to revise his system of expectations (i.e., theories), although they may still be greatly different from the supernaturalist's. An example of this is Dr. Andrew Weil's calling upon psychosocial variables rather than "magic" to account for certain altered states of consciousness.[15] Indeed, the naturalistic method challenges anyone using the "psychosocial" explanation to make his account more exact, communicative, and systematic—or else to let the account be classified as magical utterances.

The Challenge of Naturalism.   It may be that the naturalistic method is threatening to great numbers of viewpoints, including Freudian analysis and much of what passes as scientific medicine. The world is full of vague and indefinite claims, imprecise statements of conditions, careless testing, and unsystematic observations. To be sure, there is no need to be careful in cases when the issues are not particularly critical. But what is interesting about supernaturalists is their desire to receive the reputation of being credible without having met the tests to earn it.

The advantage of being vague about predicted supernatural events and the conditions for bringing them about is that if one is never quite definite, one can never quite be refuted. One appears to be saying something but not so definitely as to be precisely understood. The naturalist, however, points out that if you do not speak so that you can be tested to see if you are *mistaken*, then you really have not said anything that might be *true*.

In some cases, however, alleged supernatural claims have been gradually forced to be more definite and precise. And in some cases the specified conditions have been adhered to with the result that the expected observations have come about. Where this has happened, the supernatural is no longer thought of as supernatural but as a part of the rich and variegated world of nature and culture. Naturalism is not a dogmatic commitment to one view of what the world must be. It is a matter of investigation, argumentation, etc. What naturalism does require is that predictions and promises be made definite and that checking and testing procedures be spelled out so that they may be demystified. If a person wishes to be vague, that is his concern. But to ask to be exempted from cross-examination while being treated as a serious witness who has undergone cross-examination is asking for a special privilege, which the naturalist is reluctant to grant. If one view can be granted "diplomatic immunity" or exemption, then so can every view. And that is to render no view more credible than another, no promise worthier than another, and no human commitment more meaningful than another. There might be individuals who profess to hold to the view that all views are equally deserving of belief. But they could not consistently recommend this view over any other. Indeed, to try to make it appear more "attractive" by psychological gimmicks would be to violate what the view itself implies.

The Importance of Being Precise. We often become more precise in our communication as the need arises. The degree of precision or exactness depends on what our interests are and what distinctions we wish to make. You distinguish a piece of green paper with George Washington's picture on it from a similar kind of paper with Ben Franklin's picture. The number on each piece of green paper is important to you. Where you do not want to make a distinction, then you do not feel it necessary to be exact and precise.

In June, 1974, the evangelist Billy Graham distinguished two sources of temptation—Satan and the individual himself. Inviting certain members of the audience to "come forward," Graham warned that Satan would give them a thousand excuses in addition to the excuses that they themselves could invent for not coming forward. This assertion naturally raises the question of how Satan's excuses are to be distinguished from those of the person himself. The sermon that the evangelist had just preached was about the reality of devils and exorcism, and Graham was simply applying his theory by saying that the chief of devils was present at Graham's Crusade and was busy trying to frustrate the evangelist's preaching efforts.

Let us try to be precise about these excuses for not going forward to "accept Christ." Take, for example, the excuse, "People might see me on TV, and I don't want to be seen on TV." Or another excuse: "If I go forward, will my friends wait for me?" Or, "If I go forward, I'll miss my ride home." Or, "I do not think Graham's view makes sense." Now exactly which of these excuses comes from Satan and which from the individual himself?

The point here is that if there are no ways for making this distinction, then why did the evangelist say what he said? The evangelist needs to come up with a way of distinguishing excuses invented by Satan from those coming from other sources. If this distinction cannot be made, then the case for the influence of a real Satan in human life is seriously weakened. (Interestingly, Billy Graham seemed unable to believe that persons would have *reasons* for not "coming forward" in his Crusade. To him, they were all *excuses.*)

SOME DIRECTIONS OF NATURALISM

Methodology As Primary.   At the core of the naturalistic framework is its methodology of both rigorous criticism and open inquiry. Out of the interplay between the two ideals of critical scrutiny and experimental adventure, certain directions have developed. These are a part of the more established background of naturalism and are therefore less subject to change than are the more peripheral hypotheses. Nevertheless, nothing of the naturalistic framework is taboo in the sense that it is beyond question and perhaps revision or replacement. This is not to say that its central principles are not well-established. Rather, it is to say that the only way to know whether a principle, theory, scheme of categories, etc., is established is to keep raising specific and critical questions against it. Perhaps one of the most important differences between naturalism and some versions of supernaturalism is the former's willingness to allow *doubt* to be a major and healthy stimulus in the search for knowledge and understanding.

Some of the established background, major directions, and expectations of naturalism may now be looked at.

Location in Space and Time.   For a naturalist to say that nature is the totality of reality is not to say that he knows all about nature. Rather, he holds that anything that is real exists in space and time. To say that this is one of the directions taken by naturalism is to say that naturalists expect reality to be plural and to be located in space and time. It is with this presumption that naturalists proceed in experimental inquiry.

One reason naturalists are reluctant to believe in a disembodied soul is that to them it is meaningless to say that something exists nowhere and at no time. Even those who speak of astral-body travel contend that there is really spatial travel of some sort and a body of some sort. Which is to say that the astral body is believed to be located spatially, even if in another "world" that has no spatial connection with our everyday world.

One of the most famous alleged astral travelers of modern times, Sylvan Muldoon, held that a "cord" linked his projected etheric double to his physical body. This seems to be a naturalistic expectation on Muldoon's part. That is, he found himself resisting the thought of breaking up completely the complex "spatio-temporal continuity" that the naturalist calls "nature."

It is interesting that the apostle Paul spoke not so much of a soul as of a "spiritual body," as if at least finite existence had to be located in some spatial region.[16] (It would be unwise to insist that a finite body must be located in a predetermined limit of space. It is at least conceivable that a giant computer could be embodied in an area of, say, two square miles. It is possible to conceive of a beehive as a body composed of smaller bodies.)

Nature and Mystery.   The naturalistic framework treats all realities as "inside" nature. Nothing exists "outside" nature. This, however, should not be understood to mean that our present understanding of nature is so complete that all our new discoveries will have to fit into our present *views*. To a great extent, to say that all things exist in nature is to say that untestable supernatural claims are misleading if they are taken to be more than tentative hypotheses to be better formulated and eventually tested.

There is, however, a certain temptation to dogmatism here. Naturalism is sometimes too quick to define something as supernatural and thus as unworthy of attention. In some respects, the naturalist pays too much regard to the interpretations of those who claim to be in contact with the supernatural. The naturalist would do well to move himself into the new areas of inquiry. If he is to be true to his own central principles, he must take his scientific training into areas where previously scientists were too embarrassed to go.

Contending that everything is a part of nature is the same as saying that nothing is beyond critical inquiry. No area is deliberately reserved for pure mystification. Undoubtedly, there are whole areas, levels, layers, and dimensions (or whatever) of nature that we currently are unable to investigate. Our instruments are either not sensitive enough or nonexistent. The naturalist cannot claim to know without doubt that certain members of the universe are by their nature unexplainable, although he realizes that most aspects of nature or the universe are likely to remain unexplained.

The naturalist asks the supernaturalist to be consistent when he asserts that the universe is filled with mystery. If the supernaturalist were consistent, he would not claim to *know* which aspects of the world are beyond our human understanding. The naturalist says that we do *not know* for certain which areas of the world will remain an unknowable mystery to us. Hence, as an experimentalist he will simply sail on into the sea of mystery and gain knowledge where and when he can. He will not presume to know where the line of absolute mystery is drawn.

It is curious that the supernaturalist often claims to know a great deal about what is supposed to be a mystery. To the naturalist, this looks as if the supernaturalist wants to enjoy the status of being a propagator of special knowledge without being placed on the witness stand for cross-examination.

Plurality and Continuities. Naturalists emphasize both the plurality and the continuity of the universe. A pluralistic universe is one whose separate entities are not mere illusions or shadows of a "higher" reality. In an earlier chapter you studied the view called *monism*, which asserts that whatever is in relationship to something else is mere shadow and appearance. Naturalism rejects this depreciation of relationships. An entity is not unreal simply because it stands in relationship to other members of the universe. Indeed, naturalism has come increasingly to assert that an entity can stand in *many* relationships to other entities. This means that what an entity *is* depends on what its *relationships* are. In this sense you are many things, and your total reality may be regarded as a synthesis of these many things-in-relationship.

When stressing the continuity of the universe, the naturalist is speaking in a semi-mythological mode. It would probably be more in keeping with his emphasis on plurality if he should speak, not of the continuity *of* the universe, but of continuities *within* the universe. There are widespread themes and categories—such as causality, process and structure, events and energy (matter), relationship and entity, and field—which are modes of thinking that in some sense we impose on the universe. Because they "fit" in some sense, the naturalist does not regard them as wholly arbitrary. Probably of equal importance is the fact that naturalism claims that some modes of thinking do *not* "fit" well on the universe. Rigid dualisms such as the hard-and-fast distinctions between spirit and matter, mind and body, activity and possibility, and time and eternity are rejected as excessive impositions on nature. There is too much continuity between mind and body, for example, to allow us to make them into two altogether different kinds of substances.

In other words, rigid dualisms are rejected because every entity is connected directly, or indirectly, with the rest of the universe. Everything is what it is because it is related through others: such is naturalism's doctrine of pluralism and continuity.

Experience As the Starting Point. If nothing is real except in relationship, then nothing can be *known* by us except as it is directly or indirectly related to us. This naturalistic view of knowledge insists that experience is the starting point of knowledge. This does not mean that reality can be nothing but one's own experience or that experience is the stopping point. Rather it means that only by affecting our experience in various ways does reality become somewhat knowable to us. Knowledge increases as new experiences are predicted, expected, and brought to pass under specified conditions.

Naturalism does not suppose that every entity must directly shape our experience before we can know of it. The world is judged to be filled with entities-in-relationship that have no direct bearing on any human being's experience. But only through those realities that do directly create for us our experiences do we have data for projecting theories pertaining to a wider world of reality. This means "that all hypothetical thinking is a projection beyond [what is] actually experienced, that all so-called revelations and intuitions are extensions of such imaginative constructions," and that experience is the arena in which these constructions and projections are to be tested.[17]

Publicized Reports.   Naturalism stresses the importance of publicly reported experiences whenever the issue of knowledge is of concern. Also, the more one makes public his bold and imaginative hypotheses, the better chance they will have of being subjected to critical challenge. Naturally, when a person wishes to avoid being challenged, he will tend to profess that he just knows such and such to be the case on the basis of his own personal experience alone. Philosophers have long been debating the issue of private experience and private language. What is important to see here is that we generally allow only a very few kinds of claims to stand solely on the basis of one individual's personal experience. For example, if Bill tells us that his left arm feels sore, we do not think that we, too, should feel it before we can believe him. However, Bill may move beyond reporting information of his private or subjective world only. He may claim that yesterday he saw Mary in a bank in Santa Fe. We would not hesitate to question him on this claim if something were to make us think that he was mistaken. Or you yourself may have seen Mary in Boston at the time when she was supposed to have been seen in Santa Fe. "Perhaps you were mistaken," Bill says to you.

Naturalism acknowledges the capacity for human reports to be in error or mistaken. However, inasmuch as we must finally depend on the observations of individuals, the only alternative is to train *many* individuals to observe and to *compare* and *check* their observations. Indeed, even certain kinds of machines can sometimes be used to help human beings in the process of observation.

Except when it is a report only of his own feelings, one individual's statement is usually not regarded as a broad enough base for establishing far-reaching conjectures and theories. Naturalists can only take as tentative an individual's report that some extraordinary being from another world visited him. Like any tentative claim, it needs to establish itself on a broader basis if it is to be taken to be more than a report of the individual's own interpretation of his private experiences.

The broad definition of an "object" is that it is something available to *any* individual to experience if he is in the proper position or fulfills the proper conditions. Once again, the importance of carefully laying out the conditions of observation cannot be overemphasized.

Nature and Values.   Naturalism is sometimes accused of not being able to account for the existence of values in the world. This accusation is often a mixture of charges. In a later chapter we will confront the tough issue of whether morality in a world with no God underwriting it can justify moral behavior. For the present, it is sufficient to say that the naturalist points out that within nature people do as a matter of fact find themselves giving value to all sorts of things, persons, relationships, and experiences. Without a supernatural being, the sunset is beautiful, the apple tasty, music moving, a friendship important, and love desirable. The world is filled with the possibilities for value as well as disvalue. Value is not supernatural in either origin or reference.[18]

SOME CRITICISMS OF NATURALISM

The Charge of Hopelessness.   Supernaturalists point to the failure of naturalism to come up with a strong belief in life after death. Human life is, for naturalism, a brief candle blown out after a few years on earth. Without hope for life beyond the grave, the naturalist is reduced to dressing up this finite and mortal existence ere it returns forever to dust. One might say of each human life, "If he was so soon done for, I wonder what he was begun for." Indeed, according to the naturalist, humanity was not begun for any cosmic purpose and has no cosmic aim, goal, or meaning. The naturalist gives no hope for everlasting life but instead states bluntly that "the world was not made for us."[19]

Naturalists acknowledge that the great majority of them have no strong belief in life beyond the grave, but they charge in return that whether they be Evangelical Christians or Hindus, the believers in life after death have no *strong evidence* to support their belief. To those who demand to live after they die, naturalism stands as a reminder that children do not always get what they demand. It is not the job of philosophy to invent promises that will satisfy the wishes that people project upon the universe.

For unlike many world-views, naturalism offers no cosmic consolation for the unmerited defeats and undeserved sufferings which all men experience in one form or another.[20]

The Charge of Despair and Meaninglessness. Naturalism is accused of offering a philosophy that leads in the end to despair and meaninglessness. The cosmos, indifferent to the affairs of mortals, rolls on in its oblivion, paying no regard to the cherished ideals that make human life dear and significant. If people were to take seriously the philosophy of naturalism, they would commit suicide or at least confess that when their lives are totaled up, the sum is zero.

To this charge, naturalists concede that for many human beings who are *taught* that they are eternally and cosmically important, the philosophy of naturalism is indeed a bitter pill to swallow. It should come as no surprise that, having raised their expectations to infinite horizons, many people would fall into misery and despair if they should come to believe that their expectation of infinity is merely a pipe dream. Such a dream is born of both wishful thinking and the undisciplined, vain imaginings of a finite species resentful of its mortality.

But there are in fact a number of naturalists who either have never expected cosmic significance or have overcome most of what they regard as the illusion of self-importance. This is not to say that naturalists have never known the bitter night of despair. Like the Christian John Bunyan and other believers from many faiths, some naturalists have walked through the slough of Despond. Like their fellow human beings everywhere, naturalists ache when their dearest die, when their love is not returned, or when their most valued dreams and wishes fail to materialize. But the ideal of naturalism is to love, learn, create, and enjoy existence without indulging in self-deception regarding one's own immortality or resurrection. That a number of naturalists are able to live out this ideal in a reasonably acceptable manner gives witness to the possibility that perhaps the human species is not completely chained to all of its ancient illusions.

The Charge That Naturalism Trusts Too Much in Human Power.   A common charge that supernaturalists make is that naturalists think they can lift themselves up by their own bootstraps. For example, in the realm of knowledge, naturalists claim to need no divine revelation; in the realm of morality, they claim to need no God for direction and motivation; and in the realm of just plain survival, they claim that they can make it without God.

In response, naturalists reply that the primary question is not whether people *need* divine revelation, but whether there is *evidence and reason* to support the claim that such revelation *exists*. Naturalism holds that the world is perpetually revealing itself in countless ways and that the task is to interpret the responses that nature and culture elicit from us. To be sure, given a certain cultural or social setting, many people have come to expect divine revelations. They have learned to expect to receive divine instruction while praying, reading certain Scriptures, or performing certain other activities. In this sense, they have *come to need* revelation. That is, much of their lifestyle depends on the *belief* that supernatural interpretation or guidance is available.

But to *believe* in all this does not render it true. Our beliefs do often motivate and shape our behavior and attitudes, but this in itself is no basis for supposing that the beliefs are warranted or supported by evidence.

The charge that naturalists have no God to direct and motivate them in moral and ethical matters is an accurate charge. I will, however, deal with this issue later in this book.

The general charge here is that naturalists try to lift themselves up by their own bootstraps. The answer usually given in reply is that it is a false charge. Naturalists claim that people are so finite and utterly dependent on countless variables as to render foolish the assertion of anyone who claims to depend on himself only.

Naturalism receives its very name from *nature*. The energy system of nature, with its numerous dimensions and variables, is regarded by naturalists to be necessary to their finite human existence. Far from thinking that they lift themselves by their own powers only, naturalists believe that it is imperative to understand more thoroughly the numerous threads that bind us together socially and the ties that link us to the physical and chemical world.

The individual who says, "I depend wholly on myself" or "I have faith only in myself" is not sensitive to his involvements with physical nature and his mutually dependent relationships with his culture and society. To do so simple a task as walk across the street is to depend on countless social and physical variables that we casually take for granted. In a reflective mood, we may see how utterly dependent we are on nature in its physical forms and in its emerging cultural forms.

Keenly critical of certain institutional patterns that perpetuate supernaturalism, some naturalists desire institutional reforms. They want institutional support for lifestyles that are both naturalistic in orientation and humanistic in moral ideals. Supernaturalism has many shapes and forms. It thrives best wherever mystification is substituted for experimental inquiry and logical analysis. Supernaturalism in this sense is not so much *what* one believes as the *way* in which one protects one's beliefs from the light of investigation and critical analysis. Indeed secularism can itself become a dogma that spawns its own atrocities. The thriving naturalistic method is a steady check on secular mystifications as well as religious ones.

RELIGIOUS NATURALISM

One of the leading modern spokesmen of atheism, Kai Nielsen, makes the following statement: "In defending atheism I am not saying that religion is unimportant. It is precisely because I think religion is important that I find it necessary to argue for and defend atheism."[21] There is considerable controversy over how to define 'religion'. The controversy is less heated when the definition is broken down into various kinds of definitions. In this book I am usually defining 'religion' in only a preliminary way as core-concern with the pervasive finitude of either oneself or one's identity group. If anyone is not disposed to accept this as a tentative definition, he may call this deep core-concern what he will. It is the concern itself, not a word, that is of primary interest to me.

Professor Nielsen states very well this concern over finitude when he writes of "death, defeat of hopes, the destruction of ideals and human and sometimes even natural savagery."[22] Whether they are Buddhists, Catholics, Protestants, Hindus, or humanists, most human beings try to find some security against the ravages of time and the uncertainties of human existence. In this book I have been attempting thus far to show, among other things, that there is a variety of ways in which individuals and movements have responded to this core-concern over the finitude of oneself or one's identity group. Many classical theists, for example, insist that a changeless Perfect Being survives the ravages of time, and that this changeless Being can save us from death and final decay. Probably the notion of God's "eternity" is a response to the fears and anxieties generated by the apprently transitory state of human existence.

Naturalists see the need to face courageously and honestly the fact of human temporality and death. They believe it is possible to do so without promising everlasting life. They believe it is possible to know joy and love and meaningful existence without suffering the self-deceptions that they believe to infect classical theism and other supernatural schemes. But naturalists concede that a forthright and meaningful response in the face of death and finitude does not come easily. The art of living courageously and happily as a naturalist is something that has to be learned, both from others and in the process of living one's own life.

Almost all people responding to this core-concern have felt the need for a human group in which they may receive support, comfort, and challenge from fellow human beings who likewise face death and the deep frustrations of finitude. Naturalists are not exceptions to this human need. Some of them wish to support groups that help people in their hours of deepest struggle to rise above hate and hostility, to share with others in the achievement of value, and to take death courageously as an inevitable and final event. The universe, says the naturalist, has no overriding purpose. But so long as they live, human beings may have purpose and meaning in their shared existences. Many of those who demand an immortal life of bliss have become convinced that their demand will be met by some supernatural agent or force. But naturalists regard this conviction to be unwarranted.

The naturalistic method, of course, can never say that this issue is closed off from further investigation. It may be that some who disbelieve in life after death are indulging in wishful thinking also, since they do not wish to live an uninteresting or frightful life beyond the grave. But be that as it may, the consistent naturalist can only leave the matter open for further inquiry even if he thinks that thus far the survival hypothesis is very weak. In a later chapter we will deal more thoroughly with the pros and cons of life beyond the present life.

PERSONALITY AND NATURALISM

Naturalism does not intend to say that there is a Cosmic Person. There are only finite persons. But theistic opponents of naturalism charge that naturalism cannot account for the presence of finite persons or personality within the universe. The theistic assumption here is that personality cannot grow out of what is impersonal. There must already exist personality prior to the arrival of finite persons. And that prior personality is, says the theist, none other than the Cosmic Person, God.

The naturalist replies that the basic assumption that the theist is making is this: *Nothing finite can exist in the world unless something very much like it exists already*. The naturalist charges that the theist is not really prepared to follow the *implications* of this assumption. Why? Very simply, it would embarrass the theist. For example, there is evil in creation. Well, did evil exist in God before creation? It will not do to say that human beings produce evil, for then we would have a case of something *completely new* in the universe. In fact, the naturalist claims that personality is the emergence of something new. If nature produces persons, then the open mind simply must accept the fact. That is what intellectual humility entails.

Naturalism asserts that we can explain how persons emerge in the world. The theory of evolution, our studies of child growth, and many other natural and social sciences have given us an understanding of how persons have evolved and developed. To be sure, there are degrees of understanding. The naturalist argues that naturalism, not supernaturalism, provides the method for increasing our degree of understanding of how persons emerge.

The naturalist has another point to make. Outside his window he sees the red blossom of the oleander. It was not there last week. Where did it come from? Shall he presuppose that it must already have been there? He thinks not. Rather he concludes that there were certain *conditions* that were there making it possible for the blossom to *come into being*. Indeed, many centuries ago some of these *conditions* did not even exist. They, too, had to come into existence. The theory of evolution attempts to trace the developmental processes by which certain conditions and their products come about. Other naturalistic theories and hypotheses are used in conjunction with the theory of evolution in the attempt better to account for the emergence of consciousness and other distinctively human phenomena.

NOTES

1. Sidney Hook, "Naturalism and First Principles," *The Quest for Being and Other Studies in Naturalism and Humanism* (New York: Dell, Delta Books, 1934, 1961), p. 173. This article also appears in *American Philosophers at Work,* ed. Sidney Hook (New York: S. G. Phillips, Inc., 1956).

2. See ibid., p. 174.

3. See Karl Popper, *Objective Knowledge: An Evolutionary Approach* (New York: Oxford University Press, 1972), pp. 258–261.

4. See Gordon H. Clark, "Special Revelation as Rational," in *Revelation and the Bible,* ed. Carl F. H. Henry (Grand Rapids: Baker Book House, 1958), p. 137.

5. Gordon H. Clark, *Religion, Reason, and Revelation* (Philadelphia: Presbyterian & Reformed Publishing Co., 1961), p. 233. Italics added.

6. See ibid., p. 110.

7. See Cornelius Van Til, *The Doctrine of Scripture* (Ripon, Calif.: den Dulk Christian Foundation, 1967), p. 79. This is vol. 1 of Van Til's *In Defense of the Faith.*

8. On the matter of how the word 'fact' is used variously, see the excellent discussion in Norwood Russell Hanson, *Perception and Discovery: An Introduction to Scientific Thought* (San Francisco: Freeman, Cooper & Co., 1969), chaps. 10–13.

9. See Popper, *Objective Knowledge,* pp. 30 f.

10. See John Miller III, "Science and Religion: Their Logical Similarity," *Religious Studies* 5, no. 1 (October 1969): 52, n. 1.
11. In my own opinion, scientists have been too cautious in setting forth hypotheses. This caution has often frozen boldness of imagination, which is essential to the growth of knowledge. Perhaps we should be bold and daring in *inventing* numerous rival hypotheses to explain the same problem, but cautious in *believing* our hypotheses.
12. See Miller, "Science and Religion," p. 52, n. 1.
13. Christians sometimes say that the proper conditions exist only in the unobservable will of God. Unfortunately, this uses an alleged supernatural phenomenon to explain other supernatural phenomena (see Frank Morrison, *Who Moved the Stone?* [London: Faber & Faber, 1958]).
14. See T. R. Miles, "On Excluding the Supernatural," *Religious Studies* 1, no. 2 (April 1966): 144.
15. See Andrew Weil, *The Natural Mind: A New Way of Looking at Drugs and the Higher Consciousness* (Boston: Houghton Mifflin, 1972), p. 110.
16. See 1 Corinthians 15:44.
17. Jack J. Cohen, *The Case for Religious Naturalism* (New York: Reconstructionist Press, 1958), p. 23.
18. The above points (from "Location in Space and Time" through "Nature and Values") were drawn to a great extent from Howard L. Parsons, "Religious Naturalism in Hartshorne," in *Process and Divinity: The Hartshorne Festschrift*, ed. William L. Reese and Eugene Freeman (LaSalle, Ill.: Open Court, 1964), pp. 529–540. Having modified and amplified Parsons' exposition, I cannot claim that he would agree with my own exposition and supplement. For a useful and sympathetic examination of the naturalistic movement, see Sterling P. Lamprecht, *The Metaphysics of Naturalism* (New York: Appleton-Century-Crofts, 1967).
19. Bertrand Russell, "A Free Man's Worship," *Mysticism and Logic* (Garden City, N.Y.: Doubleday, Anchor Books, 1957), p. 53.
20. Ernest Nagel, "Naturalism Reconsidered," in *Perspectives in Philosophy: A Book of Readings*, 2d ed., ed. Robert Beck (New York: Holt, Rinehart & Winston, 1969), p. 194. This article is also found in Nagel, *Logic without Metaphysics* (New York: Free Press, 1956), and appeared originally in *Proceedings of the American Philosophical Association* 28 (1954–55): 5–17.
21. Kai Nielsen, "Humanism and Atheism," *Religious Humanism* 4, no. 1 (Winter 1970): 29.
22. Ibid., p. 31.

CHAPTER X

Morality without Supernaturalism

A REVIEW OF THE COSMOLOGICAL ARGUMENT

As you will recall, the major point of the cosmological argument for classical theism is that the world is not self-sufficient or self-explanatory; at every moment it is absolutely dependent on something beyond itself. The cosmological argument presupposes that not only is each and every member of the universe contingent, but also the universe as a whole is contingent. That is, the world might never have come into being at all, and in itself it lacks the power to prevent itself from falling into nothingness. The reason that any and all of its parts ever existed is that they are in some sense created, sustained, and supported by another Being. This superior and more perfect Being is regarded as contingent or dependent on nothing for its own existence. Unlike the contingent world, this superior Being is wholly self-contained.

If all things do in fact depend absolutely upon this superior Being, then it may accurately be designated as the *Necessary Cause* of all things. While it is necessary to *their* existence, they are not necessary to *its* existence. Classical theists argue that this Necessary Cause is really God, which is why they use the pronoun 'he' rather than 'it' when referring to this Necessary Cause.

The ontological argument, you recall, leads to a further conclusion: The Necessary *Cause* of all things is the Necessary *Being* because he exists of necessity. Hence, he could not possibly cease to exist. Furthermore, he has always existed. It is even impossible that he could have come into existence *once upon a time*. Why? Because that would entail that once he did *not* exist. According to the ontological argument, this necessary Being must *of necessity* exist without either beginning or end.

CAN MORALITY BE JUSTIFIED
IN A WORLD WITHOUT GOD?

Dostoevsky's Warning.   In a previous chapter you encountered a more thorough explication of this cosmological argument as well as some of the major objections to it. I now wish to introduce you to a view that asserts the *dependency of morality on God.* You have often heard it said that without belief in God people would do all sorts of immoral and destructive things. Many theists believe that their faith in God helps to keep the world from falling apart morally. One of Dostoevsky's characters exclaims: "If there is no God then everything is permitted." What this suggests is that without God nothing could be regarded as immoral. Any action, attitude, or deed could be taken to be as moral as any other. Murder would be as virtuous as an act of kindness.

It used to be thought by great numbers of people that nontheists in particular could not be trusted to tell the truth in court or to hold public office. According to this way of thinking, anyone who does not believe in God has no reason or justification for being moral. Why should you or I, or anyone, be moral if there is no God?

Clarifying the Issue.   It will be useful to distinguish an empirical question from a question that is not (at least is not conspicuously) empirical. The empirical question may be stated as follows: "As a matter of fact, are those who do *not* believe in God less moral than those who *do* believe in God?"

Now this looks like a question for which a sociologist might find some sort of answer. Unfortunately, he soon would see that the question is not as free from ambiguity as it first appeared. In the first place, what exactly counts as *belief* in God? There is no need to turn this chapter into a discussion about what it means to "really believe" something. For the present purpose it is sufficient to point out that, in some surveys and polls, the beliefs of people are taken to be what these people *say* they believe. What is important to see here is that the term 'belief' is sometimes too indefinite to be of practical use. Hence, in such cases it needs to be made more definite. Our sociologist friend might wish to make it clear that he is recording what people *say* they believe. *How* do they say it? By checking off certain answers on a research questionnaire. Much more could be said on this matter of recording beliefs, but there is no point in doing so here.

However, and in the second place, the question about belief in God naturally raises the further questions about the *content* of the belief. You cannot simply believe. You have to believe *something*, even if you are mistaken in what you believe. Furthermore, in order to believe *in* something or someone you have to believe *that* certain things about it or him are, to some degree, true. This leads our sociologist friend to be a bit more definite in his poll regarding belief in God. For example, *which* particular God are we talking about? Or, *what characteristics or properties* must we assert to be true of God before we can be said to believe in God? Our sociologist may wish to make a few clarifications in order to indicate that he is using the word 'God' to include certain characteristics and to exclude others.

For example, he could make up a questionnaire that would read something like the following:

If you checked that you *do* believe in God, then from the following statements check those that you hold to be true of God.
☐ He is three Persons in One.
☐ He observes or knows all my private thoughts and feelings.
☐ He cannot do evil.
☐ He could conceivably commit suicide.
☐ He literally sits on a throne.
☐ He has a permanent body.
☐ He is neither male nor female.
☐ He feels sympathy and anger.
☐ He feels tired sometimes.
☐ He revealed the Book of Mormon to Joseph Smith.
☐ He lives on another planet.
☐ He eats and drinks.
☐ He laughs and enjoys a good joke.
☐ He will send nontheists to hell.

In the latter quarter of the eighteenth century, public officials in Pennsylvania and South Carolina had to believe in one God as well as in heaven and hell. Delaware demanded assent to the doctrine that God is three Persons in One.[1] Thomas Jefferson was often denounced as an infidel and unbeliever. Actually Jefferson believed *in* God, but *what* he believed in about God was greatly different from what some of the Presbyterian Calvinists of his day believed. Hence, it is possible to say that Jefferson did not believe in the Calvinists' God, nor did the Calvinists believe in Jefferson's God. That is, neither believed that the other's God even existed, for certainly *both* of these deities could not have existed simultaneously. It is true that Jefferson was a nontheist or atheist if by that we mean he denied the existence of the God in whom Calvinists claimed to believe. By the same token, the Calvinists were atheists if by that we mean they denied the existence of Jefferson's God.

Caution is useful in interpreting what people mean when they say they do or do not believe in God. Logically, no one could believe that God is the Trinity of three Persons in One without believing that he exists. But apparently some people are not very logical. In one religious survey at Manhattan College, more people believed that God is three persons in One than believed that God exists. Perhaps some of the students at Manhattan College meant to say the following: While we have great doubts about the existence of God, we do not doubt that *if* God should exist he would surely be three Persons in One.[2]

Why Be Moral in a World without God? Having seen that the question of belief in God is not altogether unambiguous, we are perhaps ready to venture further into the question of the dependency of morality on God. Of course, if you accept, say, the cosmological argument for God, you cannot consistently talk of a world without God. The cosmological argument holds that there could not even be a world without God. However, in appealing to those who doubt or deny the existence of God, theists sometimes try to show nontheists what the denial of God's existence leads to in the realm of morality. That is, they try to show what it leads to *if* the nontheists are consistent.

It must be admitted that in fact many unbelievers are at least as overtly moral as believers. But what the believing theists—e.g., Alvin Plantinga and George Mavrodes—wish to argue is that nontheists have no *rational justification* for being moral. True, nontheists may *feel* moral obligations because of their social environment, background, or whatever. But the feeling does not *justify* fulfilling the obligation. A person may feel like hitting another human being, but the mere possession of this feeling does not justify actually hitting someone.[3]

Many theists believe that no one has a *reason* for being

moral if there is no God to guarantee that his moral efforts will have a lasting impact. Furthermore, why should someone carry out a moral obligation if it costs him to do so? Theists who talk this way are, of course, working on the assumption that no one should be moral if it does not in some way pay to do so. Other theists claim that they do not expect to be fully rewarded for their good deeds. We will leave aside this second group in order to concentrate on the first, which is composed of those who believe that an individual has no rational justification for being moral if he receives no benefit from acting morally.

Now the force of this theistic argument is as follows: We do as a matter of fact tend to regard as greatly defective those people who lack all concern for the welfare of other people. But if there is no God, why should we regard such people as defective? After all, how can we expect people to sacrifice for others when they have no grounds for expecting to improve their own welfare in doing so? Hence, morality in a world without God seems to be odd at best and stupid at worst.

Those theists making this argument are trying to force a dilemma: Either believe in God or give up the belief that morality and social responsibility are justifiable. They claim that all attempts to hold on to morality without God are as absurd as fishing in a dry lake or depositing money in a bank that has gone out of business.

Why Be *Selfish* in a World without God?   The nontheistic naturalists might try to answer the theists' tough challenge by offering a counter-challenge: "On what grounds can *selfishness* be justified?" The thrust of this simple question raises the possibility that perhaps neither pure altruism (in the sense of unrewarded moral sacrifice) nor pure selfishness can be justified. At least neither of them can be justified in the abstract.

Human beings do not live in the abstract. They live in concrete settings and in historical circumstances. Hence, the question becomes very personal and concrete: "Why should *I* with my particular circumstances in life be moral?" What is interesting in this controversy between theists and naturalists (and certain other nontheists) is that so many people on both sides seem to think it is very important that people be moral. Both sides also seem to think that some reason or justification for being moral is required.

What Is So Important about Morality?   Those who argue against the necessity of morality altogether seem in the final analysis to be arguing not so much against morality as against what they regard as the *wrong* morality. They sometimes become very moralistic in their criticisms of morality. The point here is that it is very difficult to deny that morality is a major concern of most people. Every day, people pass moral judgments against some kinds of behavior and praise certain other kinds of behavior. Scientists reproach fellow scientists who falsify their research data, and one insurance salesman condemns another for lying to his customers.

Most people probably believe that it is crucial that at least *others* act in a moral and responsible manner. Why do they believe this? Well, we may suppose that they believe that our social relationships—with their greatly diverse forms—would fall apart unless some level of moral expectations were satisfied. Very simply, a community in which everyone anticipates being shot in the back by his neighbors would be a nasty, brutish, and short-lived community unless some reform program were brought in. If a community of all-out selfishness provides a miserable and terrifying life, then why settle for it? What could *justify* supporting such a painful existence? What reward or benefit does it offer?

So, it is not clear that selfishness is the most reasonable option for people who live for this life only and who do not expect their moral efforts to count for eternity. Those theists who assume that selfishness is the only rational or justifiable choice in a world without God seem to have considerably overstated their case.

But Why Should *I* Be Moral?   Theists grant that a community would be miserable indeed if everyone—or perhaps the majority—were wholly selfish. But the point is, "Why should *I* be *un*selfish?" In other words, I might agree that everyone *else* ought to be morally and socially responsible. That is, it would be nice if they were all moral; I surely would profit from their social sensitivity and responsibility. This community would be beneficial *to me*. But does this entail that therefore *I* should be moral? The point of these theists is that it would be foolish of *me* to be moral and unselfish if I could live selfishly in a community where everyone else—or at least the great majority—is leading a life of social and moral responsibility. The assumption of the theists is, of course, that God will see to it that the unselfish will benefit in the long run, whereas the selfish will at least be denied rewards, if not punished in hell.

SOME KEY AGREEMENTS AND DISAGREEMENTS

This argument between theists and nontheists is not necessarily a fruitless one. A careful following of it indicates that the disputants agree on some highly significant points. First, they agree on the undesirability of a community whose social sensitivity and behavior fall below a certain level. This suggests, then, a second possible agreement, namely, that the individual will much more likely be happier in a community that enjoys a certain moral and social level than in a greatly selfish community. Third, theists, naturalists, and other nontheists seem to agree that the practical problem is to get *other people* to be less selfish and more socially responsible.

The theists, however, claim an advantage over the nontheists by being able to offer some inducement to morality. In essence, they believe they have the carrot and the stick to obtain better results. But the nontheists think that such an inducement is based on an illusion at best.

Now it is important to understand that just as there are differences among theists, so differences exist among nontheists regarding the question of the justification and the motivation for morality. Some nontheists take a position somewhat as follows: The trouble with theism (of a certain kind at least) is that it diverts attention and energy from the essential job of *training* people to become moral on *realistic* grounds. This includes training each individual to see that often the best—and sometimes the only—way to lead other people toward social and moral responsibility is to *obligate oneself to joining with them.*

Keep in mind that theists and nontheists agree that the individual benefits greatly by living in a socially sensitive and moral society. Even the selfish person has a *vested interest* in keeping his community somewhat socially sensitive. If too many people begin to become greatly selfish and disrespectful of certain elementary claims of others, then selfishness will cease to offer a payoff.

It may at first be humorous to think that a selfish person might very well be justified in joining with his fellow men to increase the level of unselfishness, good will, and social responsibility in his community. But humorous as it may seem, it nevertheless may be the way men do often learn to relate to each other unselfishly. In other words, in order to develop a moral community, in which they do have a *vested interest*, selfish people may actually have to become leaders (or at least participants) in exemplifying moral and unselfish behavior.

ON THE AUTONOMY OF
MORALITY AND RELIGION

Autonomy and Mutual Influence.   Some theists seem to go so far as to hold that our particular belief in God determines our morality. Other theists, as well as many nontheists, seem to want to reduce religion to morality. There is a long-standing controversy regarding the autonomy of morality and the autonomy of religion. What I propose as a way of making progress in this controversy is a new way of looking at the phenomena in question. In short, instead of trying to decide whether religion is derived from morality, or morality from religion, we might better inquire into the way they mutually influence one another. Indeed, there are points of overlapping, for certain religious responses open up avenues to greater moral sensitivity, whereas increased moral insight sometimes brings one to a more profound religious struggle with his own finitude.

Religion and morality may be seen as something analogous to a marriage wherein each individual remains himself, but not exactly the same self as he or she was before entering into the marriage. And just as there may be tension sometimes in a good marriage, as well as enrichment, so there may be tension and enrichment in religion's encounter with morality.

Argument by Stipulative Definition.   One of the greatest sources of tension comes when certain versions of theism regard belief in God and certain cognitive and ritual behaviors to be *essential moral* behaviors. For example, some theists have contended that morality for the "natural man"—i.e., the non-Christian—is impossible. They arrive at this conclusion because they have *stipulated* that belief in God and "personal acceptance" of certain theological claims are to be taken as essential moral commitments. Furthermore, these claims are made to be prerequisites to all other expressions of morality.

It is to be expected that nontheists would regard such theological claims and beliefs to be, at best, irrelevant to morality. It would be self-contradictory for nontheists to hold themselves to be morally responsible for believing in the attributes of a God whose very *existence* they deny or seriously doubt. In fact, some nontheists have fired back with the charge that belief in God counts as an immoral act. However, many, if not most, nontheists and theists agree that their opponents can be greatly moral on at least some issues. Frequently they join together in pursuit of common values.

A Clarifying Summary. On the question of the autonomy of morality, the most stable conclusion seems to be that morality cannot be absolutely autonomous for either theists or nontheists of whatever variety. Morality is not immaculately conceived, nor does it develop in a vacuum. Morality is contextual; that is, it occurs in a setting. The debate, therefore, has to do with what that wider context or setting is. All theists hold that the "ultimate" context of morality is the will of God. This entails that in order for something to count as a moral action, intention, attitude, or whatever, it must be at least in harmony with the divine will.

To be sure, theists differ greatly as to what the will of God is. Muslims, Christians, Jews, and other kinds of theists often disagree with each other very sharply on what they take to be the will of God. It follows, therefore, that they often differ as to what they take to be moral for human beings. Even among those who designate themselves as Christians, a great diversity regarding the divine will is sometimes very conspicuous.

There is an interesting shift from regarding morality to be "harmony with God's will" to regarding it to be "harmony with nature." This transition (whether for good or ill) seems to have come through pantheistic Stoics and other ancients. Pantheists, you recall, hold that God and nature (or the universe) are one and the same reality. There is no need here to review the different types of pantheism. What is important to see is that pantheism made it linguistically more convenient for Stoics and others to speak of being in harmony with nature, cooperating with nature, and even enjoying oneness and unity with nature.

Hence, it is not surprising that when astronomers and other scientists eventually began speaking of the "laws of nature," they prepared the way for a new horizon of expectations in moral thinking. That is, many people began to speak of the *moral* laws of nature. Eventually some people came to believe that a science of ethics is quite possible.

Thomas Jefferson exemplified this way of thinking. As a deist, he held that God created nature and then left it to run

autonomously according to its own endowed laws and principles. Jefferson and other deists held that God would not interfere with nature by injecting miracles and supernatural revelations. True morality, for Jefferson, consists in living in accord
with the moral laws of nature. He believed that Jesus was a
moral and religious genius who enjoyed a superior grasp and
understanding of the moral laws. He saw Jesus as a kind of Sir
Isaac Newton of morality and religion.

Nature and Social Darwinism.   Soon after Charles Darwin
expounded his theory of evolution in 1857, a view of ethics and
morality called Social Darwinism began to develop, especially
in England and the United States. According to this view, all
species in nature develop through struggle and competition.
The strong survive the competition, while the weak perish.
That is the way things are, said the Social Darwinists, and that
is the way they ought to be. Human beings, as a species within
nature, were regarded as different from other animals only in
the style and manner of their competitiveness. It was considered to be somehow "unnatural" to ask human beings to behave differently from their fellow animals—all of whom were
regarded by Social Darwinists as blood-red in tooth and claw.

Some Christian theists took Social Darwinism to be the logical outcome of the nontheistic view of the universe. Give up
God, and Social Darwinism fills the vacuum! However, many
Social Darwinists professed to be Christians and even looked
upon fierce competition as God's way of developing strength of
moral character in those individuals who were so fortunate as
to come out on top.

It is unfair to say that either theism or nontheism is logically
tied up with Social Darwinism. The mistake of Social Darwinism—a view that Darwin himself detested—was to confuse
what *is* with what *ought* to be. The fact (if it is a fact) that
animals compete ruthlessly does not entail that human beings
ought to turn such behavior into an *ideal* toward which to
strive. The fact that human beings and other animals often
become diseased does not entail that diseases should be made
into an ideal. Furthermore, the Social Darwinists were wrong
in their claim to facts. They *selected* the competitiveness
among the species in nature, but ignored the equally significant factor of cooperativeness and mutual aid within each
species.

Both theistic and nontheistic humanists contend that Social

Darwinism dehumanizes human life. They denounce it as being both unscientific and morally perverse. Recently a non-theist wrote a book entitled *The Virtue of Selfishness* in which she attempts to argue a case for selfishness as a moral ideal.[4] Theists and nontheists alike have criticized her position on numerous grounds, one of which is that her arguments are riddled with self-contradiction.[5]

Selfishness and Inconsistency.   What is of peculiar interest to any debate between theists and nontheists regarding human morality is the fact that many of the proponents of either side of the debate share a common point of strong agreement. They hold that the attempts to defend or justify selfishness cannot be prevented from breaking out in fatal *inconsistency*. Indeed, it seems to be empirically rare for someone to be totally selfish and also happy. It is as if total selfishness is not in one's own best interest. Selfishness when applied full force is difficult to carry out.[6] Somewhere along the way, people seem to have to become involved somewhat in the lives of others. They find that acting in the *interests of others* is necessary to make their own lives *interesting*.

This is a powerfully important point, not only because many theists and nontheists agree on it, but because it suggests fruit-ful avenues of inquiry. It opens up possibilities for understand-ing with greater depth the relationship between religion and morality. The Christian theologian Augustine wrote that the human heart is a restless reaching-out. It was his belief that this human restlessness can find rest or contentment only in God. Sankara of India taught that man is always partially empty and unfulfilled so long as he perceives himself as some-how outside the life of God. Both Augustine and Sankara insisted that true fulfillment comes only "in" God, but they differ greatly as to what it means to be "in" God. Sankara, you recall, was a monist who believed literally that the finite human self is unreal or is at most an "appearance" of God, who is truly real. Augustine, on the other hand, granted the human individual a reality distinct from God's reality, for this Chris-tian theologian was eager to deny that God in any way ab-sorbed the personhood of finite creatures. Granted, Augustine sometimes wrote as if he were a monist, but on the whole he wished to speak of God as enjoying self-containedness. He thought of God as existing without any dependence on finite creatures for even the *quality* of his life. Sankara, by contrast, appears to say that God's life somehow would be empty without the "appearances" filling it and giving it content.

One of the most difficult things to grasp is the position that an individual can be both a distinct reality *and* a dependent reality. It is mistakenly assumed by many monists, and even some theists, that a dependent being is somehow less than actual or real. Some seem unable to believe that a thing can be real if it is impermanent. The Christian theist C. S. Lewis complains that finite human beings "wanted to be nouns, but they were, and eternally must be, mere adjectives."[7]

It is as if sometimes people like Lewis do not know exactly how to accept human beings as real unless they are everlasting and self-contained. A less drastic approach would be simply to say that every finite entity is real both in the sense of being distinguished from other entities and in the sense of standing in essential relationship to other entities. In short, to be real is to be related to other realities.

To Be Is to Be in Relationship.   A nontheistic naturalist might argue that Augustine and Sankara, despite certain confusions, are nevertheless driving at something profoundly insightful. They are in agreement that no finite human being could be a human being unless he enjoyed some sort of social context. Things that even selfish people often claim to hold dear seem to come about only through *interpersonal relationships*. Hence, the issue is not so much pure selfishness versus pure altruism, as where we shall live along the line between them.

In some respects, total selfishness is an abstraction, an unreality. No one can *live* at such a reduced level. Or to say it otherwise, the cost of total selfishness is so great that even a slight amount of enlightened self-interest will reject it as holding no great rewards and benefits. The practical problem of human selfishness is to better motivate concrete, actual, involved, living human beings who nevertheless are selfish and even ruthless in some areas of their lives. In other words, people become selfish in certain parts of their lives whenever they believe it is more reinforcing than being socially responsible is. Hence, the skill of moral persuasion lies in finding ways to reward moral behavior and to make certain forms of greatly destructive behavior less rewarding. Instead of presupposing that in the end everything will turn out justly, with responsible people being rewarded and selfish people being penalized, the nontheistic humanist sets forth another option. Very simply, it says that human beings would do well to improve the social context in which they live so that unselfishness, rather than selfishness, is rewarded in this life.

But who will exercise the skill of moral persuasion and social construction work? In some respects, almost every human being, simply by being with others, exercises it somewhat, and with varying degrees of success and failure. It is often misleading to think that a context for moral development either exists or does not exist. In most cases it is a matter of degree—of starting with what is available and then seeking to improve on it. In moral development we more easily move from small successes to greater ones. We learn to promote the freedom and happiness of others when by doing so we find our own lives becoming more enriching and interesting.[8]

No A Priori Argument against Selfishness.   There does not seem to be a self-evident or deductive principle that somehow demolishes the thesis of selfishness in the way that a flame-thrower demolishes a tree. Those who look for such an argument or principle seem doomed to disappointment. But what consequences follow from such disappointment? Will the disillusioned individual rush headlong into selfishness (which is here defined as caring for the happiness of oneself *exclusively*)? He might embrace total selfishness if that is what he wants and if that is what will satisfy him and make him happy. In other words, the issue of selfishness becomes an empirical or factual question. The point here is that absolute selfishness does not seem to offer a very enriching and enjoyable human existence.

The "mountain people" of northeastern Uganda fell into a life of selfishness because they lacked the social and natural resources for a better way of life. Having been thoughtlessly evicted from their traditional territories and reduced from daring and prosperous hunters to hostile bands, they lost the skills of love, affection, compassion, and concern for others.[9] Far from enjoying vibrant individualism, the mountain people (the Iks) remind us that personal individuality is a *social* achievement. Such individuality comes about only through cultural and natural conditions that nourish ideals such as human uniqueness.

From Selfishness to Self-Love and Other-Love.   Even Ayn

Rand found, in one instance at least, that selfishness is arid and barren unless it encompasses concern for loved ones. Indeed, she found it necessary either to give up the word 'selfishness' or to stretch it to include at least some cases of unselfishness.[10] She chose the latter, but only briefly. Rand so stresses the need to protect oneself from other people that she fails to emphasize the equally important factor of joyous involvement with others in a shared mutuality. She seems genuinely unable to grasp the notion of the mutuality of trust and sharing. Indeed, having herself apparently failed to develop in this area of mutuality, Rand sets forth the following strange theory about all women: "The essence of femininity," she claims, "is hero-worship—the desire to look up to a man."[11] This is her basic reason for saying that she would never vote for any woman for president of the United States.

But vital self-love is to be distinguished from selfishness and the weird vacuum it leaves. Self-love includes love for both self and others. It finds effective love of others to be an immediate and direct source of enjoyment. Vital self-love, in contrast to selfishness, does not need to idolize another finite human being. A woman who loves herself rationally and with self-approval does not need to look upon a finite male as either a god or "the metaphysical concept of masculinity as such" (to use Miss Rand's grandiose language).[12]

Unselfishness comes, not in giving up one's happiness, but in finding that involvement in the lives of others is enriching, stimulating, and worthwhile despite certain risks. I will avoid here the temptation to discuss the need for unselfishness to utilize both rationality and emotion if it is to be effective involvement with others rather than aimless sentimentalism. Selfishness turns out to be a retarded version of vital self-love. Informed and enlightened unselfishness comes about as self-love develops skill, confidence, grace, and the enjoyment of mutuality. People forsake selfishness to the degree that a more socially responsive and moral way of life becomes for them available, secure, and enjoyable.

GOD AND THE VISION OF LOVE

Some theists argue that the vision of human beings living as mutually accepting brothers and sisters could not have developed apart from God. Morality, thus, is declared to be a super-natural gift to the sinful "natural man." One Christian writer states this point succinctly:

Men have no basis left in their natural condition for evaluating what is good or evil. They must have recourse to the supernatural not only for knowledge of good and evil but also for the ability to decide and act according to this knowledge. Because this knowledge cannot come by way of humanly constructed rules and laws, it must come only through faith and love and what is divine. Seen in this context, the law of God is not the command of a master to be his slave but the instruction of a father to a son.[13]

In reply, nontheists such as naturalists and humanists regard this above position to be incredibly naive, showing little awareness of how moral laws and principles do in fact develop over long centuries of human living and dying. Such a Christian view is regarded as little more than misleading Sunday-school rhetoric. Far from recalling the neat and simplistic picture given by the Christian above, the actual picture of moral development is much more complex and involved. Even in the Bible, the *complexity* of moral life cannot be completely obscured. In the book of Genesis, for example, Abraham is said to have been told by God to go up on a mountain in order to kill his only son Isaac as a sacrificial offering.

Only a few years ago, the Southern Baptist Convention found itself in a heated debate over this very account of Abraham and Isaac. It happened that the Convention was publishing some commentaries on the Bible, one of which was on the first part of the Old Testament. To make this involved Southern Baptist controversy short, I will simply note that the commentator on the book of Genesis stated that Abraham only *thought* that God told him to sacrifice Isaac's life on the altar. The commentator was trying to say that God simply would not tell someone to kill another human being—except perhaps in clear self-defense.

In the end, the Southern Baptist Convention voted to recall this commentary and to commission a new one to be written that would reflect a more conservative view of the Bible. What is ironic is that the first commentator thought that he was being extremely conservative. After all, had not God given a commandment against killing? Would he command the father to kill his own son? In the New Testament this very puzzle comes out again when the writer pictures Jesus as warning his disciples that "the time is coming when anyone who kills you will think that he is rendering a religious service to God."[14]

This thorny question as to what God does in fact reveal to people is discussed painfully but forthrightly by a Christian theist in an article entitled "Conscience and Religious Morality."[15]

The nineteenth-century existentialist and Christian writer Søren Kierkegaard wrestled with this story of Abraham and Isaac and concluded that in some way the ethical commitment must be suspended in favor of the religious. Kierkegaard promised that somehow God would make up for whatever loss might come about at the moral level.[16] Kierkegaard shows subtle insight in his analysis, so much so that the notion of divine revelation ceases to be the simple rule book that some Christian writers seem to have in mind when they attempt to show how supernaturalism saves the day by providing a remedy for our moral perplexities.

MORALS DEVELOP BY
NATURAL AND CULTURAL VARIABLES

Some nontheists hold that morality grows and develops in the process of human involvement and interaction. Like traffic regulations, morals are hammered out and shaped through considerable trial and error, through great advances and through tragedies and failures. It is a tough world, and the moral regulations that have come through cultural and natural circumstances have not been won easily. Moreover, without diligence, sensitivity, and wisdom they may be lost. According to nontheistic naturalists and humanists, morality has not dropped out of heaven into the heads of prophets who then transcribed it into documents. Indeed, many theists themselves reject this simplistic explanation of "morality out of the blue."

The nontheistic naturalist and humanist John Dewey stated a position that many theists could accept, although they would want to add some metaphysical amendments. Dewey writes:

We who now live are parts of a humanity that extends into the remote past, a humanity that has interacted with nature. The things in civilization we most prize are not of ourselves. They exist by the grace of the doings and sufferings of the continuous human community in which we are a link. Ours is the responsibility of conserving, transmitting, rectifying and expanding the heritage of values we have received that those who come after us may receive it more solid and secure, more widely accessible and more generously shared than we have received it.[17]

Note that Dewey does not say that this heritage that we prize, and which we wish to improve upon, was erected simply by human beings out of their own resources alone. Dewey is a naturalist who takes nature as the *necessary condition* of human existence. The human individual does not develop in a vacuum. He must be nourished in two wombs—the womb of nature and the womb of society and culture. Human culture and society could not emerge and develop without the incredibly vast energy system and context that Dewey calls "nature." He speaks of "a humanity that has interacted with nature."

Hence, the debate between theists (at least classical theists) and nontheistic naturalists has to do with the wider context called *nature*. Classical theists insist on having still another context for nature—namely, God. Naturalists, however, hold that nature is the sufficient context accounting for the emergence of the social and cultural life of animals and man. In Chapter VI, entitled "God, Evil, and Suffering," some of the differences between theism and naturalism were discussed. Whether you go with theism or naturalism (if either) may depend upon how you evaluate the earlier arguments for and against the existence of God. Also, you may wish to look again at Chapter II, on views of Scripture; for classical theists believe that the more complete morality could not have developed except through supernatural miraculous revelation.

According to the naturalist and the humanist, morality emerges, dies, is restored, and is sustained by a vast reservoir of natural and cultural variables. Supernatural revelation is regarded as nothing other than human interpretations and convictions that have been projected onto an imaginary cosmic scene that theists take to be eternally authoritative. Naturalists look upon the Bible, the Qur'an, and the other Scriptures of the world as nothing other than the interpretations, dreams, visions, hopes, and even rages of human beings as they respond to the numerous and complex dimensions of their natural and cultural environments. The variables by which people live and move and have their being are, therefore, not supernatural, but natural and cultural.

ROOM FOR GROWTH

Many theists as well as nontheists believe that human moral knowledge like all other forms of knowledge is still incomplete. They differ primarily on where to place the weight of authority. Some Christians say, "Turn *first* to the Bible and to the continuous experience of the church."

There is no great problem here until the Christian says, "Turn *finally* to the Bible (and perhaps also to the experience of the church) as the court of *last* appeal." Naturalists and many other nontheists have no quarrel with those who look into a Scripture for possible guidelines and fruitful suggestions. But to take the guidelines as somehow infallible or unquestionably authoritative is clearly something a consistent nontheistic naturalist and humanist cannot do.

The naturalist and humanist must turn to experience, not as if it were an infallible document, but as a stimulus for challenging human hypotheses and convictions. He must learn from experience, even though experience never stands uninterpreted (as we saw in the chapter dealing with the issue of "immediate experience"). In short, interpretations are guidelines, but they are also open for criticism, revisions, improvement, and even elimination. The naturalist cannot consistently pretend that he already has moral guidelines for every generation or occasion. This is not to say that his guidelines will be completely overthrown at the end of each day. The naturalist simply must face the conclusion of his premises that while nature and culture set the limits and opportunities for the emergence of moral structures, nevertheless nature and culture are themselves not eternally unchanging. For the naturalist, this is a chancy world.

Morality grows only in a setting, and the naturalist's complaint is that theists too easily forget that the real context for morality is not simply patterns that are pre-cut and delivered. People are born into and nourished by both nature and culture, and they are also an influential part of these two realms. It is in these realms that the moral battles are to be won or lost. Looking for supernatural guidance, as some theists do, is, as far as naturalists are concerned, a way of avoiding the responsibility for cultivating the hard-won moral garden and improving the social climate and context.

WITHOUT VISION THE PEOPLE PERISH

Some naturalists grant the possible truth of the hypothesis that without *belief* in God the moral vision of universal love and peace might never have come about in early mankind. (This hypothesis is still in need of a way for it to be broken down and tested.) The naturalist's point, however, is that now that the vision has come into human consciousness, we no longer need the God-myth that spawned it—if, indeed, it did spawn it. Sir Isaac Newton's theory was inspired and informed by the previous theories of Ptolemy, Copernicus, and Galileo. But that did not oblige Newton to hold on to these earlier theories. Rather, he gratefully accepted them, used them, and then transcended them. Similarly, naturalism need only be grateful for whatever moral vision came through theism. It need not turn theistic myths into either idols, infallible revelation, or metaphysical doctrine. Indeed, naturalism itself must stand ready to be revised, not arbitrarily, but in a manner that is informed by an understanding of the natural and cultural conditions that shape existence and the quality of human life.

The naturalist regards as misleading the saying that if there is no God, then everything is possible. To the contrary, people have to test to see what is or is not possible within the confines and resources of nature. The naturalist claims that because nature is not simply something human beings entirely invent, they therefore must realize that certain kinds of actions bring certain kinds of consequences. Nature is not a genie standing ready to fulfill whatever its master commands. Rather 'nature' is only a word referring to the vast and complex energy system of which humans are a part and out of which they develop culture and lifestyles. To disregard the structures of nature is to play the fool. People must learn from nature certain patterns in order to find the limitations and resources it provides.

CHANGE AND STABILITY

The theist contends that the naturalist and humanist cannot be sure that his moral rules and guidelines will always hold true. The humanist agrees with this point and then notes how often theists, having thought that they themselves possessed some infallible guideline, were nevertheless forced later to qualify and revise their claims. In Romans 13, Paul speaks of capital punishment as divinely ordained. But unfortunately the apostle offers no insight regarding the *conditions* under which capital punishment is to be justified. His pronouncement informs Christians neither about the circumstances nor about the level of responsibility of the society for training people to live without violence.

It is even more interesting to see how very often Christians have qualified the commandment against killing. Exemptions are so easy to find. In contrast, most Christians seem to have given little thought to the possibility of qualifying the commandment against adultery. In fact, some Christians believe that adultery is grounds for murder, but not vice versa.[18] The Bible, however, praises two women, Rahab and Esther, for practicing deceit in what was regarded to be a good cause. Many nontheistic humanists hold that Christians have grown too permissive in the way they frequently exempt *collective* killing from the moral injunction against killing. These humanists argue that the moral condemnation of killing other human beings did not start with Moses and must not be easily justified even in causes that purport to be in the tradition of Moses or Jesus.

BEYOND THEISM

Humanists believe that the moral vision is so important to the survival and enrichment of human life that it must not be tied up with theism. The possibility of human improvement in happiness and peace admittedly depends greatly on moral vision to inspire and motivate people to new heights; but human advance can do quite well without theism. Morality is difficult enough without theological interference. There is no guarantee that human moral life will advance, and humanists are afraid that whatever worth classical theism may have had in the past, it is now becoming a drain on human moral life and energy.

The Christian moralist Paul Ramsey supported the Southeast Asian war because of what he took to be a practical Christian commitment. He saw some moral justification for the killing in Viet Nam. He believes, however, that abortion is an unjustified killing of human persons. This is his view despite the fact that the Bible nowhere indicates that a fetus has the status of a human person. Some Christians claim that Ramsey does not represent "true Christianity" on such moral issues as war and abortion. This, however, merely calls attention to the great difficulty in determining in concrete moral situations precisely what the Christian answer is.

Humanists also often differ greatly on specific moral questions. This is why they have no basis for speaking of some one authoritative court of final moral appeal. Theists would seem to be in the same boat with their fellow humanists on this score, although they have been slow to acknowledge this sobering conclusion.

NOTES

1. See Sanford H. Cobb, *The Rise of Religious Liberty in America* (New York: Macmillan, 1902), p. 507.
2. See Dorothy Dohen, "The New Quest of American Catholicism," in *The Religion of the Republic*, ed. Elwyn Smith (Philadelphia: Fortress Press, 1971), p. 80. Perhaps for some of these students the phrase "the Trinity" referred not to a view of God as three Persons in One, but to Trinity High School or something similar.
3. In the following few paragraphs I draw some suggestions from a paper by a Christian theist, George Mavrodes, presented at the annual meeting of the American Philosophical Association, Western Division, May 5, 1972. Professor Mavrodes was kind enough to send me a preliminary draft of this paper, entitled "Religion and the Queerness of Morality."
4. Ayn Rand, *The Virtue of Selfishness: A New Concept of Egoism* (New York: New American Library, 1964).
5. One of the nontheistic criticisms of Rand's philosophy of morality is found in William F. O'Neill, *With Charity toward None: An Analysis of Ayn Rand's Philosophy* (Totowa, N.J.: Littlefield, Adams & Co., 1972).
6. See Colin M. Turnbull, *The Mountain People* (New York: Simon & Schuster, 1972), chaps. 10, 11.
7. C. S. Lewis, *The Problem of Pain* (New York: Macmillan, 1962), p. 68.
8. See Robert G. Olson, *The Morality of Self-Interest* (New York: Harcourt, Brace & World, 1965), pp. 33–42, 127–129.
9. See Turnbull, *Mountain People*.
10. See O'Neill, *With Charity toward None*, p. 203.
11. Ayn Rand, "An Answer to Readers about a Woman President," *Objectivist* 7, no. 12 (December 1968): 1.

12. Ibid.
13. Thomas E. Davitt, *Ethics in the Situation* (New York: Appleton-Century-Crofts, 1970), p. 17.
14. John 16:2. (Charles B. Williams' translation [Chicago: Moody Press, 1952].)
15. By John Donnelly, appearing in *Religious Studies* 9, no. 2 (June 1973): 189–199.
16. See Søren Kierkegaard, *Fear and Trembling*, trans. Walter Lowrie (Garden City, N.Y.: Doubelday, 1954).
17. John Dewey, *A Common Faith* (New Haven: Yale University Press, 1934), p. 87.
18. See J. E. Barnhart and Mary Ann Barnhart, "Marital Faithfulness and Unfaithfulness," *Journal of Social Philosophy* 32 (April 1973): 10–15. This article is forthcoming in *The Ethical Dimensions of Contemporary Human Problems*, ed. Lawrence Habermehl (Woodland Hills, Calif.: Dickenson Publishing Co., 1975).

CHAPTER XI

Miracles, Supernatural Healing, and Prayer

WHAT IS A MIRACLE?

A Problem of Meaning. In every city in the United States there are individuals who have been living months, and sometimes years, on "borrowed time." If the predictions of their physicians had come true, these people would now be dead. It is not uncommon for someone to use the term 'miracle' to characterize this extended period of life for these people.

One of the problems with the term 'miracle' has to do with what it means. For example, when someone lives beyond his physician's predictions, is it always a miracle? How can we be certain that the physician had all the relevant facts? Physicians have sometimes been in error when predicting *cures* that fail to come about. So, perhaps they can be in error when predicting specific deaths. A physician in the South recently examined a man very carefully and then pronounced him to be in excellent health. Before the patient could drive away from the physician's office he fell over and died of a heart attack. Was that a miracle?

Miracles Are Extraordinary Phenomena. Many believers hold that the major purpose of miracles is to do good, although miracles may have bad consequences for wicked people. This raises the question as to whether Satan or other wicked individuals can perform miracles. When Moses was having a confrontation with Pharaoh, he was allegedly told by God to throw a stick to the floor so that it could become a snake. This Moses did, whereupon Pharaoh had his magicians and sorcerers to do likewise. The writer of the book of Exodus describes Moses' deed as a miracle and leaves the implication that Pharaoh's men performed a miracle also.[1]

If an alleged miracle becomes too common, it runs the risk

of no longer being regarded as a miracle. If you and I could regularly pick up a pencil, throw it to the ground, and have it become a snake, it would soon become regarded as a rather normal and natural phenomenon, especially if just about anyone could perform this feat. So, it would appear that in order for something to be a miracle, it must be extraordinary and rare. Of course, sometimes people say that everything in the world is a miracle. What this often means is that the "creation" of the world with everything in it is not just a run-of-the-mill, ordinary, everyday event. Rather, it is regarded by the theist to be one of the greatest miracles of all time.

A theist might allow himself to believe that creating a universe is nothing out of the ordinary for God. For all the theist knows, God may be creating universes in the way that you and I regularly spin off daydreams one after another. So, a miracle may be quite regular and ordinary for God but extraordinary for finite human beings.

Miracles and the Laws of Nature.   One of the most persistent debates among theists who believe in miracles has to do with whether miracles are natural or supernatural. If God made the world, then in a sense the "natural world" is itself a supernatural activity. But once nature's regularities and laws were established by God, then presumably they combined to help make up the natural world. It is natural for a piece of iron to rust under certain conditions. You can predict that it will do so. Formulated laws of nature are attempts to focus on regularities within the universe.

You can count on such regularities. For example, if you nail a man to a cross, run a spear into his side, leave him hanging for hours in the hot sun, then usually you can count on his being dead before long. And you can also count on his remaining dead. Both the Christian as well as the non-Christian who believes there was a real Jesus think it was according to natural law that Jesus died. There was no miracle involved in the death of Jesus. Anyone else on the cross would have done just as he did. To be sure, many Christians think that God intervened with some miracles in order to work events so that Jesus would eventually be crucified.

Does a Miracle Violate the Laws of Nature?   Assume for the moment that this same Jesus rose bodily from death within two or three days after his crucifixion. Now, that was indeed an extraordinary event! Many Christians regard it not only as a real happening, but as the supreme miracle in human history.

But these Christians do not fully agree with one another on the question of whether this or any other miracle is to be regarded as an *intrusion* upon nature. The issue is this: Does a miracle *violate* the regularities of nature? Is it a disruption of some of the laws of nature? Some Christians answer yes; others answer no.

Perhaps help in understanding this issue can be found in the game of chess. Imagine that your opponent is losing the game. Suddenly he places on the board a new piece that makes his position in the game strong and eventually victorious. You continue to play with him through the remainder of the game, but you also eventually lose to him. Now, did he violate the rules of the game? Yes and no. He had played by the rules up to the point when he introduced a new chess piece onto the board. And even after doing that, he continued to play according to the rules.

However, it is clear that he did violate the rules once. But only once was enough to change the entire course of the game.

Some Christians contend that through a variety of miracles God may now and then violate the laws and regularities of nature without upsetting the entire system of nature. In other words, the laws of nature run according to God's direct decree (except where the evil influence of sin corrupts nature). But the creator is not prevented from occasionally overriding nature's regular runs, so to speak, in order to bring about some very good results.

Among those Christians who believe that God on occasion violates the laws of nature are two views. One view says that miracles within human history have been largely *restricted to biblical times*. This means that all the reports of miracles in the Middle Ages or in modern times around the world are to be regarded as not miracles at all. Those who accept this view think of the miracles of biblical times as special divine interventions employed, as it were, to lift the biblical revelation off the ground. In order to obtain Israel's attention and devotion, God resorted to miracles. It was important to do this, inasmuch as Israel has to serve as a very special people of God selected to give mankind the revelation recorded in the Old Testament.

Christians add that the miracles by Jesus and some of his disciples were instrumental both in initiating the special revelation (as recorded in the New Testament) and in getting the Christian church formed and motivated. This means that God ceased producing miracles some time during the early years of the Christian church. According to Christians who hold to this view, God had no need to produce miracles after New Testament times.

When the Extraordinary Becomes Ordinary.   But not all Christians agree that the day of miracles is over. Some hold to the view that God today still works numerous miracles, especially for Christians having both the need for a miracle and the faith by which one comes about. Indeed, miracles seem to be regarded as almost regular events in the lives of some of these Christians. Or, to say it differently, these people seem to *take* a number of the regular events of their lives to be miracles.

Such people appear to be claiming also that miracles can happen to anyone who meets the requirements or fulfills the proper conditions. But this claim runs the risk of undercutting the special requirements of a miracle: namely, its *extraordinary* quality. There are a number of extraordinary and difficult deeds that we cannot perform without first fulfilling certain requirements. But when we eventually do come to execute some of these deeds, we do not conclude that we have begun executing miracles. It is simply that what was once extraordinary is now normal and familiar to us.

Now, is it possible that what some religious believers regard as miracles in their daily lives are really not supernatural phenomena at all? You can drive a car without believing it to be extraordinary—certainly nothing supernatural. In driving at 50 miles per hour you are not violating the laws of nature. In fact, by understanding some of nature's regularities you are often better able to do things that previously might have been considered to be quite extraordinary if not supernatural.

Suppose you were living in the time when there were no dentures. As a boy I never heard the word "dentures." Adults were fitted with "false teeth" or "artificial teeth" after losing their "natural teeth." Back in 1597 someone made reference to "supernatural teeth."[2] (Presumably they were unnaturally, or extraordinarily, large.) This is not as far-fetched as it may sound. Suppose that before dentures were invented a man had been known for years to be without any teeth. Then one day he appeared with a new set. Extraordinary! Miraculous! Everyone knows that once an adult's teeth are lost, no new ones grow back to replace them. The man sporting his new dentures might wish to claim supernatural powers, or at least claim to have contact with a supernatural power. If asked how it happened that he received new teeth, he might wish to respond, "It's a great mystery."

There are things happening to people today that we are unable to explain with our present level of knowledge. So, are these happenings supernatural? Or are they natural phenomena for which we cannot at present account? Is "mystery" simply a sacred word for our temporary ignorance?

Do Miracles Supersede Nature without Violating It? Some writers on the topic of miracles advance the thesis that a miracle neither violates the laws of nature nor is a mere coincidental occurrence. Rather, it brings into play new factors that involve special divine causes. Take, for example, something in nature that is *not* considered to be a miracle: namely, the boiling of water. Imagine yourself attending the Mexico Olympic Games and deciding to boil some water. You discover that the water boils before reaching 100° C.[3]

What has happened? Has an ancient Aztec God put a curse on your endeavors to cook? Many people used to think in this way. Today we say that the water boils before reaching 100° C. because Mexico City is located high above sea level. According to the "law" (or regularity) of nature pertaining to the boiling of water, water will boil at 100° C. only at sea level. At higher levels the boiling point will be lower.

The point to be made is this: the fact that water boils at a temperature in Mexico City or Denver slightly different from the temperature it boils at in New Orleans is not a basis for concluding that a law of nature has been violated. Does it, however, mean that the law has been *superseded*? It depends. Suppose the law states that water will boil at 100° C.—period. Well, this law is inadequate. It will have to be qualified or refined in order to take into account varying altitudes. It is not important to determine whether this new law is to be regarded as having *superseded* the old law or as having *revised* it. Something of the old law remains; in this sense it is the same law. But new qualifications must be added; in this sense a new law is set forth. Note that the old law (or the old *version* of the law) serves as a guide to the formulation of the new or revised law. Furthermore, the revision is not made arbitrarily, but is made according to critical observations.

Some writers appear to believe that miracles are not so much violations of laws of nature as refinements of nature. That is, the report of a miracle is like the report of certain phenomena covered by a natural law, except that the phenomena in question do not behave exactly as predicted. Why? Because certain *new conditions or factors* have come about.[4]

Therefore, according to this thesis, the resurrection of Jesus came about because Jesus met certain new conditions that resulted in God's raising him from the dead. Jesus healed people because certain special conditions were met. This view suggests that anyone today could work miracles if he met the proper conditions, just as anyone could boil water in Mexico City if he did what is required.

MIRACLES WITHIN A NATURALISTIC SETTING

Augustine's Definition and Its Problems.   According to the great Christian theologian Augustine, miracles do not occur contrary to nature. This seems to be an odd thing for a Christian to say. Indeed, many Christians have insisted that miracles definitely are contrary to nature. They are not natural phenomena; they are *super*natural.

However, Augustine solves the problem in his own mind by drawing a distinction between nature as we know it and nature as God knows it. A miracle, says Augustine, is contrary to our present understanding of nature. But if we could understand nature from God's perspective, we would see that there is no conflict between miracles and nature as it truly is.[5]

The naturalist might respond to Augustine by beginning with a point on which the two could agree. He would agree that our present way of speaking of nature is very incomplete and that a more rational way of speaking may eventually be possible.

On one very significant point, however, they differ greatly. Augustine thinks that there is a Perfect Knower—namely, God—who already knows all there is to know about nature. God alone can see how miracles and non-miraculous occurrences fit together in perfect harmony. Unfortunately, Augustine is convinced that this perfect understanding is locked up in the mind of God.[6]

Naturalists, however, do not believe that there is this perfect Knower and doubt that there will ever be a mind capable of knowing all there is about nature in every respect. According to naturalism, the Perfect Knower exists only in the imagination of Augustine and other classical theists. Naturalists do not believe that the workings of the phenomena of nature depend on their being known by a Perfect Knower. Hence, nature in all its multiplicity is there to be understood by whatever minds are capable of understanding it to some degree. The hope of naturalism is that many years from now there will be human beings around to have a more profound understanding of the workings of nature than we now have. But there is no absolute guarantee that this will come about.

The point is that the human species may perhaps grow in its knowledge and understanding of the structures and processes of nature. For example, what today appear to some Christians to be miraculous healings may in coming years be explained more thoroughly as phenomena existing in accord with certain regularities of nature. In times past, faith healers have insisted that miraculous cures usually require faith on the part of those persons with disabilities and diseases. Today we understand more fully that faith in the therapist's good will and effectiveness is usually required for the healing of what is designated as a mental disturbance or a profound emotional problem.

Faith As a Natural Phenomenon.   Each school of religion and therapy has tended to claim that faith in its doctrines, rather than in the doctrines of other schools, is essential to miraculous healing or the overcoming of the disturbance in question. But studies seem to indicate that in many cases the psychosocial factor of faith is itself more important than the particular doctrines believed in. This conclusion would seem to fit with the fact that around the globe people of very divergent views of reality are healed in ways that we do not fully understand (or at least are only beginning to understand). Hindus and pagans are healed as well as Christians. Faith itself seems to be a natural psychosocial phenomenon that is the exclusive property of no religious, political, or therapeutic group. It is possible that this phenomenon of faith can be more systematically studied.

According to one psychiatrist who has spent years in research on the nature of healing, there are three distinguishing factors involved in successful therapy. They may be found in the therapeutic work of both the shaman and the psychiatrist. They are: (1) the patient's faith or belief in the efficacy of the method used by his shaman or therapist; (2) the therapist's belief in the efficacy of the method; and (3) the acceptance of the method by the society of both the patient and the therapist.[7]

HEALING

The Eighteenth-Century Exorcist.   The most celebrated exorcist of the eighteenth century was Johann Joseph Gassner. The fame of this modest Catholic priest as a healer reached into the homes of peasants and noblemen alike. Gassner's first patients were two nuns whose convulsive fits earned them a dismissal from their community. Believing that their fits were the activities of evil spirits within the two women, the priest commanded the spirits to activate themselves upon his command, upon which witnesses saw the women fall into convulsions. Then after further special verbal and bodily actions on the part of the priest, the nuns became quite normal in their behavior. Abbé Bourgeoise asked one of them to tell whether the ordeal was painful to her, and she replied that her memory of the incident was vague. A third patient was then treated; she was a woman afflicted with melancholia. Gassner told her what to do in case she was overcome again by her malady.[8]

In a booklet, Gassner explained the principles of his method of healing. He considered himself to be something of a specialist in illnesses produced either by the Devil (or his assistants) or by sorcery. But those illnesses that he took to have natural causes he referred to physicians; he did not pretend to be able to deal with these.

This raises the question as to how he distinguished a disease brought on by natural causes from a disease brought on by demonic agents or sorcerers. The first thing that the priest did was to require the patient to profess faith in the name of Jesus. Then he sought to establish communication with the evil spirit residing inside the patient. He simply spoke to the demon and entreated him to manifest symptoms of the disease in the patient's body. If these symptoms were then produced, Gassner took for granted that the demon was communicating with him. Jesus is supposed to have said that the devil is the "father of lies," but Gassner simply assumed that the demons were telling him the truth by producing for him their characteristic symptoms in the body of the patient and thus exposing themselves as truly residing in the patient's body. If no symptoms were forthcoming, Gassner took this as evidence that no demon was residing in the patient and sent him to a physician.[9]

There can be little doubt that this priest effected startling and significant changes in the behavior and outlook of many of his patients. To deny this would be to hide from evidence. This is not to say that the priest's own *explanation* of either the causes or the cures of the maladies was warranted. Many good performers—whether in music or other arts—are unable to give a credible explanation of how they perform so skillfully.

In fact, a physician at about the same time as Gassner was able to bring about some equally sensational changes in the behavior of some people, but he did not hold to the Jesus theory of cures or the Devil theory of afflictions. Rather, this physician—Mesmer—preferred the theory of "animal magnetism," which he claimed was his own discovery.

Animal Magnetism. In 1775 Franz Anton Mesmer was invited before a governmental commission of inquiry in Munich to give a demonstration of his reported ability to perform marvelous cures. The Secretary of the Academy in Munich was suffering from convulsions, and Mesmer proved that he could control the Secretary's convulsions at will. Unlike Gassner, however, Mesmer made no attempt to connect his practice with religion or God.[10]

In 1776, Mesmer had earned a medical degree in Vienna, having completed a dissertation on the relationship between plants and human diseases. After a few years of practice as a physician, he came to experiment with magnets in the treatment of diseases. Eventually he became thoroughly convinced that everyone had a certain magnetic field in and about his body. Diseases, he felt, come when the magnetic field loses a certain measure of harmony or balance. This idea of health as harmony and balance is, of course, an ancient view going back at least as far as Greek medicine and the Pythagoreans. Mesmer's innovation, therefore, lay in extending this notion of balance into the magnetic field that he believed to encircle each organism.

Mesmer believed that people like Gassner and himself possessed an extraordinary degree of magnetism. This may be compared to the notion of "mana" of which some anthropologists write when they describe beliefs of various cultures.

Mana is believed by some societies to be an impersonal force that resides in larger-than-average amounts in some special persons and even some things. Those possessing this mana are regarded as forceful and influential. Or, to say it otherwise, those individuals who demonstrate unusual influence and control over certain aspects of their environment are regarded as possessing mana.[11]

Mesmer thought of the magnetic field as a physical fluid pervading the universe. This should not be ridiculed, for even in the late nineteenth century, physicists, asserting that light waves must have some medium through which to travel, postulated the existence of "ether" as this universal medium.

There is no doubt that Mesmer changed the lives of many people. Many of the best minds of his time acknowledged that he had actually eliminated a great variety of disturbing symptoms in people. His fame was exceeded only by the monetary fortune that he received for his services. Even for a physician, his earnings were excessive, but Mesmer was convinced that he not only was one of the world's greatest physicians, but also was the Copernicus of the science of healing. Learned physicians who rejected his *theory* sometimes explained his *cures* as the result of "imagination." This vague hypothesis should have been pursued with greater boldness and rigor, but it was not.

Like any physician, Mesmer had his tragic failures. Perhaps the most disappointing was his claim to have restored sight to an eighteen-year-old girl who had been blind since the age of three. She and Mesmer had magnetic sessions together. He came to believe that she could see, and she also professed to being able to see. Unfortunately, this newly restored sight did not last long, and complaints were raised over the fact that the young woman seemed to be able to see only when Mesmer was present with her.[12] Modern psychiatrists, drawing upon their own experiences with patients, would explain the allegedly restored sight as suggestion, transference, and counter-transference.[13]

Science and Animal Magnetism.   Mesmer was accused of desiring to keep his secret to himself and of resenting having his skill and theory tested. This accusation is only partially true. Actually, he welcomed the opportunity to demonstrate his skill. Every success he had in changing people's symptoms of illness he took to be support for his case. But he was not willing to concede that anything could conceivably count as evidence *against* his view.

This attitude is doubtless characteristic in varying degrees of most human beings. That is why science as a critical process is usually not embodied in one person only. The imaginative creator of a theory may not be able to criticize his own speculations. Other people of his scientific community pressure him to keep accurate records. They also offer their own criticisms, and this sometimes advances the growth of scientific knowledge. It is essential that science cultivate doubt as a part of its method. Religions, on the other hand, have often insisted on belief and denounced doubt.

Mesmer was a scientist in setting forth a bold and imaginative theory. He was like a shaman, however, in covering up his failures and refusing to entertain the thought that perhaps his theory might be superseded by a better theory not yet conceived.

Science and Religion.   What is important in comparing Mesmer with Gassner is Mesmer's attempt to produce an explanatory theory without reference to God, Christ, demons, and other supernatural beings. This does not imply, however, that Mesmer, the physician, was less dogmatic than Gassner, the priest. Rather, Mesmer's theory simply reflected the rising secular outlook. It is a mistake to think of religion as dogmatic, and science as open-minded. Such a contrast is too simple. It seems more likely that religion emphasizes belief, whereas science emphasizes questioning and suspension of judgment. Yet even this comparison is misleading. It is more accurate to say that science is interested primarily in knowledge as an end in itself, whereas religion has "salvation" (in numerous forms) as its primary concern. Knowledge in religion is *instrumental* to receiving salvation. If the believer is convinced that he has salvation, then his concern for growth in religious knowledge may not be very intense. Indeed, many religions take for granted that the human problem is not so much one of knowledge as one of finding salvation or one of living out the implications of one's salvation.

However, because human beings are sensitive to many cues and contingencies, their motives are usually multiple and intertwined. The same individual may be passionately concerned both to enjoy salvation and to grow in knowledge and understanding. In some cases, the passion for knowledge will lead him into areas where his religious convictions are forced to undergo critical inquiry and severe testing. But because his love for knowledge is nothing short of a profound commitment, his dearest religious convictions are not given diplomatic immunity from periodic scrutiny and critical evaluation.

In the process of living out the implications of their commitment to the ideal of truth, many religious believers have been forced to revise their understanding of what salvation is, sometimes to the point where the revision is a drastic replacement of one version for another. While the new way of looking at salvation may have grown out of the old way, the similarities between them may now be slight.

But in some cases much of the old continues into the new, despite denials that this is the case. A good example of this is Karl Marx's new view of the salvation of the human species through new methods. Some ingredients of the old way—e.g., history as teleological—seem nevertheless to survive in his new way and to control it to a great extent.

Contemporary Speculations.   Very much like Mesmer, a number of laymen today use the words "vibrations" and "vibes" to express the notion of quasi-physical magnetic waves flowing back and forth between individuals. Doubtless this way of speaking is to some extent a shorthand way of referring to certain patterns of "body language" (which is only beginning to be studied systematically and contextually).[14] Also there are various verbal expressions, tones, inflections, patterns, etc., that laymen sometimes corral under the vague heading of "vibrations."

An avenue of fruitful research lies in the possibility that every living thing possesses a radiant energy field (or fields) that the normal eye cannot detect. This need be taken as neither an ultimate mystery nor a supernatural phenomenon. We do not regard microbes to be supernatural agents simply because we need instruments in order to detect them. One instrument currently used in detecting the outflow of energy from living things is Kirlian photography, also known as electrophotography, radiation-field photography, and corona photography.[15] This corona or outflow of energy may eventually be given a more definite title as systematic research continues.

Summarizing the current status of Kirlian photography,

Steve Aaronson quotes Dr. Michael Schachter of Rockland County Community Mental Health Center in New York State:

"There are claims that the phenomena which we're dealing with go 'beyond science.' I think it's obvious at this point that the things we're observing are within science; they are observable. The picture is a physical, measurable phenomenon. What's giving rise to the picture is still in question, but it's something that affects the physical world in a physical way."[16]

From Occultism to Science.   It may very well be that some individuals possess certain abilities for bringing about quick cures in other people. It is not the business of science to say that this could not be the case. If it is in fact the case, then the task of science is to learn, if it can, what the conditions and variables are by which remarkable healings do come about.[17]

The systematic and open-minded study of the relationship between human health and the environment of words, body cues, social cues, and other daily inputs is still on the runway, so to speak. The sciences of psychology, sociology, physiology, as well as new scientific fields that are not yet formulated, will hopefully move us from occult utterances to scientific understanding. A strong warning needs to be sounded, however, against those who in the name of science would set up a new occultism. It is imperative to see that science cannot be science unless all of its theories and hypotheses are regarded as temporary human responses to the world. The occult mind may insist that nothing could ever conceivably falsify its convictions. But the scientific mind not only defends its hypotheses but also seeks to expose them to the light of critical inquiry. In this way, the advance toward more powerful and profound theories becomes more likely.

Occult minds insist that all sorts of "spirits" and "forces" pervade numerous dimensions and planes of the environment. Unfortunately, occult claims are notorious for their doubletalk, which serves as a device for exempting them from the court of critical inquiry. Occultists make all sorts of statements and pronouncements about supernatural phenomena, but when pressed to spell out what they mean by their statements, they often reply that statements cannot be made about such matters.

Doubtless, some occultists have become sensitive and responsive to aspects of the world to which many people are insensitive. But not everyone who makes pronouncements about the "other dimension" can be regarded as a significant witness. Furthermore, even those persons who are especially sensitive to "other dimensions" may be very poor interpreters and describers of what they are in contact with.[18] Given our present state of knowledge, we would do well to keep in mind the metaphorical and mythical quality of such words as "energy," "agents," "vibrations," "spirits," and the like. Indeed, it is not useful to try to nail down the "essential nature" or "inherent property" of something. It is more useful to discover the "relational properties," that is, the consequences and reactions of phenomena on one another, and the patterns of these interactions. It is of no practical or theoretical worth to attempt to establish the "true nature of man." It is more important to discover the interrelationships among the relevant phenomena that come under the heading of "human personality."[19]

Following through with One's Claims.   If, say, a Southern Baptist insists that there is a God who works miracles today, then he may find the following to be a problem. In 1858 a girl named Bernadette Soubirous had visions that she took to be of the Virgin Mary. This was near Lourdes, a town in southern France, where throngs of people now come for healing each year. Near the place where young Bernadette's vision occurred flows a spring that is regarded as having something directly to do with the remarkable healings. Various Catholics and non-Catholics have been convinced that some instantaneous healings have come about at Lourdes.

Having been checked out, these healings give every reasonable indication of being authentic and instantaneous. A three-year-old girl with terminal cancer whose bones had been eaten away by the disease was immersed in the waters at Lourdes. Her condition continued to deteriorate for the next two days, but on the third day, not only was the disease arrested, but the bones in her skull grew back. Her doctor, a Protestant, said that "miracle" would not be too strong a word to use.[20]

Since 1858 there have been sixty-two authenticated cases of instantaneous cures at Lourdes. To be sure, this is only a very tiny percentage of the great numbers of people who have gone there and have had to return home without being cured. But this fact should not disqualify these sixty-two cases from being carefully considered.

The reason that the cures at Lourdes might pose a problem

for a Southern Baptist who believes in miracles is that it was the Virgin Mary who appeared to the young girl at Lourdes. If the Baptist rejects the *Catholic* interpretation of the cures at Lourdes, then will he follow through by converting to a *naturalistic* interpretation? If he opts for a third interpretation, it will have to be a supernaturalistic interpretation stripped of Roman Catholic overtones.

This third option is not an easy one to accept for a Southern Baptist or any Protestant believing in miracles today. It looks as if the Protestant view will have to be something like the following: God works miracles of healing, but very often people who witness the healings *imagine* that certain saints or the mother of Jesus are somehow instrumental in bringing about these cures. This comes, says the Protestant, only from their imaginations and not from special illumination from God.

Of course, Catholics must face the fact that Protestants sometimes witness what they regard as miracles. These Protestants do not see visions of Mary or saints, and in fact they often regard such visions to be at best the product of false teachings and doctrines, if not inspired by Satan. Hindus also profess now and then to witness miraculous cures, but they do not regard them to be particularly Christian in origin.

A naturalist will, of course, seek to discover *common variables* in all of these remarkable cures—whether among Protestants, Catholics, Hindus, Christian Scientists, humanists, Buddhists, or whatever. The naturalist may point out that if one group asserts that remarkable cures are only natural phenomena unless done in connection with the "true faith," then that group must face the possibility that even its own supernatural miracles are really not supernatural after all. The naturalist asks the supernaturalists of each group to follow through consistently with their own logic. If Oral Roberts doubts that it was a divine miracle that once brought seagulls into Utah to devour the insects that were destroying the Mormons' crops, then Roberts must himself face those who, while acknowledging his remarkable healings now and then, nevertheless doubt that Roberts' cures are to be explained according to his hypothesis of supernaturalism. If Roberts can explain in a non-supernaturalistic way the arrival of the seagulls in Utah, then why cannot Roberts' cures and redemptive works be explained in a non-supernaturalistic way?

PRAYER

The Promise of Jesus to Answer Prayer.   Jesus is reported to have told his disciples that some people will do works greater than even he himself had done. However, he mentions two conditions that must be met. First, these people must believe in him. Second, Jesus must himself return to the Heavenly Father.[21] Before departing, Jesus gave his disciples the following promise:

Whatever you ask in my name, I will do it, that the Father may be glorified in the Son; if you ask anything in my name, I will do it.[22]

Specifying the Conditions.   Unfortunately, there is a great dispute even among Christians as to exactly what is meant by asking in the name of Jesus. Presumably this is not a magical formula to be attached to the end of a prayer. Some Christians regard the phrase "in the name of Jesus" to be synonymous with the phrase "according to the will of God." If this is acceptable, then Jesus is to be understood as saying that he will positively answer any request that is offered in accord with the will of God.

There is, unfortunately, a certain endless circularity in this sort of condition. If a Christian prays for something—for example, the restored health of his young daughter—what is he to say if the prayer is not positively answered? If his minister tells him that Jesus failed to answer because the prayer was not in accord with the will of God, the man may wish to ask how the minister knows this to be true.

To say that a prayer was not answered because it was not in accord with the will of God is the perfect loophole. If God fails to answer, then someone can always claim that the request was not in accord with the will of God. It was not really "in the name of Jesus." And how do we know that it was not? Well, no positive answer was given! This may be called Christianity's "Catch 22." It is a bit like talking with a bureaucrat who does not quite grasp what it means to have precise specifications. Or it may be compared to those politicians who promise in vague terms so that they can never be charged with failing to deliver as promised. Another advantage of the vague promise is that it allows the politician or the religious leader to latch onto any good thing that happens to come about and to claim that this is "really" what he was promising all along.

Try the following experiment: Every day, pray to a pencil sharpener. Do so faithfully. Then look about and you will see some good things happening. Do this every day and say to yourself what Oral Roberts says: "Something good is going to happen to you!" And something good will happen, if not to you, then at least to one of your relatives.

Archbishop William Temple is said to have once remarked, "When I pray, coincidences begin to happen." I have heard people give glowing testimonies of how their lives have changed after beginning Transcendental Meditation. Often things will seem better for you if you begin emphasizing the good things that happen and ignoring some of the bad things. Praying to a pencil sharpener each morning may help remind you to look for the good things throughout the day. Or if this seems too superstitious to you, then perhaps a minute of constructive meditation each morning will be sufficient to help you start your day in a creative frame of mind.

Prayers of Request.   Most theists believe that prayer is not simply a psychological or sociological phenomenon. For them, prayer has some cosmic significance. Those theists who feel uncomfortable about asserting its cosmic significance are prone to play down the view of prayer as "asking and receiving." Such a view seems somewhat unsophisticated to those who have an appreciation of the complexity of human purposes in the world. How can someone ask for something which, if granted, would frustrate the purposes of other people?

The world is so complex that some people feel that they are not quite fair in asking God to put them at the head of the line or to treat them with special consideration. If a businessman prays for his own success in getting a certain desirable contract, he is in effect praying that God will see to it that his competition will not receive the contract. Indeed, prayers of request have an air of lobbying about them. And some believers find it very difficult to play the role of lobbyist before God.

So, it is not surprising that many theists tend to regard the element of *asking* as not central to prayer. Asking must be reserved for rare, critical times of severe illness and the like.

Also, the more general the request is, the more room it leaves for God to work in. Prayer requests that are too specific will presumably have to be restated by God anyhow if he is to act on even half the requests he receives daily. During the

Crusades in the Middle Ages, many prayers were offered by Muslims and Christians requesting the defeat of the other. Perhaps a prayer of thanksgiving would now be appropriate for theists everywhere. It would consist in thanking God for not answering many prayers of a competitive or military nature.

Experimental Prayers.   Now and then a Christian will ask a non-Christian to engage in what is essentially an experimental prayer. Such a prayer is supposed to serve to make the non-Christian more willing to believe, or at least less willing to disbelieve. Looked at from a naturalistic viewpoint, this device is simply a way of initiating certain behaviors that have desired associated behaviors. The Christian hopes that the non-Christian, by his performing the initial behaviors, will then become more susceptible to performing the desired associated behaviors.

Sometimes the Christian will claim that if the non-Christian refuses to participate in experimental prayers, then he is not being open-minded. In reply, the non-Christian might work out an arrangement with the challenging Christian. He might ask the Christian to experiment with certain non-Christian behaviors or practices. For example, a Hindu could ask the Christian to pray to Krishna rather than Christ. Or the naturalist might ask the Christian to experiment open-mindedly with naturalism by repeating twice a day the following meditation:

"Today I will seek to live a life of intellectual honesty. I will not indulge my infantile wishes by professing belief in a God. Rather, I will cultivate intellectual humility, moral responsibility, and joyfulness. With the help of my fellow human beings and with my own abilities and skills, I will not be so arrogant as to demand from the universe a place of cosmic fame. Rather I will endeavor to discover joy, peace, truth, and contentment in my finite situation. I will look for opportunities to grow and develop my own potentials, and also to share with others in their endeavors to make life more enriching, gentle, and interesting."

A very eager naturalist might even keep in his home a few photocopies of articles stating the general naturalistic position. Then, when the Jehovah's Witnesses, Presbyterians, Mormons, and the like come by to deliver their literature, the naturalist might invite them in to sit down and read the naturalistic position while he reads their theistic literature. Doubtless, there are many naturalists who would feel embarrassed to do this, perhaps because they naively assume that somehow naturalism, being the natural view, simply grows without cultivation.

Prayers as Miracles. If thousands of prayers were answered every day, and if these answers were miraculous interventions into nature, then things might very easily become chaotic. The theist, therefore, must believe that God simply will not give answers to certain prayers if they would create too much confusion on earth. Or the theist may wish to postulate certain "spiritual laws" that work somewhat in harmony with the laws of nature as we presently formulate them.[23] A more careful formulation of these laws would specify what the conditions are which must be fulfilled if prayers are to be answered. For example, must the Muslim become a Methodist? Or must the Methodist become a Hindu? Indeed, are there perhaps "spiritual dimensions" to the universe that may be tapped by people who do not believe in God? Indeed, it may turn out that in some cases belief in God (of whatever version) will prove to be an unnecessary burden in addition to the endeavor to live in accord with the "spiritual laws." This is already the position that Theravada Buddhism has been taking for centuries.

Some theists insist that God freely bestows his grace and illumination on whomever he chooses and that it is wrong to specify conditions that God must meet before he can come to human beings in a special way. In response, however, it must be said that the insistence on conditions did not begin with science. For centuries, religions have specified certain conditions that human beings must meet if they are to approach God. To attempt to approach him without meeting these conditions is sometimes regarded as blasphemy or as dangerous.[24] This is simply a way of saying that doing certain things under certain conditions will more likely produce certain consequences. The more these conditions, procedures, and consequences are spelled out systematically, the more they may be classified as a part of scientific experimentation and understanding.

The Common Unconscious. One writer puts forth the hypothesis that there is an unconscious level that human beings share more or less in common. It is not God or a divine reality; rather, it is a kind of reservoir that can be tapped by self-suggestion, telepathy, and other methods. Prayer, on this view, could be thought of as a kind of S.O.S., which a sinking ship sends out in general and which is picked up by whatever ship happens to be in the area.

According to this hypothesis, a communication flow goes on in the world at the unconscious or semiconscious level. If this view is correct, the word 'God' may be simply a picture-thinking way of symbolizing the Common Unconscious. Clearly, this view calls for further investigation, more definite formulation, and more empirical testing.[25]

MIRACULOUS CONVERSION

The Inner Sanctum.   In the early 1840's William Miller and some of his fellow Christians came to believe that Jesus would return to earth in 1843. They prepared themselves for the eventful day. We can only imagine how they felt on December 31, 1843, as the hours ticked by. Shortly thereafter, one of the members of this group of Christians reexamnied Miller's calculations, which he took to be based on the Bible. After this reexamination, Miller became convinced that he himself had made slight miscalculations. Thus, the date of the coming of Jesus was reset for 1844 instead of 1843. But again the great event failed to materialize.

A word needs to be said about specific predictions of this sort. First, they deserve respect because they are not mystified or hidden predictions. Miller made it clear that Jesus would come to earth and that he would come at a definite time. Second, the prophecy was actually testable. When he realized that it had not come true and thus had failed to meet the test, Miller did not resort to verbal trickery or mystification. He simply revised his prophecy, which again failed to be fulfilled. So, Miller retired from prophesying.

Hiram Edson, however, was not content to say that Miller and his followers had been wholly wrong. Drawing from a vision that he claimed to have experienced, Edson said that Miller had correctly predicted the *time* of Christ's coming but had wrongly stated the *place* of Christ's coming. According to Edson, the place was not to be earth at all, but the sanctuary of heaven. The Seventh-Day Adventists took over this explanation and made it a part of the Seventh-Day Adventist doctrine.[26]

The peculiar thing about Edson's prophecy lies in the fact that he lifted it out of the realm of the *observable*. Whereas Miller had placed his prediction on the line, Edson resorted to mystification by making it impossible to check his claim in any way. If someone says that Christ did not go to the heavenly sanctuary at the time that Edson claimed, who is to say that he is wrong? When we start talking about the activities of heaven, anyone can describe them in any way he pleases because there is no way to prove him wrong—or right.

Similarly, classical theists sometimes speak of supernatural conversions taking place "inside" an individual. This is important because what takes place "inside" the soul is supposed to be sealed off from every form of observation. It is like Edson's heaven. All sorts of things can presumably happen there, but no one can observe them in any way. No one can check to see if claims about what goes on "inside" the soul is really going on.

Naturalists and theists who reject supernaturalism are not impressed with talk of *miraculous* conversions taking place in some mysterious temple of the soul. They point out that conversions seem to be brought about by natural and social variables, not by supernatural causes.

Conversions without Supernaturalism.   Orthodox Christians have said on numerous occasions that unless people are converted and transformed *within*—in their hearts—there cannot be moral reform. "It is absolutely impossible," says Billy Graham, "to change society and to reverse the moral trend unless we ourselves are changed from the inside out."[27]

Graham and Orthodox Christian theologians insist that this inside conversion is a supernatural work. They also say that it cannot be received except under certain specified conditions. For example, one must believe that there is a God, that Jesus is the Son of God, that Jesus rose from the grave, etc. (There is some disagreement even among orthodox Christians as to what conditions and beliefs are absolutely necessary for conversion.)

Two points that naturalists, personalists, and panentheists would make in response are as follows: (1) This orthodox Christian conversion is not a miracle; rather, it is the product of natural and social conditions and variables. (2) This particular form of conversion is not a necessary prerequisite for moral and social reform. Let us explore these two points.

Orthodox Christians are forced to place the conversion "inside" in order to keep it mystified. "Inside" the believer all sorts of supernatural forces are said to be at work. Also, Christ and the Holy Spirit are both said to be "residing within" each believer. If we ask *where* this inside is located, we are given a stone for an answer. It is not inside the skull, nor inside the body. In fact, the word "inside" turns out to be a metaphor.

It would be a mistake to shun metaphors, for they often carry a good deal of truth, even if in a confused manner. In this case, however, the metaphor seems to be more a veil to conceal than a light to illumine. Doubtless there are important experiences that are in some sense private to each individual, but this does not seem to be what the orthodox Christians have in mind when speaking of the conversion taking place "inside" the convert.

Are the Conditions of the Conversion Identical with the Conversion Itself?   From a naturalistic viewpoint, the miraculous conversion seems to be identical with the conditions or requirements that are supposed to make the conversion possible. Take, for example, the requirement of repentance. A person must repent in order to be converted. But how does one know when repentance has come about? Orthodox Christians do not look "inside" the soul to see if repentance is going on there (wherever "there" is). Indeed, when examined carefully, it is doubtful that this way of speaking of the "inside" of a soul can remain intelligible.

Orthodox Christians test their converts in a number of ways to see whether repentance has come about. The candidate must in some way communicate something like the following: "I recognize myself to be a sinner in need of God's mercy. I repent of my sins and accept Jesus Christ as my Savior." This may be compared to getting married. The bride and groom repeat their vows and say, "I do." But no one looks "inside" each of them to see whether they are "really" married. Suppose that one of them does not mean what he says, but rather is only pretending to be married. Well, we do not x-ray his soul to determine his sincerity. Rather, we *observe still more of his behavior*. If he giggles during the ceremony, we might wonder whether he is sincere. Or if he leaves his new bride on the day after the marriage ceremony, then we might wonder whether he will come back. If he does not come back, then we might say that while legally married, he is not "really" married.

To be really married is to exhibit certain marital behavior.

Similarly, to repent within an orthodox Christian setting is to engage in certain designated observable behavior. This specified behavior *is* the repentance! It is a part of the conversion. It is not a mysterious miracle, but rather is observable behavior brought about by cues, stimuli, words, etc.

What upsets orthodox Christians is finding someone who, having for years been exhibiting repentance and faith behavior, now takes a wrong turn. Billy Graham, for example, had for years heard his friend Richard Nixon speak the language of repentance and manifest the behavior of an orthodox faith. Indeed, in the book *Great Reading from Decision* both Graham and Nixon speak this language.[28] But the evangelist was shocked when reading some of Nixon's language in the White House tapes. Not only was Nixon not speaking the "language of Zion," he was speaking the kind of language that many orthodox Christians had classified as contradictory to the language of orthodox Christian faith and repentance.

Now, is Nixon "really" an orthodox Christian? Most orthodox Christians would agree that Bertrand Russell was not, for he expressed views that clearly contradicted Christian belief. To be sure, Russell's language was not of Nixon's inelegant sort, but it was definitely in opposition to orthodox Christian language. Nixon, however, is perhaps a borderline case in the eyes of many orthodox Christians. Some of his behavior is sufficiently orthodox, but much is definitely not. Orthodox Christians have disagreed for centuries on where to draw the line between the true believer and the mere professing believer. Some have been willing to say that a person is a true believer if he simply produces the appropriate language and some other behavior to suggest that he "really means" what he says even though he is too weak in the flesh (or wherever) to provide still other appropriate behavior.

The basic point here is that *repentance in the orthodox Christian sense turns out to be not an "internal" miracle after all.* Rather, it consists of behavior—observable and detectable behavior. To be sure, accompanying this behavior are also feelings, which are regarded in some sense as private and personal. But this is not what orthodox Christianity has in mind when speaking of the individual's "inner self," where the supernatural lightning is supposed to strike and the miraculous forces are supposed to be activated. Like Hiram Edson's heavenly sanctuary, this "inner being" is forever removed from any form of detection. It belongs to the land of mystification, wherein dwell hosts of beings and forces forever locked up from investigation.

In opposition to supernaturalism, the naturalist's view is that the orthodox Christian conversion is not something taking place in some supernatural realm. Rather, this conversion *is* a host of *natural and social phenomena* that may be studied; hopefully this study will become increasingly more sensitive and systematic. The conversion is not something in addition to specified conditions and requirements; rather, it is *identical with* them. The impact of this conclusion is that the behavior to be classified as "conversion" is brought about, not supernaturally, but by natural and social causes.

Is Orthodox Christian Conversion Behavior Essential to Moral Reform? The orthodox Christians claim that moral and social reform is not possible until a conversion "from within" comes about. This claim is regarded by naturalists to be very misleading. It diverts attention from the real issue. What orthodox Christians are actually advocating is *their own moral and social reform program.* Contrary to what they assert, the issue is not one of "inner" conversion versus social reform. The orthodox Christian's "inner" conversion is itself a social reform program. To call it a miracle taking place "within the heart" is to draw attention away from what it in fact is. It is an elaborate program for changing an individual's social, verbal, etc. environment in order to change his behavior. This program, furthermore, seeks to influence political and institutional behavior as well as the private behavior of an individual when he is alone. Orthodox Christian efforts to enact legislation to punish prostitution and gambling are political and social programs. The same is true of the efforts to ban what the orthodox regard as pornography. Orthodox Christians will often say that moral reform cannot come except through inward conversion to Jesus Christ, but their actions show that they are eager to legislate moral behavior as they see it.

Practically every group has some interest in legislating certain kinds of moral behavior. Murder, thievery, rape, fraud, and other victimizing behavior is felt by many diverse groups to demand political and social control. Legislation against these forms of victimizing behavior is more widely approved, whereas legislation favoring the devotional reading of Christian Scriptures in public schools is not so widely approved. The point here is that while there are numerous orthodox Christians who assert that moral and social reform comes through miraculous conversion, their actions indicate that they do not take this view very seriously.

Is Conversion Essential to Reform?   It is very important to make a distinction between (1) conversion and (2) supernatural or miraculous conversion. The naturalists and the panentheists are not denying that the former is an important element in a person's life. What they are denying is that the conversion is a miraculous phenomenon coming about supernaturally. Conversion is, rather, a natural and social phenomenon brought about by a great complex of variables. The new convert is given new reading material, new associates, new vocabulary, new responsibilities, new cues and expectations, new rewards and privileges, new goals and means of achieving them, new meetings to attend, new things to do at the meetings, new activities, and numerous other challenges and reinforcements that he previously did not enjoy.

Far from being a miracle, this conversion *is* this program. The more fully and extensively the individual follows the program and extends it into the various dimensions of his life, the more fully is he being converted—by definition. There is nothing going on in some supernatural heavenly sanctuary of the soul. This is not to say that the human repertoire of behavior and experience is not open to novelty, depth, and creativity. To the contrary, the reform program, when it is liberating as well as disciplining, increases depth, creativity, and novelty of experience and behavior. The only denial being made here is that there is an "inner heart" where supernatural powwows are taking place beyond the realm of all possible observation and systematic investigation. Conversion as understood in a nonsupernatural context is indeed essential to social and moral reform because it is a part of that reform. (This leaves open here the question of *which* reforms are more moral and worthy of commitment. For a treatment of this question see Chapter X, entitled "Morality without Supernaturalism.")

NOTES

1. See Exodus 7:8–12.
2. See *Oxford English Dictionary*, s.v. "Supernatural."

3. See Robert Young, "Miracles and Epistemology," *Religious Studies* 8, no. 2 (June 1972): 122.

4. See ibid.

5. See Augustine, *Reply to Faustus the Manichaean*, trans. Richard Stothert, in *The Works of Aurelius Augustine*, 15 vols. (Edinburgh: T. & T. Clark, 1872), vol. 5; bk. 26, par. 3.

6. See ibid.

7. See Jacques Mousseau, "Freud in Perspective: A Conversation with Henri F. Ellenberger," *Psychology Today* 6, no. 10 (March 1973): 60. The above analysis of the three factors is the result of Ellenberger's research. For a profound study of psychic healing and related topics, see Ellenberger's large book, *The Discovery of the Unconscious: The History and Evolution of Dynamic Psychiatry* (New York: Basic Books, 1970).

8. Ellenberger, *Discovery of the Unconscious*, p. 54. This book is heavily documented.

9. Ibid., pp. 53–57.

10. See ibid., pp. 56–57.

11. See Eric Sharpe, *Fifty Key Words: Comparative Religion* (Atlanta: John Knox Press, 1971), pp. 37–38.

12. See Ellenberger, *Discovery of the Unconscious*, p. 60.

13. See ibid., p. 892.

14. See Ray L. Birdwhistell, *Kinesics and Context: Essays on Body Motion Communication* (Philadelphia: University of Pennsylvania Press, 1970). See also various writings of Erving Goffman.

15. See Steve Aaronson, "Picture of an Unknown Aura," *The Sciences* 14, no. 1 (January/February 1974): 15.

16. Ibid., p. 22.

17. For an interesting and popular summing-up of some possible lines of future research in parapsychology, see Peter Gwynne and Charles Panati, "Parapsychology: The Science of the Uncanny," *Newsweek*, 4 March 1974, pp. 52–57.

18. See Robert E. Ornstein, *The Psychology of Consciousness* (San Francisco: W. H. Freeman & Co., 1972), pp. 152 f.

19. See Karl Popper, *Objective Knowledge: An Evolutionary Approach* (New York: Oxford University Press, 1972), p. 195.

20. See Malcolm L. Diamond, "Miracles," *Religious Studies* 9, no. 3 (September 1973): 312; "Miracles at Lourdes," *Newsweek*, 9 August 1971, p. 48.

21. See John 14:12.

22. John 14:13 (RSV).

23. See H. H. Price, *Essays in the Philosophy of Religion* (New York: Oxford University Press, 1971), pp. 46, 54 f.

24. See Ninian Smart, *The Phenomenon of Religion* (New York: Herder & Herder, 1973), pp. 89–93.

25. See ibid., pp. 46–55; Montague Ullman and Stanley Krippner with Alan Vaughan, *Dream Telepathy* (New York: Macmillan, 1973).

26. See Jan Karel Van Baalen, *The Chaos of Cults* (Grand Rapids: Eerdmans, 1938), pp. 164–166.

27. Quoted in Julius R. Mantey, "Repentance and Conversion," in *Basic Christian Doctrines*, ed. Carl F. H. Henry (New York: Holt, Rinehart & Winston, 1962), p. 192; cf. Billy Graham, *The Secret of Happiness* (Garden City, N.Y.: Doubleday, 1955), pp. 2, 29, 64; idem, *The Jesus Generation* (Grand Rapids: Zondervan, 1971), pp. 90, 125–127.

28. Ed. Sherwood Wirt and Marvis Sanders (Minneapolis: World Wide Publications, 1960), pp. 3–42, 357–360.

CHAPTER XII

Myth and Salvation

THE JESUS MYTH

The Mormon Deliverer. Mormonism is one of the fastest-growing religions in America. You might wonder how the conservative Mormons of Utah could today claim to follow the teaching of a man such as Joseph Smith, whom many historians regard as one of the most daring tricksters and deceivers of the nineteenth century. This man claimed to have received from God's angel information and guidance that Mormons today rank with the Old and New Testaments as God's infallibly revealed message to mankind. Furthermore, Smith convinced great numbers of his followers not only that he enjoyed divine approval of his numerous wives, but that God had commanded other Mormon men to practice polygyny.

Skeptics have felt that Smith's imperative to take many wives was more an impulse from his own sensual id than an injunction from the deity. But confident that God moves in wondrous and mysterious ways, Smith and his followers have merely turned a deaf ear to the skeptics. The evidence seems to indicate that Smith was indeed gifted with the skill of deceiving other people. Yet in the households of every devout Mormon the name Joseph Smith evokes deep and profound emotions and inspires young and old alike to carry out the teachings of their faith in sincerity and dedication.

Mormons think of Joseph Smith in the way that Jews think of Moses or Joshua. Smith is their deliverer. He delivered them out of darkness into light. In his own youth, Smith encountered churches racked with schism and diversity. Between 1814 and 1830 the Methodists split four ways. The Baptists splintered into Reformed Baptists, Hard-Shell Baptists, Freewill Baptists, Seventh-Day Baptists, Footwashing Baptists. With its pride in religious liberty, America in its pioneer spirit created new religions the way it created new trails in the wilderness. Just twenty-five miles from Joseph Smith's home was a woman —Jemima Wilkenson—who thought that she was the Christ. As an adolescent, Smith was greatly confused as to which religion was the true religion. Eventually he was delivered from his confusion by what he took to be a special revelation from the Almighty himself.[1]

The Power of Belief.   The heroic efforts of such a patriot as William Tell have long served as a model of virtue for Swiss youths. Today, however, the evidence strongly supports the conclusion that Tell was not a historical personage at all, that he was no more a real person than was Hercules.

To be sure, in times past many people believed that Hercules was an actual person whose marvelous and kind deeds reflected his great divinity. Once he was extensively worshiped by people who would have scoffed at the idea that he was only a mythical character. The stories of his life were considered a part of history until, as time rolled on, what was once seen as genuine history became regarded as simply another instance of human imagination. To tell a devout worshiper of Hercules that the object of his worship was a mythical being would have been like telling a Christian today that Jesus never did exist and that Jesus is the product of various historical developments and of human imagination.

Is Jesus a Mythical Being?   The hypothesis to be considered in this chapter is that Jesus Christ did not exist in the first century, and therefore did not suffer under Pontius Pilate. Nor was he crucified and subsequently raised from the dead. The teachings attributed to him came mostly from Jewish history, and over a period of time the "story" of Jesus, like many legends, was woven together from numerous pagan and Jewish sources. In short, the movement of Christianity came about without a historical Jesus. A believer in the Dionysian religion might have been angered had you told him that his God, Dionysus, was only a mythical being. Similarly, Christians today might become angry upon confronting the suggestion that their founder, far from being a God, was in fact not even a mortal man. Christians easily reject the ancient religion of Osiris, even though many people once regarded Osiris as a real divine person.

The anger of Christians who confront the suggestion of the

mythical nature of Jesus is quite understandable, for under the category of "Jesus" they have arranged many of their deepest hopes, visions, convictions, and moral ideals.

A vital myth has a certain coherence to it in that it has its own verbal and ritual scheme that makes possible a certain communication among those who participate in it. For example, people who watch the soap opera *As the World Turns* can converse at length about the interactions within the play itself. Indeed, they can share emotional reactions, expectations, and moral judgments, and in general they have a certain intense involvement in the story. To be sure, the story of *As the World Turns* is make-believe. Yet it is sometimes typically true in the sense that it rehearses human problems and in ritual drama plays out the problems in detail.

Very often people write to the television station to express an opinion about the story itself. Strange as it may seem, there are a number of people who share in the life of this soap opera to the extent that it becomes for them something real and very significant. It moves them and influences their lives. One of the characters in the story has actually been attacked on the street by viewers who could not distinguish between the reality within the myth and the wider reality beyond the myth.

The Compassionate Buddha.   The Buddha, Siddhartha, probably did exist in India in the sixth century B.C. Unlike Jesus and Hercules, Buddha is definitely not to be regarded as wholly mythological. Yet there are many tales and claims about him that must be classified as without foundation, although they are still taken by many devout Buddhists to be actual accounts of the life of the Compassionate One. Today Buddhism is divided over the question as to whether Siddhartha was and is in fact a supernatural, divine being.

There seems to be a tendency on the part of great numbers of people to idolize someone, to create a divine being, to project a supernatural personality who is far more than mortal life itself. Many theists have argued that this is simply the deep and underlying human longing for God. And they take this desire or longing as evidence for the existence of God. It should be noted, however, that human beings have an ancient and powerful tendency to tell lies. It would be foolish indeed to conclude that this is supporting evidence for the objective reality to which these lies purport to refer. The strong tendency to tell lies under certain conditions may very well be universal among human beings. If it is, it is evidence of a universal weakness on their part. Similarly, the universal tendency toward belief in Gods is regarded by many naturalists to be a universal human weakness, although an understandable weakness.

THE QUEST FOR THE HISTORICAL JESUS

Every View Is a Hypothesis.   Every view about Jesus as a historical personage is a hypothesis. Furthermore, not one of these views accepts as true *every* claim in the New Testament about Jesus. To be sure, so-called orthodox Christians tell themselves and others that they accept the entire New Testament, which, they assert, offers a perfectly consistent picture of Jesus, with no contradictions whatsoever. But this conclusion is regarded by most New Testament scholars as unreliable. Orthodox Christians nevertheless reply that their opponents hold to a "presupposition" that blinds them so that they are unable to agree with the orthodox claims.

Unfortunately, this orthodox reply turns out to be nothing more than the charge that those who do not agree with the orthodox view are those who do not agree with the orthodox view. Whether we use such words as "presuppositions," "conclusions," "assumptions," or "methodology" is of no fundamental importance. The point is that there is considerable and strong disagreement about the details of the life of the alleged carpenter of Nazareth who is said to have made claims to divinity.

Everyone who reads the New Testament must either carve out for himself a picture of Jesus or accept the picture that others have already carved out. Except for those who believe that the Bible is the infallible revelation of God, serious students of the Bible acknowledge openly that some of the New Testament assertions pertaining to Jesus cannot be accepted at face value. It is very clear why the infallibilists or orthodox believers cannot admit that they, too, do not accept at face value some of the details of the life of Jesus that the New Testament sets forth as true. Very clearly, these orthodox Christians see that if *some* of these details can be called into question, then *every* detail is open for debate, including the question of *whether Jesus even existed at all.*

The Real Jesus.   It will be impossible in this book to venture at great length into the debate regarding the historical claims of the New Testament pertaining to Jesus. I will try, however, to show why it might be plausible to accept the thesis that Jesus never really existed. To be sure, some writers tell their readers that this thesis is not even worth considera- tion, which presumably justifies their not even considering it in their books.

What is most interesting, however, is the great diversity among those who claim that there was a real Jesus of Naza- reth. Indeed, for some he was not even from Nazareth but was a Nazarene, which, they say, was mistakenly taken to refer to the city of Nazareth. New Testament scholars differ greatly in forming their pictures of Jesus. To agree that he *existed* is of no significance if they do not agree on a number of the impor- tant *details* or ingredients of his life.

Let me give an example. Some scholars hold that Jesus be- lieved in hell. Others say that he definitely did not. Rather, they say, some of the New Testament writers *attributed to Jesus* some of *their own* personal beliefs about hell. Now, it seems difficult to deny that the Jesus who taught that the masses of people will go to hell because they do not believe in him is very different from the Jesus who rejected the whole idea of hell. To be sure, if a Jesus did exist when writers say he did, he must have heard of the doctrine of hell. So, either he accepted it or rejected it. And the choice here is basically between two very different kinds of persons—Jesus A and Jesus B.

Take another "detail" of Jesus' life. Some Christians hold that he thought that the end of the world was just about to take place in his own lifetime. The trouble with this view is that it leaves Jesus as a fallible person somewhat like the rest of us. But that is not all. If Jesus was in error about this significant question, then it is very possible that he was in error about other matters—including such issues as salvation, God the Father, heaven, and other supernatural phenomena.

Even orthodox Christians seem to be divided on this issue of Jesus' view of the end of the world. Some think that Jesus believed that the world would become increasingly worse until God the Father would send Jesus Christ back to earth to clean up the entire mess. However, other orthodox Christians look upon the death and resurrection of Jesus as the real victory over Satan and sin. Everything thereafter is regarded simply as a matter of waiting until Satan makes a few last struggles before realizing that his defeat has already occurred.

The former group pictures Jesus as believing that some time in the future he will return in the flesh to the earth to "rule with a rod of iron" over the planet for a thousand years. The second group of Christians, however, does not believe that Jesus believed any such thing. The first group thinks that Jesus will return and locate himself in the Middle East—in or about Jerusalem—in order to set up headquarters there. But the second group regards this as pure fiction. Yet each group claims to be talking about the same Jesus. This is, of course, the old question of how many differences we can permit between two assertions about something before concluding that the subject under consideration is actually *two* subjects. A few years ago a Christian author wrote a book entitled *The Real Jesus*. The fact that he claimed that his picture of Jesus was "true to the New Testament accounts" does not mean that his claim was warranted. Rather, the claim suggests that the man was greatly insensitive to much of the research going on in the field of New Testament scholarship.

CHRIST AS A SAVIOR-GOD

Paul the Apostle and the Cosmic Christ. The early Christian documents have all been lost. But among the material of which the New Testament is composed, the letters of the apostle Paul are judged by most scholars to be the earliest. The so-called Gospels—Matthew, Mark, Luke, and John—were written somewhere between forty and a hundred years after the time when Jesus was supposed to have carried out his mission. Even the apostle Paul wrote no earlier than a quarter of a century after the alleged resurrection of Jesus. What is of profound interest is that Paul had almost nothing to say about the details of the earthly life of Jesus. Paul is almost exclusively concerned with a cosmic Christ and his cosmic achievements.

This should not be surprising for someone who is familiar with the religious thinking of Paul's time. Both pagans and Jews were greatly concerned with cosmic figures who were supposed to be influencing and controlling human destiny in some powerful way. The Jews, for example, had developed a very elaborate angelology. In the book of Daniel (ca. 165 B.C.) angels are given individualized names, and in Jewish literature about fifty years later all heavenly beings are ranked and classified in a hierarchy. Written about a century before Paul's writings, the *Book of Enoch* divides the angels into seven classes. The Dead Sea (or Qumran) scrolls of the Essenes, a group of religious ascetics who lived south of Jerusalem, speak of an all-out war among the celestial spirits. The Essenes, already in existence before Paul's time, thrived until at least A.D. 69. Paul simply absorbed his culture's prevalent notions of celestial beings.

Paul had on his mind the threat that cosmic spirits, angels, demons, and powers held over his life and the lives of others. This way of thinking is very foreign to the modern secular outlook (although some of the younger generation today seem to be plagued by fears of demons and other supernatural forces). The genius of Paul lay in the way he confronted this cosmic threat. According to his letter to the Colossians, he came to believe that he no longer had to deal directly with mediating angels and spirits.

Apparently, Paul had felt terribly uncertain of his status before God. He had kept the law of the Old Testament, which he thought had been revealed through angels.[2] But this law still left him insecure and in painful doubt about his own salvation. Hence, like many of the pagans of his time, Paul came to believe that there is a cosmic savior-God who died and was resurrected. Paul was able to identify this savior-God with the Messiah. His cosmic Christ, therefore, was both the promised Jewish Messiah and the cosmic savior who would break not only the power of Satan and all the powers and principalities of the universe, but also the enslaving power of the Hebrew law.

Many of the pagans believed that the death of the savior-God was something of a substitute death and resurrection on behalf of human mortals. The dying God died *for them.* By mystical union with the dying God, the believers could share, not only in the God's death, but also in his resurrection. Much of Paul's writings are filled with his "in Christ" doctrine. That is, he pictures the Christian believers, like the pagans, as living "in and with" the savior-God.

Originally, the dying and resurrected God was associated with the death and rebirth of crops, but in an urban environment this farming motif became subordinate. Yet Paul retained the agricultural metaphor when he referred to the resurrected cosmic Christ as the "firstfruits" of the dead.[3] That is, he was saying that the Christ is the first of the new crops to appear. The crops are symbolic of human beings who have been buried in the ground, like seed, and are to be brought to life like new fruit and vegetation.

Paul and Baptism.   The rite of baptism was not invented by Christians. Many sects of the Jews—including the Qumran community—and various pagan *mystery religions* used baptism as a dramatization of their faith. For Paul, immersion in water represented not only purification and cleansing from sin, but also being plunged into the life of the cosmic Christ himself. Immersing the believer in water is a graphic representation of death and burial, and raising the believer out of the watery grave is a dramatic symbol of the resurrection of both the cosmic God and the believer who has become mystically unified with him.

In his letter to the Romans, Paul writes the following:

Do you not know that all of us who have been baptized into Christ Jesus were baptized into his death? We were buried therefore with him by baptism into death, so that as Christ was raised from the dead by the glory of the Father, we too might walk in newness of life.

For if we have been united with him in a death like his, we shall certainly be united with him in a resurrection like his. We know that our old self was crucified with him so that the sinful body might be destroyed, and we might no longer be enslaved to sin. For he who has died is freed from sin.[4]

No one can read Paul's writings without receiving the impression that a major concern in his life was that of deliverance and freedom, especially from sin, which he believed was caused by his "lower self." In baptism, Paul could think of his lower nature ("old self" or "sinful body") as being destroyed. Then in the resurrection, the new or converted self could blossom forth in freedom. For Paul, baptism not only dramatized the believer's present death and resurrection, but served as an installment toward the time in the future when the completed resurrection would come about. He believed that his literal earthly body would in the near future perish and be replaced by a fully "glorified body."

Paul and Freedom.   Paul longed to be freed from the mortal body, the curse of the law, the power and control of cosmic spirits, and the power of sin. Indeed, it is no exaggeration to say that he was obsessed with freedom from such curses. He believed that he had received a special revelation from God through Christ informing him that Christ Jesus was indeed the dying Lord who would free him. The word 'Jesus' *means* "the deliverer or savior." In essence, Christ Jesus was, for Paul, both the Messiah and savior-God or Lord. In this one doctrine of the Messiah as savior and Lord, Paul was able to resolve in his own mind the distinctive pressures that both his Jewish and pagan backgrounds had brought to bear on his life. When he says that Christ has set him "free from the law of sin and death" he is speaking as a "twice born" believer (to use William James' words).[5]

The Christ of Paul, therefore, was born not in Bethlehem or Nazareth, but in many towns and cities of the Mediterranean world of Paul's day. Paul was no different from leading figures of the pagan mystery religions in that the pressures of his life demanded a dying savior who would be resurrected from death. Many Jews have rejected Christianity because of its conspicuous pagan elements. Yet it must not be thought that the Jews of Paul's time were all of one mind. Jewish life—as the Qumran scrolls show—was not wholly cut off from pagan influences, and vice versa.[6] Indeed, there was in Paul's time a vast cultural movement in expectation of a great deliverer of some kind. Some Jews longed for an earthly Messiah who would rise up to overthrow their oppressors. Other Jews, having given up on earthly Messiahs, longed for a cosmic deliverer to come with supernatural power to bring freedom, justice, and salvation.

The Son of Man.   Jesus is supposed to have referred to himself as the "Son of Man." But this phrase, coming originally from the book of Daniel and then from the *Book of Enoch*, refers to a cosmic figure or group in contrast to the heathen powers of the earth. In Daniel the phrase "a Son of Man" refers to the Saints of the Most High, who descend from heaven to set up an everlasting Kingdom of God. The *Book of Enoch*, written a few years later, refers, not to *a* Son of Man, but to *the* Son of Man. This latter book pictures an individual cosmic person, a supernatural being, who is perhaps connected with the Jewish Messiah.[7] It seems plausible that Christian beliefs about a cosmic savior were drawn from the *Book of Enoch* and other such literature, which existed long before the New Testament letters and books were composed.

One New Testament book, Jude, quotes from *Enoch* and even treats it as if it were divinely revealed Scripture. Indeed, the author of Jude mistakenly assumes that the *Book of Enoch* was written by Enoch himself, which would have made the book many centuries older than in fact it is. The *Book of Enoch* was written only a few decades before Jesus was supposed to have been born. It seems likely that over a long period of time Jesus was born in the hearts and minds of Paul, the author of *Enoch*, and numerous others whose expectations were of cosmic dimensions. Only later, when the cosmic Christ failed to deliver the goods, did interest develop in his *earthly* ministry.

Christians today sometimes imagine a kind of Maginot Line between Jewish and pagan thinking. But recent discoveries and literature reveal the constant cross-fertilization that went on between them. Christianity developed as a product of many factors, both pagan and Jewish. Paul says that Christ came in "the fullness of time." A naturalist would agree with this in one sense by arguing that the social, historical, cultural, religious, etc., variables were such as to make the birth of something like Christian beliefs and practices very likely. But this explanation is natural and cultural in character, not supernatural.

Paul's Jesus and the Cosmic Powers.   In Paul's time many people were of the opinion that earthly affairs were more or less run by what was taking place in a multi-layered universe, which, according to the *Book of Enoch* and the *Testament of Levi*, was inhabited by angels and other supernatural beings. Much of the popular religious thought of Paul's time pictured the universe as scaled and graded; the material level was supposed to be low on the scale and under the control of angelic agents whose concern for human welfare seemed to be greatly lacking. Indeed, like many of his neighbors, Paul felt that the earth was under the control of evil cosmic agents or "elemental spirits."

But cutting through the endless deals that an individual had to make with these evil angels and agents, Paul asserted that it had been revealed to him that deals with these intermediate cosmic agents were no longer required. This is where Christ Jesus—Christ the Deliverer—comes into the picture. As with the author of the book of Hebrews, Paul was eager to assert Christ's superiority over all the angels.[8] And because this cosmic Christ became available to sinful and mortal human be-

ings, the angels and other such agents could for all practical
purposes be ignored. Christ simply moved them out of the
picture. A later book in the New Testament refers to Christ as
"the mediator between God and man."[9] Angels are subsidiary
at best.

What early Christianity represents is a profound *simplifica-
tion* of religion in a world weary with endless deals with supernatural agents and weary with a multiplicity of rules and regulations the following of which was deemed essential to
salvation. What Paul told his fellow Jews and pagans was
that there is now only one agent to deal with, namely Christ
Jesus. Furthermore, there is no endless sequence of requirements necessary before the benefits of this savior can be enjoyed. Indeed, the genius of Paul resides in the simple assertion that the benefits of forgiveness, resurrection, redemption,
and eternal happiness are available to those who simply ask for
them in sincere trust. Instead of requiring that this and that
deed be performed, Paul's Christ demands only one thing from
his followers: *faith, or trust.* In essence, Paul was giving up on
the endless religious rat-race. He threw in the towel, so to
speak. He said in effect that either God must be trusted to save
mankind or there is no hope at all.

Paul's Background of Belief.   But how can a person be sure
that trust in *Christ* is the same as trust in *God*? How can one be
certain that Christ is the true representative of God? Paul's answer was simply to assert that this is the case. Like others in his
time, he was convinced that he had received a revelation that
assured him that he was on the right path. As a Jew, Paul
could hardly believe as some of the pagans did that God could
literally die and be resurrected. But a number of pagans had
believed that various *sons* of Zeus had died and been resurrected. Paul, therefore, could believe that the son of the Hebrew God could die and be resurrected. The pagans did not
worry greatly about the historical details of the earthly life of
the sons of Zeus, and Paul seemed not greatly concerned with
the historical details of Jesus' earthly life. It was sufficient that
he died on earth and rose from death itself.

The Logic of Paul's Belief.   You might ask how Paul could
be so convinced that Christ is a full representative of God. A
naturalistic reply would point to Paul's background and setting, as well as to the logic of his thinking. If we simply presuppose, as Paul did, that there is a God and that he demands

atonement or sacrifice for sin, then we can see how the pagan notion of a dying God could fit into Paul's thinking. Not being able to atone for his own personal sin, Paul was driven logically to the position that God would have to supply the atonement himself. The pagan notion of a dying God was perfect. Paul does not clearly refer to his cosmic Christ as God. But over and over he uses the title *Lord* in referring to his Christ. This is a kind of compromise on Paul's part. On the one hand, as a Jew he could not easily believe in two Gods. On the other hand, Paul had to have a divine being to deal with the cosmic spirits, demons, and angels, as well as with the curse of sin and death. Hence, the Messiah of God is not simply an earthly figure but is "the Lord Jesus Christ." In him, says Paul, "all the fullness [pleroma] of God was pleased to dwell."[10] This Lord of the cosmos is regarded as none other than God's own Son.

Paul claimed that God the Father "has delivered us from the domain of darkness and transferred us to the kingdom of his beloved Son, in whom we have redemption and the forgiveness of sins."[11] Like many Jews of his time, Paul expected God to bring about the end of the world very shortly. Paul imagined that the Lord Jesus Christ would return again before some of his own readers would die or "sleep." Paul explains:

Lo! I tell you a mystery. We shall not all sleep, but we shall all be changed, in a moment, in the twinkling of an eye, at the last trumpet. For the trumpet will sound, and the dead will be raised imperishable, and we shall be changed.[12]

The early Christians expected the world to end and Christ to return to redeem and to bring justice. But because this supernatural phenomenon failed to materialize as the decades went by, the Christians began to give up their intense expectation that the immediate future would usher in a revolutionary change. By the time 2 Peter was written, the author of the book was forced to give a reason for the failure of Christ to return. While the explanation given is pathetically irrelevant, it does indicate that the Christians were indeed suffering a crisis of faith. The promise of Christ's appearance and his universal and cosmic transformation had not been kept.[13]

The First Coming of Christ. The earlier Christian literature made no attempt to provide details of the coming of Christ to earth. The emphasis was upon his death and resurrection and his expected return to put things in proper order. But as the Second Coming of Christ failed to come about, the Christians had little choice but to turn to what Christ had already done on earth.

Unfortunately, the earthly Jesus had to be constructed in the way that the cosmic Christ was constructed—namely, out of the belief and literature already available and the desires and longing of the believers. Having become convinced that there was a Christ who suffered, died, and was resurrected, the early Christians seemed to have placed all their hopes on the Second Coming of Christ. Consequently, the details of the First Coming were originally of no great concern to them.

But now the First Coming was becoming increasingly important as prospects of the Second Coming faded. This change of emphasis did not, however, come all at once. It was a gradual transition. Christians came to talk less about what Christ *would* do, and more about what he *had done* already. Indeed, Paul had already emphasized the past death and resurrection of his savior-Lord, although he had failed to give details of Jesus' life on earth.

In the Gospel of Matthew, which was written decades after Paul's life, there is still talk of the Second Coming and the resurrection of the dead in the future and the end of all things on earth. But in addition, the author of the Gospel of Matthew looks backward to the time when the Christ must have defeated death at his own resurrection. Indeed, the author provides the following utterly sensational story connected with the death of Jesus:

And Jesus cried again with a loud voice and yielded up his spirit.

And behold, the curtain of the temple was torn in two from top to bottom; and the earth shook, and the rocks were split; the tombs also were opened, and many bodies of the saints who had fallen asleep [i.e., had died] were raised, and coming out of the tombs after his resurrection they went into the holy city and appeared to many.[14]

It seems incredible that as frequently as Paul refers to the future resurrection of the saints, he makes absolutely no reference to this undeniably sensational resurrection of saints in the past. Neither do the other writers of the New Testament. But if we assume that the event never actually happened at all and hence was never a part of Paul's knowledge, then it is quite understandable that he did not make any clear reference to it.

It is not likely that most early Christian believers would ask themselves *whether* Christ once existed on earth at all. They were more likely to ask themselves what he did and what he was like. Quite naturally, they would wish to have some account of *events leading up to his death*, inasmuch as the death of the savior-God was crucial and central to the Christian outlook.

It is not surprising that the four Gospels would each contain the Passion narrative, although, to be sure, it seems impossible to harmonize these four accounts. Because Paul and the earlier Christians had made the resurrection central to the Christian faith, Christians gradually felt the need to have some kind of account of the *events surrounding the resurrection*. Also, such a God on earth would doubtless be expected to perform *miracles and have a special supernatural birth*. (Orthodox Christians today like to boast of the uniqueness of the virgin birth of Jesus, but actually the notion of such a birth for sons of Zeus and other deities was common.) A great savior would, moreover, be expected to make some *wise statements* and offer *words of moral excellence*. Hence, the Gospels provide the "teachings of Jesus."

The Teachings of Jesus.   There is nothing particularly unique about the teachings of Jesus in the New Testament. His "Beatitudes" were already in existence, as were the Golden Rule and other notions about the Fatherhood of God. All in all, it must be said that the ingredients for the life of Jesus were already available before the first century A.D. It was well known, for example, that Pontius Pilate was just the kind of person who would have murdered the innocent savior-God when he was on earth.

Indeed, Pilate was greatly detested by the Jews of his time. Such Jewish writers as Philo and Josephus accuse him of brutality, atrocities, and savagery. Toward the last quarter of the first century A.D., Christians could very easily come to think that Jesus was one of the numerous innocent Jews to suffer under Pontius Pilate. The timing was perfect also. Paul, a major force of Christianity, had certainly spoken of the earthly death of Christ and the imminent Second Coming. Hence, it would seem to have been rather easy for Christians after Paul to assume that their Christ was killed by some wicked oppressor at some time just before Paul, but not too long before him. Paul does not claim ever to have met Jesus in person when Jesus was presumably on earth. This, then, might have suggested to later Christians that Jesus did live a generation or so before Paul, which is precisely when Pilate was in power in Jerusalem. (I will not go into the possibility that Jesus was confused with the Jewish "Teacher of Righteousness" of the Qumran community just south of Jerusalem. There is some evidence that this Teacher might have been crucified or murdered by political forces.)

There are numerous passages in the Old Testament referring to suffering and dying on the part of innocent people. In fact, the suffering of the innocent seems to be a widespread theme. Plato, also, speaks of one who, though righteous, "will be whipped; . . . racked; . . . bound; . . . have both eyes burned out; and, at the end, when he has undergone every sort of evil, . . . be crucified."[15] Isaiah 53 speaks of the Suffering Servant whose death brings healing and salvation to the heathen. Jews have tended to regard the faithful among the Jewish people to be this Suffering Servant. But Christians came to regard it as their own cosmic Christ, whose death would atone for the sins of the world. In fact, it is pretty well agreed by the great majority of New Testament scholars today that the Gospel writers and the other New Testament writers also were often quite loose in their treatment of the Old Testament. The Christian writers claimed that the Old Testament was filled with "prophecies" pertaining to their savior, Jesus Christ; but it is clear to all scholars except the orthodox Christians that the early Christian writers found prophecies in the Old Testament that were simply not there. In short, the Christians twisted and distorted numerous passages in order to make a case for their predicted savior. (The fact that non-Christians conspicuously distorted passages of the Old Testament is hardly grounds for denying that Christians did it.)

Furthermore, in pagan literature much material similar to that in the New Testament may be found. Indeed, some Christian writers felt it necessary to come to terms with the numerous *similarities* between their own views and pagan views. In a book entitled *Refutation of all Heresies*, the Christian writer Hippolytus says in his introduction that he is going to divulge the secrets of the Egyptian and Chaldean mysteries. But both the parts of his work where he does this and also the summary of their contents in the epitome (which is otherwise intact) are missing.[16] This suggests that a Christian copyist might have feared that other Christians reading this material might see too many striking similarities between Christianity and the pagan mysteries.[17]

Furthermore, Christianity could have emerged without a historical Jesus or even a Paul. The cultural patterns and tendencies in the time of Paul were already in play, and Paul was a manifestation of some of them. This is not to underrate the role of Paul, for Christianity would not have been quite the same without his doctrines and influence. But the new faith would have been somewhat similar and just as real. After all, there were other Jews and pagans at that time who were wrestling with the questions and problems that Paul faced. And they, like Paul, were of a mixed Jewish-pagan background.

Hence, Christianity is larger than Jesus or Paul, which is one reason why its influence has continued to this day. Indeed, to say that *it* has continued is to be somewhat misleading, for Christianity is not some frozen doctrine and institution that continues unchanged throughout the centuries.[18] It has changed and broken up into numerous parts and pieces. To be sure, each piece tends to regard itself as the essence of Christianity, but this is to presuppose that there really is such an irreducible essence. I myself find fruitless all debates that try to decide what the "true essence of Christianity" is. It is much more fruitful and practical to ask whether there is in reality a God, whether there was a Christ Jesus, what God is doing to solve the problems of human life, what is morally required of us, whether miracles are possible today, and whether we shall live after this earthly existence. In this chapter and previous ones I have attempted to deal with some of these issues.

The Emergence of Christianity As a Multi-Colored Phenomenon. Books have been written on the way Christianity developed out of its cultural setting. Perhaps the best work defending the hypothesis that Jesus was not a historical person is G. A. Wells' book *The Jesus of the Early Christians*. Wells goes into great detail in order to present his case and defend it against objections, and I can only recommend his book as one with which Christian scholarship has thus far failed to come to terms. It will be interesting to see whether Christians will take up Wells' challenge and engage him in forthright debate. The debate could prove fruitful to all who are interested in the quest for the historical Jesus.

The fact that many people have *believed* in the historicity of Jesus is of little importance in the debate as to whether Jesus actually lived. What is important *historically*, however, is that people have believed that he once lived on earth. For the sake of convenience and dramatic appeal we sometimes like to believe that great inventions, ideas, and movements come about by means of one great man or woman alone. But a careful study of great inventions, ideas, and movements reveals that they come because of numerous historical and cultural variables.[19] In this connection, New Testament scholars have long debated whether the true founder of Christianity was Jesus or Paul. The hypothesis that I advance in this chapter is that Christianity is not *one* thing, but a very broad collection of movements, ideas, institutions, etc.

THE CHRIST OF KIERKEGAARD

There are many theologians within the Christian tradition who are very hesitant to make claims about details of the historical Jesus. They regard these alleged details to be incidental to the essence of Christianity. This, of course, raises the fruitless question as to what the essence of Christianity is. Even if the disputing groups could agree on what the essence of Christianity is, this agreement would in no way be evidence in support for or against the conclusions agreed upon. The hypothesis that I have advanced in this chapter is as follows: Even though a vast number of people have come to believe that there was a Jesus who died and rose from the grave, they are mistaken in their belief.

The influential nineteenth-century Christian Søren Kierkegaard felt compelled to conclude that we know almost nothing about the life of Jesus. He writes:

The historical fact that God has existed in human form is the essence of the matter; the rest of the historical detail is not even as important as if we had to do with a human being instead of with God.[20]

In other words, what is important for existential Christians like Kierkegaard is what they regard as the historical fact of God's becoming a man. All other details about the man Jesus are considered to be relatively insignificant. In fact, Kierkegaard says that he encounters the *contemporaneous* Christ and has no interest in the life of a Nazarene who long ago walked the streets of Jerusalem.

Of course, Kierkegaard is presupposing (1) the existence of the God of classical theism and (2) that this God did in fact become a man. It is extremely interesting that Kierkegaard concedes that the traditional arguments for classical theism will not do the job required of them. Furthermore, he concedes that historical inquiry will not lead anyone to conclude that God became a man.

So why does this existential Christian believe that God did become a man? Because, he says, the idea is so absolutely absurd! He refers to it as the "absolute paradox." Behind this sensational way of writing, Kierkegaard is saying the following: The idea that God became a man is true because no human mind could possibly have thought of it! It "did not arise in the heart of any man." Therefore, it must have originated in the mind and activity of God alone.[21]

This chapter, however, has advanced a contrary thesis, one that is more in harmony with either naturalism or panentheism than it is with classical theism of a Christian variety. According to the argument of this chapter, the world in which the apostle Paul and the other early Christians lived was filled with notions either of God's becoming a man, or of a man's being promoted by God to divine status. Far from dropping in from heaven, the idea of Jesus as divine Lord and Christ arose as two major religious fronts (the Jewish religion and pagan religions) came together. Indeed, we now have solid evidence that within these two broad fronts were greatly diverse beliefs surging and stirring within the Greek and Roman world before and during the rise of Christianity. Christianity is a continuation and development of various patterns of belief and behavior that already had their source in a cultural and historical setting. It sprang from natural, not supernatural, soil. Like adherents of most other religions of the time, Christians only imagined that their myths of cosmic splendor were supernatural in source and essence.

JESU, JOY OF MAN'S DESIRING

In the beautiful chorale "Jesu, Joy of Man's Desiring," Johann Sebastian Bach captures the best of the Jesus myth. In many ways Jesus is a mythical projection of some of the noblest desires and aspirations that enter into human life:

> Jesu, joy of man's desiring,
> Holy wisdom, love most bright;
> Drawn by Thee, our souls aspiring . . .

People need a vision of sublime passions, wisdom, and love. In music, poetry, and story form these supreme values are often personified. The being onto which these values are projected can attract people toward gentleness instead of rage, toward hope rather than despair, and toward kindness in place of revenge.

It is likely that Jesus as a historical being never lived at all; yet he, like Buddha in the Far East, has lived as a powerful myth and hopefully will continue to live for many as a vision of wisdom, love, compassion, and peace. It is difficult for some people to live by principle and by the evaluation of circumstances. They need stories and parables, and the New Testament has provided great numbers of people with examples of morality embodied in flesh and blood.[22] Indeed, imitating a model is one of the most effective means of learning.

The vision of the New Testament is, however, not sufficient for everyone as a moral and religious ideal. There is too much hatred and revenge in the Jesus of the Gospels. Furthermore, there are moral and social issues today with which the Jesus of the Gospel tales does not pretend to deal. One of the great dangers of the Jesus myth is that it has become a kind of final authority for some people. It is especially dangerous when they *select* what they desire from it or even read into it what they choose, and then treat their selection as a divinely instituted pattern. The Jesus myth is *used* by some to give the stamp of approval not only to the highest values, but also to the most depraved activities. The advantage of a powerful myth such as that of Jesus or Buddha is that it motivates people. But the disadvantage is that it can motivate for evil ends as well as good.

THE LOGIC AND MYTH OF CHRIST'S ATONEMENT

A Ransom to the Devil.   For about a thousand years, among Christians the dominant or orthodox theory of Christ's atonement or sacrifice was the *ransom theory*. This dogma was finally challenged by Anselm in the eleventh century. It has its roots in Paul's notions of angels and personified cosmic powers who threaten the lives of mortals. In the writing entitled *Ascension of Isaiah* we have materials that are both Jewish and Christian in origin. The Christian section purports to tell how Christ traveled through the various levels of the universe before reaching earth. At the upper levels, Christ did not need to disguise himself because the angels there were friendly and righteous. But at the lower levels he had to appear as an angel in order to slip through unnoticed. Finally, on earth he came as a man. Fortunately, he remained unrecognized by Satan and other evil spirits until it was too late.

In other words, many Christians believed that Jesus served as a kind of bait to lure the Devil into a contest so that Christ could defeat him. One of the fathers of the Eastern Church, Gregory of Nyssa in the fourth century referred to Christ's humanity as the bait concealing the fishhook of his deity. Slightly later, Augustine spoke of the Cross as a mousetrap baited by Christ's blood; Satan took the bait and was caught. In this sense, Jesus served as a ransom to the Devil, but the Devil never collected.[23]

This Christian myth may be compared to a Hindu version of divine atonement:

At one time the world and the gods were threatened by a powerful demon. The demon was particularly hard to defeat since everything he put his hands on turned to ashes. It was [the God] Vishnu who succeeded in destroying the demon by assuming the form of a beautiful woman, Mohini ('the deluding one'). The demon, infatuated, was asked by Mohini to anoint himself before coming to her. In anointing himself, he could not but touch himself, and thus he became ashes.[24]

There is here and in the Christian ransom theory something of the fable of the greedy dog who, in grabbing at the reflection of a bone in the water, loses the bone he has in his mouth. Both the Devil in Christianity and the powerful demon in the Hindu myth are regarded as greedy. But the point is that God has the power and means of outwitting and defeating such cosmic terrorists. God became incarnate in a human person in order to deal with the Devil. And that is the good news ("the gospel") that Paul and others wanted to believe in.

The Satisfaction Theory. Many centuries later, Christians began to believe that the ransom that Jesus paid was to God rather than to Satan. This is a sad commentary in some ways, for it shows that many Christians have inadvertently admitted a demonic side to their deity. It turns out that the real cosmic enemy of mankind is God's "holiness," which must be appeased and satisfied. Anselm regarded the sacrificial death of Jesus to be a logical implication of "the very givenness of God's nature."[25] God's holiness must either be satisfied or the sinner must be punished. Jesus' death, then, was treated by Anselm as the logical means of satisfying God's holy demand for blood sacrifice.

Apparently it never occurred to Anselm to think of the universe as having a tragic dimension. The atonement myth, therefore, became for him a device for perpetuating human guilt at a cosmic level and thus making human actions more cosmically important than they are. In many ways, Christian myths have served to project human beings onto an infinite stage where they wrestle with supernatural agents and even move the heart of God. Thus, on the one hand Christianity has inflated human importance to infinite proportions, while on the other it has tormented numerous human beings with unreal guilt and obsession with metaphysical spooks.

New Testament scholars today are usually very eager to say that the New Testament literature does not offer one consistent theory of the atonement of Christ. These scholars wish to leave some way open to explore a more humane and less barbaric view of Christ's death than many Christians in the past have managed to do. Perhaps what is behind the atonement myth is that human sin is costly—perhaps even to God. When orthodox Christians more fully acknowledge this, then they will perhaps see that life has its tragic element and is not a simple morality play wherein righteousness is all on one side and evil on the other.

Paul was driven to the conclusion that he must trust the grace of the deity. Unfortunately, his Christological mythology was a fruitless attempt to explicate the cosmic mechanics of the workings of divine grace. Perhaps he could have learned more of grace had he remained less preoccupied with his own cosmic sinfulness and cosmic importance. Human grace is not divine grace, but the Christian myth of Christ's atonement has often portrayed divine grace with an undercurrent of aggression disguised under the pious name of "holiness."

NOTES

1. See Fawn M. Brodie, *No Man Knows My History* (New York: Knopf, 1945), pp. 12–15.
2. Galatians 3:19–20.
3. 1 Corinthians 15:20–23.
4. Romans 6:3–7 (RSV).
5. See Romans 8:2.
6. One New Testament scholar notes that it "is easy to see how some Gentiles could have mistaken Judaism for an Oriental mystery religion" (James L. Price, *Interpreting the New Testament* [New York: Holt, Rinehart & Winston, 1961], p. 328).
7. See Norman Snaith, *The Jews From Cyrus to Herod* (Wallington, England: Religious Education Press, 1949), p. 114.
8. See Hebrews 1:2.
9. I Timothy 2:5.
10. Colossians 1:19.
11. Colossians 1:13.
12. 1 Corinthians 15:51–52 (RSV).
13. See 2 Peter 3:3–4, 8–10.
14. Matthew 27:50–53.
15. Plato, *Republic*, 362A. This quotation is based on the translation of Allan Bloom in *The Republic of Plato* (New York: Basic Books, 1968), p. 39. Like Paul Shorey, Bloom uses the translation "crucified" rather than "impaled." However, it is not clear that the apostle meant by crucifixion anything more definite than what Plato had in mind. Originally the word "crucifixion" did not necessarily entail impalement on a cross.
16. G. A. Wells, *The Jesus of the Early Christians: A Study in Christian Origins* (Buffalo, N.Y.: Prometheus Books, 1971), p. 308.
17. For a scholarly defense of the view that Paul was *not* greatly influenced by pagan religions, see W. D. Davies, *Paul and Rabbinic Judaism: Some Rabbinic Elements in Pauline Theology*, 2d ed. (London: S.P.C.K., 1955). I must admit that this book seems no longer as convincing to me as it once did. The Qumran or Dead Sea scrolls as well as more recent New Testament studies indicate that rabbinic Judaism was not a completely self-contained system of thought. Also the pagan-Jew interchange seems to have been more fluid than it was once believed to have been.
18. See Robert L. Wilkin, *The Myth of Christian Beginnings: History's Impact on Belief* (Garden City, N.Y.: Doubleday, Anchor Books, 1972).
19. See R. P. Cuzzort, *Humanity and Modern Sociological Thought* (New York: Holt, Rinehart & Winston, 1969), pp. 220–226.

20. Søren Kierkegaard, *Philosophical Fragments, or a Fragment of Philosophy*, trans. David F. Swenson (Princeton, N.J.: Princeton University Press, 1936), p. 87.

21. Ibid., p. 92. Cf. Søren Kierkegaard, *Concluding Unscientific Postscript*, trans. David F. Swenson with notes and intro. by Walter Lowrie (Princeton, N.J.: Princeton University Press, 1941), pp. 187–193.

22. See R. B. Braithwaite, *An Empiricist's View of the Nature of Religious Belief* (Cambridge: Cambridge University Press, 1955).

23. See *Baker's Dictionary of Theology*, ed. Everett F. Harrison (Grand Rapids: Baker Book House, 1960), p. 72.

24. Ninian Smart, *The Phenomenon of Religion* (New York: Herder & Herder, 1973), p. 100.

25. *Baker's Dictionary of Theology*, p. 73.

CHAPTER XIII

Is There Life after Death?

ORTHODOX CHRISTIANITY AND MEDIUMS WHO COMMUNICATE WITH THE DEAD

The Old Testament Methods of Repression.   Orthodox Christianity believes that when people die they either go to hell or go to be with God. Some of the Old Testament writers seemed to believe that at death the individual descended into Sheol, a place of inactivity, vagueness, darkness, amnesia, and obscurity. Only in the second century B.C. did Jewish thinking seem to move clearly toward a view of the resurrection of those in Sheol. By the time Christianity began to be formulated, the doctrine of the individual's resurrection from the grave had already come to full bloom (although the more conservative party among the Hebrews—the Sadducees—still rejected such new ideas as resurrection, angels, and devils). The apostle Paul and the other New Testament writers seemed to share in the more popular notion of individual resurrection from death.

However, orthodox Christianity has been most reluctant to encourage any empirical or experimental inquiry into the question of the survival of individuals after death. It is enough for these Christians that the promise of life after death is set forth in the Bible. In fact, they strongly discourage all attempts to communicate with the dead. When Bishop James A. Pike sought to communicate with his "departed" son, Jim, a number of Christians thought that he was engaging in something obscene and anti-Christian. The infamous witch of Endor, whom King Saul was said to have consulted, belonged to a class of mediums who attempted to communicate with the dead. In his earlier years, King Saul was praised because he "had put the mediums and wizards [i.e., sorcerers] out of the land."[1] According to the Old Testament book of Leviticus, mediums and wizards were supposed to be stoned to death.[2]

The Old Testament is insistent that those who specialize in making contact with the unseen world are simply not to be tolerated. The best they could expect was banishment from the community. This probably gives us some insight into the politics of the time. Those prophets and priests who made contact with the God Yahweh were surely dealing with the "unseen world." So, what it boiled down to was an attempt on the part of the Yahwists to gain a religious monopoly. They were set on stamping out all interpreters of the "unseen world" but their own. The prophet Elijah is said to have killed all the prophets of the God Baal.[3]

Indeed, there seems to have been great jealousy among some of the priests and prophets of Israel. And the priest Samuel was very concerned to keep King Saul from performing some of the religious rituals that only the priest was supposed to perform.[4] It seems clear that those who sought to communicate with the dead were seen as a great threat to the prophets and priests of the Yahwist religion.

Today, many orthodox Christians fear mediums who seek to talk with the dead. In fact, the assumption among many Christians is that the mediums are really playing with a kind of spiritual dynamite; for the persons with whom they make contact are regarded, not as departed loved ones, but as demons, if not Satan himself.

Scientific Inquiry in a Critical Area. There is, of course, good reason to be skeptical of mediums and others who claim to do business with the spirit world, for the number of frauds in this area is exceedingly great. But neither orthodox Christian taboos nor the deceit and self-deceit among mediums is sufficient reason for preventing a more honest and rigorous inquiry into the possible evidence for life after death.

There are some mediums who have been completely honest with other people; such mediums should be tested and used in the attempt to explore the possibility of communicating with the spirits (or whatever) of those persons who have died. There are also perhaps other avenues of research to be taken in dealing with this crucial problem. Recent research in telepathy and clairvoyance has proved promising; indeed, it is regarded by many to be a better hypothesis accounting for the relevant data than is the hypothesis of personal survival after death. In this chapter some attempt will be made to evaluate the debate regarding the hypothesis of survival.

Can a Brief Life Be Meaningful?   One reason people wish for life after death is that they find human living today to have such great intrinsic value that they long to see life continued. (On the other hand, mere everlasting endurance after death could be regarded as undesirable for those who, receiving little joy in this present life, suspect that the next will be a continuation of the same drab existence.)

There are also some people who insist that without everlasting existence, life as we have it today would be wholly "meaningless." While this may be true for their own personal lives, it is not true for everyone. Many people believe that their life now is worthwhile and meaningful at its own level even though it is not everlasting. One orthodox Christian writer goes so far as to tell his readers that Christianity alone offers "meaning in personality."[5] This assertion appears at first glance to be an empirical statement that could be put to the test, but a careful analysis reveals that its author has no intention of submitting it to such inquiry.

A major fallacy of orthodox Christianity comes in thinking that human living is somehow without intrinsic qualitative value unless it endures forever. My wife and I have been married for twenty-one years. According to orthodox Christianity, this marriage will eventually cease to exist because in heaven there will be no marriage. So, shall my wife and I conclude that our marriage is void of intrinsic qualitative value because it will not endure forever? We do not think so. Similarly, there are other ingredients of earthly life that are of great intrinsic value even though they will in time perish. There is a certain cruelty in the Christian attempt to make people believe that their present happiness and joy is somehow "unreal" just because it is not endless.

It is often because some joy and happiness has been experienced in this life that people wish to continue to live without ceasing. I am among those who wish to continue to live after the earthly body decays, provided the afterlife is interesting and reasonably enjoyable. But whether I or anyone will have the opportunity to live forever is something that cannot be determined by either personal wishes or Scriptural promises.

Not a Supernatural Matter.   Supernaturalism has to do more with our *attitudes* toward inquiry than with the content and objects of our inquiry. A primitive person would tend to take a supernatural *attitude* toward a radio until he learned some of the variables by which the radio works. If someone had told a Medieval Christian that there are little animals moving about in a drop of water, he might have taken a supernatural attitude toward the water. But with the coming of the microscope and other instruments and techniques, scientists today have a more naturalistic attitude toward microbes and other such animals. It is very possible, therefore, that the question of life after death can be approached with a naturalistic rather than a supernaturalistic attitude.

NATURALISM AND LIFE AFTER DEATH

The Risk of Experimentalism.   Earlier we saw that in contrast to supernaturalism, naturalism stresses the methods of critical inquiry and experimentalism. By experimentalism is meant the practice of expressing one's hypothesis in observational terms. This is a risky practice because it leaves open the possibility that new observations will falsify one's hypothesis. We saw that a hypothesis or theory is, among other things, a horizon of expectations. That is, the theory leads us to expect certain observations to come about under certain specified conditions. Furthermore, the theory will lead us to expect that certain kinds of observations will not come about under these conditions. To put a theory to the test is to bring into existence the appropriate conditions for determining whether or not the predicted observations will come about as specified.

Naturalism and Spatial Continuity.   Central to the view of naturalism is the method of critical experiment. If this method of inquiry is forsaken, then naturalism is forsaken. Another doctrine that has traditionally been associated with naturalism is that of spatial continuity. But twentieth-century physics has seriously challenged this doctrine. Indeed, commitment to the more central naturalistic doctrine of critical experiment has led to observational reports that count strongly against the established position of spatial continuity.

Very briefly, this established position asserts that everything that is real must somehow manifest itself in a specific location in space. Furthermore, whatever is both real and moving must go through an unbroken series of points in space. For example, if a football is to travel from the quarterback's hand to the hands of the right end, then the ball cannot upon leaving the passer's hand disappear until it reappears suddenly in the hands of the receiver. The doctrine of *spatial continuity* leads us to expect to find no point along the way that is missed. Every point, no matter how close to the previous point, may be thought of as a kind of station through which the ball must pass before it reaches its destination.

Problems of Spatial Continuity. Naturalism leads us to expect this spatial continuity. But the expectation is disappointed in some cases. For example, at the subatomic level we confront the fact of electrons that seem to pass from one location to another without going through the intervening points of space. Needless to say, this new phenomenon proved upsetting to the established expectations of almost all physicists, until they became adjusted to the novelty.

To say that a subatomic particle can "travel" without actually going through space is not entirely accurate. It is more precise to say that the possible points between the departure point and the arrival point do not seem to be passed through. But this does not mean that *all* spatial points are bypassed; for, after all, the points of departure and arrival are themselves spatially located. Hence, what we have here is a question of the measure of distance between points of departure and arrival.

Let me spell this out a bit. Suppose that a given particle moves from point C to point M. Prior to the new experiments in physics, the naturalist would normally expect to be able to detect this unit at points D, E, F, G, and so on until the unit arrives at point M. But at the level of subatomic physics this expectation seems no longer wholly justified. To be sure, there are still some physicists who challenge this new view. The challengers insist that the subatomic particle does in fact pass through every point along the way from C to M even though we do not yet have the instruments for detecting it at these points. These challengers are expressing their faith in the old naturalistic doctrine of complete spatial continuity.

Other naturalists have had to say that their own method of inquiry will not permit them to indulge themselves in this faith. They must, therefore, follow the upsetting observations that the method of critical experiment has encountered.

Spatial Order. It must not be imagined that the new hypothesis about location in space has entirely eliminated the notion of spatial order and regularity. Each subatomic particle may not be completely tractable and predictable in its *individ-*

ual journey from one place to another, but there does remain lawfulness, that is, statistically predictable *clusters* of particles. What has happened is that space has more "loose play" in it than was previously thought. This is to state the matter very poorly, however. Indeed, it cannot be stated very well except in mathematical terms. Nevertheless, the reason for raising this issue can still be made clear. It is this: we can no longer expect at least subatomic particles to travel through every point of space between the position of departure and the position of arrival. Nevertheless, given this important qualification, we must still talk of spatial location and of lawful patterns of units within space. Spatial order is not entirely thrown out even by those who believe that the human person survives the death of his own body. *Even alleged surviving spirits, ghosts, minds, or whatever we may call them, are said to be located in some spatial order.*

The Problem of Relating Spatial Orders.   I now ask you to imagine that you have a kind of spirit-body allowing you to travel from, say, where you live now to a thousand miles out at sea. And you travel suddenly. That is the best way I can put it at present. Your usual body is asleep, let us say, in your bed where you live. While it sleeps from 2 to 3 A.M., you in your spirit-body are at sea a thousand miles away. Needless to say, in order to have arrived there you had to travel either incredibly fast or somewhat in the way that a subatomic particle travels. That is, you did not necessarily pass through every intervening point of physical space in order to arrive at your destination.

Those who believe in this kind of spirit travel will often prefer to use the phrase "astral travel" because they believe that the individual cannot travel except in a body—an "astral body." This raises a question as to what kind of space this astral body travels in, and the answers given do not always seem to be consistent with one another. For example, on the one hand, the astral body travels in astral space, which is presumably different from the ordinary everyday "physical space" by which we orient ourselves. On the other hand, the astral body is thought to *relate to* objects that exist in our more ordinary physical space. If an astral body travels to a ship at sea, the ship is not regarded as an astral ship floating on an astral ocean. Rather, it is a ship and an ocean belonging to our ordinary spatial order. In his remarkable article "Six Theories about Apparitions," Professor Hornell Hart relates the case of a woman who is supposed to have traveled astrally from Connecticut to the side of her husband far out at sea on the steamer *City of Limerick*.[6] He also provides what he takes to be evidence corroborating the claim that this extraordinary event took place.

The problem is that of showing how the various kinds of spaces are "related" to one another. How do they plug into one another? We seem on the surface to have little trouble with what may be called "dream space" because it is regarded by most people as simply subjective or private. Our so-called ordinary space is said to be objective because it is public rather than wholly private. But what if it came about that our "dream space" were to be shared by more than one person? Then would it not be a kind of new spatial order that is neither ordinary (i.e., completely public for everyone) nor completely private? How would this "in-between" spatial order fit in with our ordinary spatial order?

Indeed, it is still a matter of heated debate as to *where* the dream is located. Is it simply inside the skull of the dreamer? If in a dream you see a yellow rose you can locate the rose over to, say, the right. Also it is down near the ground rather than up in the sky. But this is all within *dream* space. We still have the problem of determining where the rose and the ground are located in ordinary *public* space.

Is dream space as such simply *not located at all*? If it is not inside the dreamer's skull somewhere, then where in ordinary space is it? If it exists nowhere, then how can we say that it exists at all? We can hardly deny that dreams "exist," but this poses a problem because the word 'exist' often entails spatial location. We say that dreams are not real, and yet we know that they are real as dreams. Presumably, a dream is real only as a private experience. And this brings us back to the question of dreams that are shared by two or more persons.

Shared Dreams.   Professor Hornell Hart, who is one of the most respected and thorough researchers of paranormal experiences, relates the case of three individual dreamers, each of whom remembered his own part in the dream. The following is from a letter written by Henry Armitt Brown, who later became a brilliant lawyer:

In the fall of 1865 . . . while I was studying law in the city of New York, I retired to my room about midnight of a cold and blustering evening. I remember distinctly hearing the clock strike twelve as . . . drowsiness crept upon me and I slept. I had hardly lost consciousness when I seemed to hear loud and confused noises and felt a choking sensation at my throat, as if it were grasped by a strong hand. I awoke (as it seemed) and found myself lying on my back on the cobble-stones of a narrow street, writhing in the grip of a low-browed thick-set man with unkempt hair and grizzled beard, who with one hand at my throat and holding my wrists with the other threw his weight upon me and held me down. . . . Over and over we rolled upon the stones. . . . Presently I saw him reach forth his hand and grasp a bright hatchet. . . . I made one more tremendous fight for life, for a second I held my enemy powerless and saw with such a thrill of delight as I cannot forget the horror-stricken faces of friends within a rod of us rushing to my rescue. As the foremost of them sprang upon the back of my antagonist he wrenched his wrist away from me. I saw the hatchet flash above my head and felt instantly a dull blow on the forehead. I fell back on the ground, a numbness spread from my head over my body, a warm liquid flowed down upon my face and into my mouth, and I remember the taste as of blood. . . .

Then I thought I was suspended in the air a few feet above my body, I could see myself as if in a glass, lying on the back, the hatchet sticking in the head. . . . I heard the weeping of friends, at first loud, then growing fainter. . . . With a start, I awoke. . . . My watch told me I had not been more than half an hour asleep.

Early the next morning I joined an intimate friend with whom I spend much of my time. . . . Suddenly he interrupted me with the remark that he had dreamed strangely of me the night before. . . . "I fell asleep," he said, "about twelve and immediately dreamed that I was passing through a narrow street when I heard noises and cries of murder. Hurrying in the direction of the noise, I saw you lying on your back, fighting a rough labouring man, who held you down. I rushed forward, but as I reached you he struck you on the head with a hatchet and killed you instantly. Many of our friends were there and we cried bitterly. . . ."

"What sort of a man was he?" I asked. "A thick-set man, in a flannel shirt and rough trousers; his hair was uncombed and his beard was grizzly and of a few days' growth."

Within a week I was in Burlington, New Jersey. I called at a friend's house. "My husband," said his wife to me, "had such a horrid dream about you the other night. He dreamed that a man killed you in a street fight. He ran to help you, but before he reached the spot your enemy had killed you with a great club."

"Oh, no," cried the husband across the room, "he killed you with a hatchet."[7]

There are, of course, other alleged cases of shared dream experiences. The hypothesis of a kind of common unconscious from which are drawn various common elements of experience is sometimes used to explain shared dreams. In other words, the hypothesis of telepathy rather than that of the existence of astral bodies or spirit bodies is called in to "explain" a number of experiences of extrasensory perception that apparently cannot be explained by ordinary sensory perception.

Even if the common pool of consciousness does exist and is available to at least some human beings, the questions that remain are: Where does this ESP reservoir exist? Is the common unconscious located anywhere? Apparently it has some "connection" or "relationship" with us mortals who find ourselves living in ordinary space. But what is the nature of the relationship between nonspatial ESP phenomena existing "within" a common unconscious, on the one hand, and our personal selves existing in the ordinary spatial order, on the other hand?

Perhaps it is a misleading question to ask where the collective or common unconscious is located. Is it not like asking where the power of a cause exists when we say that a cause produces an effect? But if it is misleading to speak of the *location* of a common unconscious, then perhaps it is misleading to speak of its *existence*! Why not talk of telepathy, shared dreams, astral travel, and apparitions as simply *experiences* that some people enjoy?

A Question of Something's Conditions Rather Than Its Intrinsic Nature.   No reference need be made to the so-called "spiritual location" of astral bodies and the like. If people have extraordinary experiences, then they have them. To ask whether an astral body "really" exists or "really" travels may be a confused question that cannot be answered. Instead of worrying about the "intrinsic nature" or "metaphysical status" of these unusual experiences, we find it far more fruitful to spend our time uncovering and specifying the detectable procedures and conditions by which extraordinary experiences come about.

The importance of this approach lies in the repeatability of the experiments. If we can designate certain conditions and procedures to be either necessary, sufficient, or at least highly contributory to the occurrence of certain extraordinary experiences, then we will have increased our understanding. For to understand a phenomenon is at least to be able to predict that it will come about under certain specified conditions or circumstances.

Without denying that some wider theory will eventually be needed to connect the hypotheses and experimental data, I think that it is still premature to demand a sweeping cosmic or metaphysical scheme that will coherently connect all our statements about astral travel, telepathy, and the like. The time is now ripe for greater imagination in coming up with fruitful experimental designs. There is a need to develop a *number* of theories that can be put to the test before we endeavor to lace together all the smaller theories into one neat supertheory. This is a way of saying that an attitude of experimentalism presently requires more than the skeptic's wooden-headed dogmatism. It also requires the true believer to indicate what sort of observations would count *against* the hypothesis of life beyond the grave.

We may say that the skeptic has lost the value of his critical skills if he refuses to entertain new and revolutionary experiments. And the true believer is still a fearful soul if he is unwilling to entertain the possibility that the extraordinary experiences may be produced under conditions greatly different from what he has asserted to be the case.

The Hatchet in the Dream Body.　Earlier we read of a shared dream in which a dream body was murdered by a dream hatchet. The hatchet, you recall, sank into the skull of Mr. Henry Brown's dream body. Now, an experimental question may be stated as follows: "If a dream body is killed in a private dream, then will that body remain dead? That is, will it cease to appear in subsequent private dreams? Does a dream body have also a dream soul or spirit that survives after a dream death?"

Let us suppose that we could discover the procedures for having not just private dreams but also shared dreams. We might then seek to learn whether there are certain things that can be said about private dream bodies that cannot be said of *shared dream bodies*. For example, it may be that a *private* dream body can be killed and then reappear in a later dream as if nothing had happened to it. But we might discover eventually that the *shared* dream body cannot appear again in subsequent shared dreams after it has been killed. Of course, this is all a matter for experimentation. Indeed, we have yet to learn how to produce shared dream experiences.

PERSONAL SURVIVAL AFTER DEATH

How Immortal Is the Immortal Soul?   Scientific explanations seek to establish relationships between conditions and specific consequences. For example, let us assume that in some sense there is at least the *experience* that has been classified as astral travel. Then let us seek to reproduce this experience in order to elicit a variety of responses from the astral body. In this way the numerous *responses* of the astral body can be charted and studied experimentally. We can ask what behavior the astral body will demonstrate under certain specified stimuli and conditions of reinforcement. Are there certain things in "astral space" that more readily attract the attention of the astral body? Are some things repulsive to such a body? Can such a body be damaged or hurt? Indeed, can it be destroyed in the way that our so-called ordinary body can be destroyed?

Such a line of inquiry raises the further question of the endurability of the soul, spirit, or "spiritual body" that presumably lives on after the ordinary body dies. Can the self or person surviving death do whatever he wants without being harmed or destroyed? For all we know, there might be a life after death that itself is still a mortal life. In other words, even though the surviving soul, or whatever, lives after the ordinary body dies, this surviving soul may not be immortal under *all* conditions. It is conceivable that if there is a surviving soul or something similar, it could under certain circumstances meet death and cease to exist. Or it might go insane or undergo all sorts of wild and terrifying experiences whenever certain conditions come into play. This is a way of saying that the immortal soul may turn out to be not immortal or not what traditions have declared it to be. It may endure longer than the earthly body but eventually die or become enfeebled or deranged.

What of the Reports of Surviving Souls or Spirits?   There are some accounts that seem to fit well with the hypothesis that there is personal life after death for at least some people. The case for survival after death rests primarily on the reports of apparitions and of the messages that mediums seem to receive. A careful student of apparitions and mediumistic messages will have to admit two things: (1) Some of the claims can be explained in accord with our present understanding of things and without resort to the survival hypothesis. (2) But there are some claims that cannot be explained by our present scientific knowledge. This, then, leaves the survival hypothesis as at least one of those worthy of respect and further testing.

Reports through mediums and reports of those who claim to have experienced astral travel agree with one another on some points but contradict one another on other points. For example, in her 1927 book entitled *My Travels in the Spirit World* Caroline D. Larsen says that she has often journeyed into realms beyond the earthly dimension. The famous astral traveler Sylvan Muldoon, on the other hand, says that his "conscious projection" always took him to places on the earth and never into any other realms. Larsen claims to have had a spirit guide and to have encountered numerous "new citizens of Spirit Land," whereas Muldoon never even saw a spirit guide and seldom met anyone in his astral travels. Also, Muldoon insists that his astral body is always connected by an astral cable or cord to his ordinary physical body so long as the latter lives.[8] Larsen, however, denies the existence of the cord.

In attempting to harmonize the discrepancies between these two famous astral travelers, Hornell Hart says that much of what is perceived in the astral world depends on what the individual pays attention to and is prepared to receive.[9] Critics of astral travel deny that it is something publicly verifiable and charge that astral travel depends greatly on the imagination and wishful thinking of the so-called travelers. Presumably Hart means to say either that Muldoon chose to travel in isolated places or that he simply neglected to see the great numbers of people all about him. As for the astral cord, are we to believe that Mrs. Larsen had one, but somehow was unable to detect it or perhaps had even disposed of it without being aware of so doing?

Muldoon writes, "It seems that the mind *creates* its own environment yet the environment is *real!*"[10] Critics of the notions of astral travel and soul survival are of the opinion that these are both nothing more than creations of the wishful mind. Indeed, if an individual could by thinking bring into existence astral trees, then could he bring into existence also other astral *persons?* If he could, there would be the problem of whether these other astral persons have any existence *of their own.* If Mrs. Larsen should create a number of spirits like herself, would they cease to exist the moment she turned her attention from them? Indeed, is she herself a mere creation of the mind of another astral spirit? And so on.

Animals and Clothes in the Spirit World.   It is interesting that very few apparitions and astral bodies appear in the nude. We may presume that in the spirit world the reason for wearing clothes is not that of inclement weather, but rather a sense of modesty. Even spirit bodies are still something to be covered up. This, of course, raises the question as to whether there exists astral spiritual clothing. Presumably such things as clothing, walking-canes, and the like are mental creations in the spirit world.

In one mediumistic sitting the medium coughed asthmatically in exactly the same recognizable way that a particular deceased asthmatic Scotchman had done when he was still living in his ordinary physical body. Whether this fact suggests that spirit bodies can suffer bronchial asthma is not altogether clear. A believer in spirit bodies might say that in this particular case the medium picked up by telepathy that the Scotchman had once suffered asthma. Hence, in serving as the voice of his spirit, the medium unconsciously supplemented her act by coughing as she engaged in her semi-dramatic performance.[11] Professor Hart is eager to point out that often the medium confuses the information that he receives from the spirit with the information that he picks up in other ways.[12]

Animals have appeared in apparitions and in alleged astral journeys. This suggests that if there is life after death, then perhaps it includes at least some domesticated animals that have come greatly to love and be loved by certain individual human beings. Moreover, there is at least one case in which an earthly dog seemed to detect an apparition:

It is on record that an apparition of a child was perceived first by a dog, that the animal's rushing at it, loudly barking, interrupted the conversation of the seven persons present in the room, thus drawing their attention to the apparition, and that the latter then moved through the room for some fifteen seconds, followed by the barking dog.[13]

This raises the question as to whether spirits and astral bodies have a special scent similar to the scent of the ordinary body.

CAN CONSCIOUSNESS EXIST WITHOUT THE BRAIN?

There is considerable evidence that drugs as well as electrical stimulation of the brain can create for a person sounds and sights that others beside him neither hear nor see. By electrically stimulating a mild-mannered woman in the region of the amygdala, an experimenter was able to turn her temporarily into an aggressive person who verbally abused and threatened the experimenter. When the switch was turned off, the woman became again a gentle person who apologized for her hostile behavior when she was informed of it.[14]

Surgery, drugs, electrical stimulation, reinforcement schedules, etc. are various *physical* means by which a number of human motives, attitudes, feelings, and responses may be changed drastically. Apparently, such physical means can even *bring into existence some new attitudes, feelings, etc.* If this is true, then the survival theory is seriously weakened. How is this so? Well, many proponents of the survival theory insist that the brain is only a transmitter or receiver and not a *generator* of personal consciousness.[15]

It seems clear that personal consciousness is not simply transmitted through the brain, but rather that the brain is at least instrumental in producing or generating consciousness or certain aspects of it. This fact does not rule out the survival hypothesis, but it qualifies it rather profoundly. Professor Hart is sometimes prone to treat consciousness as some kind of substance existing beyond our feelings and experiences. But this is to reduce consciousness to something that it is not—namely, an abstraction. There is some evidence in support of the survival of at least some conscious states after the death of the body, but it is still insufficient, and there are other data that seem to count against the theory of survival. Further experiments need to be done.

The Oxford University philosophy professor H. H. Price has for years been a student of "psychic phenomena." He tells of one of his ancestors, Peter Price, who had been rendered unconscious by an illness for several days. During this time he visited, he said later, the next world. To his surprise, he observed that it was not at all like what Roman Catholic priests had told him it was. Upon recovering from his unconscious state, he gave up his Catholic beliefs and persuaded his family to do likewise.[16]

DOES EACH PERSON HAVE MANY BODIES?

If each person has many bodies of various kinds, then some way of showing how the connecting bodies are related to one another may be discovered in the future. That is, the conditions by which the journey from one body to the others occurs may eventually be spelled out with a good amount of exactness.

In fact, it may be that both out-of-the-body experiences and apparitional experiences are best explained by some hypothesis other than the multiple-embodiment hypothesis. Apparitions of the living might be regarded as a combination of telepathy and other phenomena. Out-of-the-body experiences might prove to be the work of clairvoyance. Professor Price writes with characteristic balance:

We might suppose that clairvoyantly-acquired information manifests itself in consciousness by means of a vision or a dream, in which it seems to the percipient that he is seeing some distant person or object and thereby acquiring information which turns out later to be correct. Nevertheless, I venture to suggest that this concept of 'multiple embodiment' deserves more consideration than it has usually received.[17]

Professor Price does not mean to say that we should give mere lip service to this notion of multiple bodies, but that we should do all we can to find ways to formulate it in more intelligible ways and to test the hypothesis to see how well it stands up under logical analysis and experimental scrutiny. In other words, he is advising us neither to ignore the hypothesis (in the hope that nothing will come of it) nor to pretend that it has been so firmly established that only inferior people reject it.

UNNECESSARY ASSOCIATIONS

There is a temptation to presume uncritically that the belief in survival entails belief in any one or a number of the following: God, astrology, monism, reincarnation, karma, Buddha's eightfold path, prayer, witches, Satan, demons, etc. It *may* be that one or more of these above beliefs is required by belief in life after death, but it is not obvious that such is the case. One of my own philosophy professors, C. J. Ducasse, believed in life after death, transmigration, and some version of karma. But he was an atheist, and he regarded astrology to be nonsense. He also rejected such ideas as Satan, witches, and demons. Indeed, Professor Ducasse was very much opposed to a great deal of behavior traditionally described as "religious." He denied the supernatural but felt that mystical experiences are valuable except in certain pathological cases.[18]

On the other hand, there are many classical theists whose particular view of God implies belief in Satan, demons, witches, and prayer. But they reject belief in transmigration or reincarnation. Many Christians believe that the body of a carpenter named Jesus once died and then was resurrected to life, whereas most people who try to base their belief in survival on empirical or observational grounds are of the opinion that our present ordinary bodies will not be resurrected at all. Rather, our surviving spirits will presumably tenant *other* bodies of various kinds.

Professor Charles Hartshorne is a theist of the panentheistic variety. But he does not believe that the case for immortality is very strong. He thinks that when he dies, he will no longer exist at all. In his view, when the human species eventually perishes, only God will survive and live forever. The impact that other beings make on God will abide forever, but as conscious subjects, they themselves will no longer exist.

Many outstanding classical theists believe in life after death, not because there is empirical evidence for such a belief, but because a good and powerful God would not be likely to create a being such as man and then cut him off forever. One noted theist, while sympathetic to the idea of a resurrection of some sort, thinks that the notions of karma and reincarnation cannot stand as they are.[19]

The point here is that caution should be employed in hooking beliefs together. It is not always true that certain ideas ranging from astrology to Satan must be accepted because of either a belief or a disbelief in life after death. Although belief in reincarnation logically entails belief in survival after death, the converse does not follow of logical necessity; in fact, it may not follow at all.

There are numerous questions to be answered before a neat package of connected religious beliefs can be put together. Our conspicuous ignorance in these areas reminds us painfully of our human finitude. But dogmatic belief will not make us less finite; on the contrary, it will tend to make us more foolish and excessively vain.

PREPARING FOR THE NEXT LIFE

There are books upon books offering advice on how to prepare for the life to be lived after we die. Needless to say, it would be wise to prepare for the next life if there is one and if it is possible to prepare for it. Unfortunately, I cannot see that any of this long train of advice is of great use.

Some writers contend that the next world brings pain to those who try to maintain contact and interest in their friends, relatives, and loved ones on earth. If this is true, then a person in this life might try to avoid strong attachments with anyone so that after death he will have nothing greatly to interest him on earth. Thus, through forgetting his spouse, children, brothers, and sisters on earth, he can journey on to new relationships and activities.

For some writers, sex in the next life is only a great and painful temptation. Hence, if one arrives there with a little or no sexual desire, he is more likely to be happy. If this is the case, then sexual suppression on earth might be excellent training for the next life.

Another view has it, however, that in the next world our unconscious desires will well up with great force, and that those persons who have ignored and restrained their strong passions in this life will be the ones to suffer most. To prepare for the next life, the holders of this view recommend practice in leading a life of passion and intensity of feeling while on earth.

By contrast, some writers hold that the evidence indicates that the next life will have little intense pleasure and joy. It will be a low-key kind of existence, nothing grand and glorious. If this is true, then many Christians and Muslims are going to suffer a great deal in the next world. Going into the next world with incredibly high expectations, they will meet with overwhelming disappointment. Indeed, such a gap between the reality and the high expectations of heaven could mean that Christians and Muslims will be the ones to suffer the agony of hell. Those who will gain the most from the next world will be the ones who have learned to live with modest expectations.

There are, of course, many other versions of what the next world is like. But I find none of them to be greatly compelling of belief. Hence, I can only recommend enjoying the life that we have here and now and sharing with others in this present life venture. It would seem mistaken to live one's present life as a preparation for the next world if we cannot be sure what exactly to prepare for. Indeed, there may not even be a next world. There is, however, the present life, which provides us some opportunity to enjoy, love, and create.

NOTES

1. 1 Samuel 28:3 (RSV).
2. See Leviticus 20:27.
3. See 1 Kings 18:40.
4. See 1 Samuel 13:8–14.
5. See Francis A. Schaffer, *The God Who Is There* (Chicago: Inter-Varsity Press, 1968), p. 156.
6. This lengthy article appears in *Proceedings of the Society for Psychical Research* 50 (1956): 153–239.
7. This report of this case may be found in Hornell Hart, *The Enigma of Survival: The Case For and Against an After Life* (London: Rider & Co., 1959), pp. 237 f.
8. See Sylvan Muldoon, *The Phenomenon of Astral Projection* (London: Rider & Co., 1951).
9. See Hart, *Enigma of Survival*, p. 244 f.
10. Cited in ibid., p. 244.
11. See C. D. Broad, "The Phenomenology of Mrs. Leonard's Mediumship," *Journal of the American Society for Psychical Research* 49 (1955): 47–63.
12. See Hart, *Enigma of Survival*, pp. 126–133.
13. Quoted from C. J. Ducasse, "Is Life After Death Possible?" delivered at Berkeley, California, in 1947 as a Foerster Lecture. Ducasse is referring to Sir Ernest Bennett's *Apparitions and Haunted Houses* (London: Faber & Faber, 1945), pp. 145–150. This case also appears in Ducasse, *Nature, Mind, and Death* (LaSalle, Ill.: Open Court, 1951), pp. 474 f.
14. See Perry London, *Behavior Control* (New York: Harper & Row, 1969), p. 149.
15. See Hart, *Enigma of Survival*, p. 262.
16. See H. H. Price, *Essays in the Philosophy of Religion* (New York: Oxford University Press, 1972), p. 91.
17. H. H. Price, "Death in the Secular City," *Religious Studies* 9, no. 3 (September 1973): 355.
18. See C. J. Ducasse, *A Philosophical Scrutiny of Religion* (New York: Ronald Press, 1953).
19. See John Hick, *Philosophy of Religion*, 2d ed. (Englewood Cliffs, N.J.: Prentice-Hall, 1973), chaps. 7, 8.

Epilogue

SCIENCE AND RELIGION

Scientific Encroachment.   Contemporary anthropologists and sociologists of religion are often eager to disclaim any attempt to evaluate religions as to the credibility of the beliefs or the worth of the religious rules and regulations.[1] Those engaged in the scientific study of religion are advised to resist any temptation to evaluate "the ultimate truth claims of religion."[2]

Two things may be said in response to this appearance of scientific modesty. In the first place, one anthropologist who makes the above disclaimer argues, nevertheless, that anthropology must come to the aid of "moral philosophy" by providing it with empirical data and even a "conceptual framework."[3] This means that moral philosophy engages in analysis and evaluation because it is able to draw on scientific research and theorizing. Because science has influenced philosophy (and vice versa), it follows that through philosophy (at least) science will have some influence on the way that morality is studied and evaluated. If in this indirect way science does have a significant impact on the evaluation of morality, there is good reason to believe that it will have a similar impact on *religion.*

In the second place, scientists are sometimes put off by such a formidable phrase as "the ultimate truth claims of religion." Scientists usually say that they cannot deal with the "transcendent." Which raises the question, who *is* to deal with it? There are numerous priests, shamans, preachers, and theologians who are quite eager to stake out a claim to this area in order to make it their exclusive domain.

The philosopher may take a dim view of both theologians

and scientists on this matter. He notes that, despite their disclaimers, scientists are steadily coming forth with conclusions and hypotheses that directly invade what some theologians regard as their private domain of the so-called "transcendent." Like it or not, theology is forced perpetually to come to terms with the various sciences. Biology, geology, astronomy, and other sciences have certainly changed the tunes of theology during the past hundred or so years. Furthermore, today the sciences of sociology, psychology, and anthropology are stripping to a bare frame many religious views around the globe, views that for centuries have passed as ultimate truths.

The philosopher, therefore, is not impressed when scientists claim that they do not deal with the "transcendent" realm. Indeed, as the above chapters on supernaturalism and naturalism indicate, the very notion of the "transcendent" is at best clumsy and at worst systematically misleading.

To be sure, the world is doubtless far richer than our poor intellectual nets will ever be able to take in. But this hardly makes a foothold for supernaturalism, unless supernaturalism is to be reduced to the role of becoming the spokesman for our human ignorance. As noted in a previous chapter, supernaturalism is paying mere lip service to "mystery." What it is really doing is using the term "mystery" to protect its own assertions from scrutiny. Philosophy calls the bluff of theology when theology plays this fruitless game.

Perennial Religion. It is often said that religion is a perennial phenomenon of the human species. It is more precise to say that the dominant religious *concerns* that prompt religious *responses* will probably continue, if we mean by "religious concerns" our struggles with death, chaos, injustice, and in general our *finitude*. But while these concerns will doubtless continue to accompany our mortal journey in the world, the *responses* that we make will (for some individuals) vary from responses elicited in previous times. The naturalist or panentheist is certainly religious in his concern about finitude, but his particular religious *response* is different from that of the devotees of the Ghost Dance or of Calvinism.

Indeed, science itself as an attempt to deal with the terrors and threats of chaos and with the finitude of our understanding may be viewed as profoundly colored by the religious concern. To say this, however, is not to say that science is controlled by a dogma independent of its own dictates. To be sure, the snake of dogmatism lies also in the path of science. In desperate moments, a scientist may turn his own quest for knowledge into a quest for a total "salvation" that will deliver him from his cognitive finitude. In this desperate state, he may imagine that science either has saved him or will eventually save him from all ignorance. Such a faith seems no more justified than the Christian's expectation of the Second Coming of Jesus.

Human beings need be no more ashamed of having religious concerns than of having sexual desires or hunger pangs. The important issue has to do with whether the religious concerns will be dealt with in a profound, forthright, and open manner. There is nothing unscientific about having abiding religious interests, although the particular *responses* that deal with these interests may or may not conflict with the legitimate attempts of science to deal with the need to increase our knowledge and understanding. I hope that in this book I have made it clear that, because "religion" manifests a multiplicity of responses, it cannot be judged simply as one phenomenon. The challenge of philosophy lies partly in drawing out the great differences among responses to the religious concern with finitude. Some responses may indeed prove worthy of strong commitment, whereas other responses may be exposed by philosophical inquiry and analysis as no longer worthy. It is to be expected that human beings, finite as they are, will have need to grow and develop in the area of religion.

SAVIORS

Belief in saviors is not as harmless as the conviction that we must live forever. Saviors have a way of draining us of much of the finite intelligence that we have. In June, 1974, I listened to the American evangelist Billy Graham preach to a vast audience at the annual meeting of the Southern Baptist Convention. Besides speaking of King Jesus' returning on a white horse from heaven to earth, the evangelist made the following declaration:

Our world is longing for an answer. . . . Our world is longing for reassurance, longing for peace, certainty, the voice of authority. At no time in history has the world been so eagerly looking for a Messiah, a Führer, a leader, . . . a Mr. Clean . . . the Perfect Man.

After noting that the Nazis in the 1930's committed themselves to the "wrong leader," Graham offered his audience the true leader, Jesus. Of course, Jesus was not conspicuously present to accept the leadership, but Mr. Graham has for years been referred to as "God's man with God's message." There are other finite mortals who also seem prepared to speak on behalf of the cosmic Jesus and to interpret his divine preferences for the entire human race. Graham continued:

Once again there is a crisis in leadership. All nine of the Common Market countries have lost their leaders in the last six months. Our own leader is under a cloud. The whole world is looking for a leader.

If the arguments that I have offered in this book are reasonably sound, then the longing for a universal leader, while understandable, is a costly and misguided way of dealing with human finitude. The lust for an infallible savior—whether it be a computer, Jesus, or the Führer—is a part of the problem of the human condition rather than its solution.

Indeed, what is the solution? Well, there is no one solution. Human beings have *numerous* problems, which require a number of different kinds of solutions. In fits of dramatic passion we doubtless expect to gain *the total solution*, even when we are not clear as to what the question is. Evangelist Graham is only one among many who speak of "the sin problem." By lumping most human problems together under this category, such preachers in their more grandiose moments hope to offer one stupendous, whiz-bang cure-all, which they designate as "the Lord and Savior Jesus Christ." But this one-shot solution turns out to be a code name for a highly elaborate behavior modification program. It would be wise, therefore, to make further inquiry into the designs of this program, whose leader is said to be the cosmic Christ, but whose implementers are discovered to be our fellow fallible mortals.

The atheist Ayn Rand, with her awe of metaphysical maleness, and Billy Graham, with his talk of surrendering everything to Jesus, seem to share in common a longing for the super-hero—some Christological Roark—who is destined to make straight the crooked way.

The tendency of popular religion is to project its ideals and values onto personal models; and then, having personified these ideals, to proceed to deprive its heroes and models of flesh and blood until they become neither human nor symbolic of great ideals. Like the Lone Ranger (another popular savior), hero-gods seem to mask their humanity. Is Superman really Clark Kent? Or is Clark Kent really Superman? Perhaps they are one in two, or two in one. In any case, even Clark Kent (the human form of Superman) is hardly human. Human existence may indeed be all too brief and tragic, but the craving for super-heroes, when taken as something more than the playful invention of art, tends to make us ambivalent about ourselves because we are only mortal. Because we are not always larger than life, some religions would treat us as unfit for happiness. The doctrine of original sin as taught by orthodox Calvinism says in effect, "Because you are not Perfect Man, you are therefore accursed."

Consider the enormous amount of hatred of humanity among some of the biblical writers. Joseph Campbell, the noted student of comparative religions, once remarked: "Think of the Apocalypse of the biblical writers, how they hated everybody—the Assyrians, the Babylonians, the Greeks, the Romans."[4] The writers of the Apocalypse seem to despise outsiders, doubtless because some outsiders had greatly abused them.

In summary, the notion of saviors and hero-gods too frequently becomes a childish wish for a superman or superwoman. As a bit of childish wish-fulfillment or escapism, the preoccupation with super-heroes may be harmless. But when it begins to shape our view of reality and our relationship to it, then the fantasy ceases to be harmless. It becomes instead a derangement of thought and a displacement of human love and devotion. If there is a hero in the book of Job, it is not God or Satan. It is Job himself. Yet even he is made to repent in dust and ashes for simply being a finite mortal being. The self-hatred and other-hatred that some of the Bible too often breeds seems hardly to be an ideal by which to live. Hitler projected his grandiose ideals onto a mythical German super-hero. But Hitler detested real flesh-and-blood Germans as much as he hated non-Germans. In short, like many Christians, he loved his savior-god, his super-hero, more than he loved his fellow human beings.

To reject the saviors of the world need not lead to the worship of mediocrity. Empirical men and women are capable of great change and growth. Finite heroes, rather than super-heroes, can serve to remind us of "what might be." But hero-worship is idolatry, which deprives both the idol and the worshiper of the chance to be more fully human.

CHAOS AND BELIEF SYSTEMS

The Threat of Chaos.   Every person when he faces the threat of a chaos has an opportunity to be a finite hero.[5] Both religion and philosophy, as well as science, in many ways arise from the driving activity of human beings to erect walls against the giant waves of chaos. Idolatry is born of the need to transform our ignorance of the wild chaotic forces above and beneath us into something that we can grasp and use. An idol is a tool that evokes responses and feelings that are inappropriate to mere tools. The folly of idolatry lies in the misdirection of its frantic make-believe. It is a misdirected short cut to knowledge of, and power over, chaos or nothingness.

Some students of religion have gone so far as to regard our sense of dread and terror (the "numinous" experience) in the face of chaos to be the essence of religion. But religion is too complex, too woven into the fabric of human life, to have so simple an essence. It is more accurate to say that, historically, religions have been largely conditioned by the finite agent's dreadful realization of himself (or his identity group) as standing before chaos and the possibility of nothingness.

Much of the story of various religions could be written in terms of how they encounter chaos. The twentieth-century existential philosopher Martin Heidegger stresses the need of "letting oneself go into Nothing, that is to say, freeing oneself from the idols we all have and to which we are wont to go cringing."[6] But this is, unfortunately, easier said than done.

Courage amid Belief.   The religions of the world, as well as science and philosophy, have in one way or another endeavored (sometimes fruitlessly) to make it possible for human beings to gain courage. After all, the courage to face the threat of nothingness does not arise out of nothing. Classical theism says that God created the world out of nothing, which presumably was possible for him because he was both omniscient and omnipotent; but you and I are not. Indeed, the critique of classical theism should not be that it tried to climb onto God's coattails. It cannot be condemned for trying to hook on to a

Necessary Being who is thought to wade through chaos and nothingness like a zestful boy dashing through fields and creeks. No, the justified criticism of classical theism is that it too greatly confuses wishes with reality, mirages with substance. The same criticism may be also leveled at monistic Absolutism, which laughs off risk, chance, and chaos as so much petty illusion and mere appearance.

By contrast, both naturalism and (especially) Brightman's panentheistic personalism are belief systems that insist that chaos is not merely a passing phase of things. Nothingness is not a cosmic hiccup that can be cured once and for all. Rather, chaos is regarded as an ultimate dimension of reality, which is to say that the shape of the future will never be wholly stable, corralled, and tamed. Existential courage is that part of faith which faces chaos without absolute assurance of personal victory over it.

Placing Chaos in Perspective.   It is interesting to see how the everlastingness of chaos has been admitted by various belief systems and myths. Brightman says that you can apparently count on the presence of chaos and risk in whatever form the world happens to take at any "time." Naturalism very similarly speaks of the existence of cosmic randomness. And even classical theism's belief system neatly blocks off cosmic chaos into a kind of everlasting ghetto called hell. Despite all talk of divine omnipotence, this God cannot be thought of as eliminating all chaos. So he simply ropes it off, in the way that the city of Boston marks off an area wherein "questionable" literature and practices are allowed to exist with minimum interference. In hell, all the wild, crazy, chaotic forces are said to be turned loose to play out their terrors on one another forever. It is projected as an eternal bazaar of the bizarre.

The myth of heaven and hell is important to orthodox Christians and Muslims because it offers them the assurance that chaos will be put in its place and that it will eventually be perfectly controlled even if not eliminated. In Christian theology, although God's "holiness" will not let him destroy Satan altogether, nevertheless Satan is chained in the Lake of Fire where he will be tortured forever. God in his weird holiness may be pathological, but at least his is thought of as a kind of predictable lunacy. "The strange work of God," to use Martin Luther's phrase, is something that we can at least keep away from, for there are said to be certain revealed directions for getting around God when he is in his rage. Indeed, the full wrath of God, oddly enough, is seen only by the "ungodly." His enmity is for outsiders only. For insiders, he is the perfect cosmic host, whose orderly celestial home welcomes the elect guests who have prepared themselves for the heavenly feast.

The Role of Mythologies. The purpose of an intellectual belief system is to gain at least some control and structure through the *symbols* that "represent" reality. We long to symbolize chance and uncanny appearances, for just to *speak* of them in a coherent and rational manner is to take the first step in controlling chaos, or at least in controlling our own human responses to it. One writer expands this point brilliantly: "The thing we seem least able to tolerate is a threat [that] our powers . . . to create, grasp, and use symbols may fail us."[7]

The power to conceptualize or symbolize is our essential tool for becoming human. Without it we are a "formless monster with neither sense of direction nor power of self-control, a chaos of spasmodic impulses and vague emotions."[8] Indeed, without symbols and concepts the human animal is more random and aimless than other animals, because for him systems of symbols replace the guiding instincts that man has lost in the twists and turns of evolution. It is, therefore, no incidental thing that the human animal has his symbols sewn together into elaborate belief systems and mythologies. The myth is more than a mere fiction to be put aside once it has been found out. Mythologies have served as a useful network of conceptual highways, which throughout the centuries man has been continually laying out over a primitive terrain.

It is no wonder, therefore, that individuals, groups, and societies have bitterly resented those who would dig up their mythologies as if they were mere weeds or useless stones. Our mythologies are not, for us, obstacles in our paths but the very sod and forest which sometimes prevent the waters of chaos from washing in to carry away ourselves and everything we hold dear. To tear out the doctrine of hell in orthodox Christianity, for example, is not, for the true believer, an exercise in intellectual and moral sanitation. To him, it is a demolition job done by idiots or perverts who do not see (or care) that the doctrine of hell and the doctrine of heaven are connected. Eliminate one, and you eliminate the other. Destroy belief in Satan, and you destroy belief in God. Destroy belief in Christ as the Son of God, and you destroy belief in the God who

made the sun to shine. Such is the way the committed orthodox Christian thinks—and feels. To ask him to give up some of
his beliefs—no matter how absurd they may seem to you—is
like asking a person to jump from his boat or to throw away
the only map that he has in a strange land.

Exchanging Myths or Beliefs. Nevertheless, as a matter
of fact people do often give up at least some parts of their
mythologies. It is important to understand why or how. The
myth may simply fail to do what it promises, like a map that
keeps misleading its readers in certain areas. These people may
throw away the whole map; or, more likely, they will tend to
turn to those other parts of the map that have not yet proved
to be disappointing. So also with belief systems and mythologies. From their culture, people receive many myths, some of
which become so well tested that they may be reformulated
and elevated to the status of scientific knowledge or its equiva-
lent. But other myths seem to frustrate the believer in his
intellectual quest more than they help him. Yet instead of eliminating these myths or beliefs from his system, the believer
may retain them out of loyalty, habit, or "just in case."

Of course, mythologies and belief systems are far more complex than maps and boats. The point to be made here is that
people change or modify mythologies for a number of reasons,
one of which is that they are presented with another mythology that seems to have fewer central problems, or seems to be
more credible. But problems can be emotional in nature, as
well as moral and intellectual. A person may become a Roman
Catholic, not for any intellectual reason, but for emotional or
aesthetic reasons. Or a Catholic may become a naturalist or
personalist for intellectual and moral reasons. And so on.

In this book I have tried to present naturalism, personalism,
and panentheism in general as a kind of broad alternative to
either classical theism or Absolutism. The latter two views I
have judged as too filled with contradiction, fantasy, and wishful thinking to be taken as serious mythologies. They lack a
sufficient touch of reality, except for the reality of subjective
human desire, which is not enough for constructing a credible
position worthy of intellectual and moral commitment.
Whether or not naturalism, personalism, and panentheism will
be *emotionally* satisfying and healthy will depend upon the
programs and institutions that they maintain and develop. Religion cannot survive unless it has ritual, programs, and organi-

zation. To be sure, these may stifle a religion as well as imple-
ment it, but such is the risk that any finite religious response
must take.

Openness to Chaos.   Chaos can sometimes be used. Fire
is not merely a destructive force. Dynamic religion may be
able to cope increasingly with chaos without fleeing from it or
pretending that it is wholly under the control of the deity.
Doubtless the doctrine of "free will" has served some classical
theists well as a symbol to cover a large area of chaos in
human affairs. "Sin" is another term that has sometimes called
attention to the chaos that the deity has presumably not—at
least not yet—brought wholly under control.

A phenomenon may be chaotic in some respects but not in
other respects. It is inaccurate to lump all religious responses
together under one category, "religion," as if they all conceived
of chaos in the same way. Freud was mistaken to think that
religion *must* be a sickness.

Indeed, a careful philosophical analysis of the language of
chaos reveals that it is a concept or symbol of many shades and
hues. It is only because sentient creatures have goals and patterns of reinforcement that the term 'chaos' could have any
meaning. Threats come only to those who already have something to be threatened. Courage as a component of most
commitments of faith comes only if the commitment has not
proved to be a total failure. Courage, then, rises out of some
experience with success. A religious commitment that would
*en*courage its believers to journey into areas of honest intellectual inquiry must already have provided them with some success in the venture.

The risk of committed intellectual honesty is overwhelming
and threatening to those whose practice at this kind of honesty
has been quite limited. Those who fear that the foundations of
their established commitment may well be shaken by new intellectual ventures are often caught in a double bind. They
want to escape the guilt brought on by a sense of intellectual
cowardice, and yet they seem to be without the means of
gaining the courage to launch into frightful intellectual waters.
To them, the new horizon appears as chaos; it is like sailing
off the edge of the earth.

Perhaps the least disturbing way of venturing forth is simply
to sail out only a little at a time, departing at first from more
familiar shores, and in general increasing one's success in sail-

ing close to the shores of one's established beliefs. The secret is simply to keep at it, to practice the intellectual ventures, opening oneself gradually and regularly.

Disappointing Belief Systems.   Perhaps one of the most tragic aspects of religion lies in a system of beliefs that generates problems that seem to demand a solution but at the same time permit none. In northern Rhodesia a woman suffered the great misfortune of losing her parents while she was yet a child; all her other kin eventually died, leaving her alone in the world. Even her grandchildren were taken from her. Having watched all her relatives perish before her, she decided to journey to where the earth ends. Her system of beliefs had long taught her that God resided there. Journeying from country to country, she never arrived at her destination, where she hoped to inquire of God why he had inflicted so much suffering on her. Like Job of the Old Testament, she wanted to know what great sin she had committed to deserve such punishment. In the course of her journey she would talk to people about her loneliness, and they in turn would tell her that God causes trouble to come to everyone. Finally, the old woman died of a broken heart, having never achieved her desire.[9]

Making the Most of a Myth.   It is interesting to see how the old woman's belief system functioned at two levels. At one level it proved to be a source of great disappointment and frustration. Today many religions are suffering from this same frustration born of the double bind. But people think that they are bound to go along with the belief system anyhow, as if they had contracted for a role in a play that is no longer wholly right for them but which they must out of duty play to the hilt.

At another level, however, it is very possible that the old woman found an ingenious way to make use of her culture's myth in coping with an otherwise intolerable situation. That is, she professed a need to confront her God who dwelled in some remote and obscure region. But it is very possible that she wanted to visit a number of people. By saying that she was searching for God, she in fact obtained social sanction for going about visiting and finding people with whom to converse and live out her days. It was her way of traveling rather than staying at home alone.

Now if we had asked this woman what she was doing, she would not have answered, "I'm traveling about and visiting with people." She would doubtless have said that she was seeking God. It is useful to ask whether she actually knew that she was journeying in order to be with people. This is a difficult question. It is like the woman who finds some evidence that her husband is having an affair, but who cannot acknowledge boldly to herself that he is. So, is she pretending? Yes and no. There are doubtless many believers today who have some evidence that certain elements of their belief system are no longer credible, but who cannot actually acknowledge this clearly to themselves. So, in a sense, they pretend. But it is a serious pretense. The child playing under the table says that he is in his tepee. For him it *is* a tepee. But not in all situations. When it is time to eat, the tepee is a table.

Similarly, some people move in and out of their religious beliefs according to the circumstances of their lives. At church they may talk to children about "gentle Jesus meek and mild" and then support collective murder on Tuesday. In a certain western city a married man who was a member of the Church of Christ was involved in an affair with a woman not of his own faith. During the affair he kept trying to convert her to the Church of Christ. Now this particular religious denomination is very conservative and most certainly looks upon adultery as a sin that will send anyone to hell. Is it possible, then, that the man was convinced that his affair was not a case of biblical adultery and thus would not prevent his being a true and faithful member of the very conservative Church of Christ? Or was he only pretending to himself that he was a committed member of this church? These questions are not easy to answer with a simple yes or no. The dynamics are too involved and too multi-layered for a one-level answer.

Preachers sometimes denounce those laymen who move in and out of their religious beliefs as if the beliefs were roles to play. But sometimes people use the word "fanatic" to label someone who does bear his belief-role from one setting to another. In some cases, the intense believer's attempt to expand his belief system into other areas of life creates a crisis in his life and the lives of those associated with him. He comes to see that he is bordering on pretense. He must either give up his belief system—or much of it—or else bear it with him no matter where he goes. He cannot let the same object be both table and tepee. He cannot play the game once he has seen that it is a game, even if it is a very serious one. If there is no other belief system that he can embrace, he stands at a momentous and crucial point in his life.

Myth Both Reveals and Conceals.   A father, busy at his desk, was obliged to deal with his four-year-old daughter, who kept coming to him because she had nothing better to hold her attention. Finally, the poor man gave her three burnt matches to play with. Sitting upon the rug, she began to play; one match was Hans, another Gretel, and the third the witch. After a considerable time of quiet and play, the child suddenly shrieked in terror. Jumping up, the father sought to discover what was wrong—why his little girl, now running to him, was so terribly frightened. "Daddy," she cried, "take the witch away! I can't touch the witch any more!"[10]

Students of mythology sometimes argue that there are times when we cannot think certain thoughts because they are too threatening to us. But if they come to us couched in mythological form, then we are better able to confront them, to even play and tinker with them. The mythical forms not only conceal, thus involving us in pretense and deception, but also reveal in disguise what we otherwise might not be able to face at all.

If, in our moments of burning awareness, the myth melts, the force behind the myth may hit us as it did the little girl pretending that she was playing with a witch. This is not to say that there are witches, but rather that the world is filled with grotesque surprises and shocks. To denote these, I have used the half-mythical term "chaos."

Our myths, then, are neither pure truths nor pure fictions, but an elaborate mixture of the two. Indeed, in religion, the myth, having once gained a kind of public license, sometimes invades the mind as a guest might take over the household. Instead of being the tool of reality, in the setting of a society, a myth takes on a reality of its own. Indeed, a myth is a social reality, but often it claims to be far more—a cosmic reality. When this happens, then human beings are made to suffer the tyranny of mythology.

Consider, for example, the Roman Catholic Mass. When pronouncing the formula "This is my body," the priest and his fellow traditional-minded believers do not think that they are dealing in mythology or even fiction. Nor do they see themselves as engaging only in an elaborate psychosocial phenomenon. Rather, they believe that the natural elements of bread and wine do become the miraculous supernatural flesh and blood of God. Similarly, in India it is thought by many that the deities respond to the sacred formulae by infusing their divine substance into temple images.[11]

There is no easy short cut to separating the credible from the incredible within our mythologies. One of the tasks of philosophy is to compare myths and to engage their devotees in discourse. It is perhaps often overlooked that every *de*mythologizing program gives birth to a *re*mythologizing venture. But the new myths need not be as misleading as the older ones. At the same time, in following the urge to cut away the error, to trim the fat from every myth, we must not forget that myths do open up new dimensions of experience and reality. But what the newly discovered reality is is a matter of perpetual inquiry, experiment, and bold speculation rigorously put to the test.

WHAT CAN WE BELIEVE?

Naturalism and Panentheism. I have tried to show that naturalism and panentheism offer a better way of thinking and investigating than do some of the alternative ways. Naturalism and the panentheism of Brightman, Hartshorne, and Whitehead subscribe both to open experimentalism and rigorous logical analysis. Bold new hypotheses are thus encouraged and subsequently brought forth to be checked out for coherence and sensitive, growing empirical relevance. Naturalists and revised theists converge in criticizing the claims of various Scriptures of the world to be infallible, divine revelation. Panentheism and naturalism agree further that morality grows out of human beings' interacting with one another in the setting of pervasive natural and cultural variables. Allegedly supernatural moral commandments are regarded as human projections which, while worthy of careful consideration, are also subject to critical testing.

If a person insists on seeking only what he has already found, knowing only what he has already known, and believing only what he has already believed, then he is doomed either to despair or to enormous self-deception. Naturalism and panentheism offer more-or-less stabilized belief systems that provide orientation. But they are systems that remain open to new additions and revisions. The risk of any belief system that is sensitive to revision is that it will be revised to the point where it is no longer anywhere near the same view.

Indeed, growth is a kind of death for those elements and beliefs that have been transcended. But the failure of a belief system to grow leads to a more tragic death. If the arguments of this book make sense, then classical theism and Absolutism are two belief systems that are already dead intellectually. Nevertheless, because classical theism and Absolutism are more than belief systems, they continue to thrive in virtue of the powerful momentum of their institutions as well as the emotive dimension of their myths.

Intellectually speaking, classical theism and Absolutism represent a dangling dead hand of the past. Unfortunately, the living have often permitted the dead to run their lives unnecessarily, like a lover who lives on the memories of a past love because he is unable to embark upon a new one. I have presented naturalism and panentheism as perhaps a new love for some to discover.

An Extension of Paul's Faith.   The study of religion is useful and informative for a number of reasons, one of which is that it tells us much about how the struggling human species has responded to the contingencies of life. Fortunate are those who can still learn something from the religious responses that they personally reject either in part or whole.

Many writers have characterized the apostle Paul as an arrogant man riddled with serious complexes and emotional disturbances. But other writers have regarded him to be a great instrument of divine information. A more realistic picture, however, would portray Paul as a man who, though indeed deeply disturbed, was in many ways victimized by the crosswinds and contradictions of his own culture. He stands as one who was extraordinarily sensitive to the great agony and promise of his time.

His doctrine of "justification by faith" is still an enormous advance in the moral and psychological struggles of human beings. In essence, Paul is saying that he cannot fully measure up to the prescribed moral standards. His only recourse, if he is to avoid absolute defeat and despair, is to trust in God's goodness to accept him as he is. This trust in divine graciousness is "justification by faith."

On this point many critics have altogether misunderstood the problem that Paul was trying to solve. His primary and

fundamental concern was not with a human morality in relation to a social system on earth. To be sure, in his letters, Paul
dealt with many practical problems of morality; but his insights at this level are of no long-lasting importance. What is of
importance is his insight regarding morality as it pertains to
one's relationship to God. Call this vertical morality rather
than horizontal morality, for this is a very useful distinction.
Whether or not you agree with Paul on his theism and Chris-
tology, it is important to grasp that for him God is involved in
human morality. This means that human beings have to answer to God for their actions. The brilliance of Paul lies in the
conviction—painfully arrived at—that human beings cannot
greatly impress the deity with their moral performances. If
they are to avoid the wrath (chaos) of God, then they must
trust in his goodness and not in their own actions. They can
neither buy nor earn acceptance before God; it is entirely up to
the deity and not to themselves to determine whether they are
to escape his wrath.

Today, the very existence of God is a profound problem or
question. It was not a problem for Paul, for he simply pre-
supposed the existence of God. Today, many people seem to
be caught in the pretense of belief. They say they believe in
God, or perhaps want to believe, but they also know that such
belief is not altogether possible for them. On the question of
belief in God's existence, some classical theists still roll the
drums of morality, as if the only issue here were that of sin and
righteousness. But this is a diversionary tactic.[12]

Doubt about the existence of God is an epistemological
problem. That is, it is a question of what can and cannot be
known by mortals. It is a question of evidence, of logic, and of
the criteria of belief. No matter how hard some classical theists
try to use the point of morality to cover up the epistemological
difficulties, the difficulties still show through.

But Paul's doctrine of justification by faith (or trust) in
divine grace can throw some unexpected light on even our
epistemological dilemma. The dilemma is this: How can we
come to terms with God if we think that there might *not even
be a God*? By extending Paul's insight we come to the following resolution: We cannot trust absolutely in the accuracy of
our concepts or hypotheses of God. We can at this fundamental level say only that a good God (if he/she exists) will not
torment us as a consequence of our considerable ignorance and

finitude. If God is *not* good, however, then he is hardly to be trusted anyhow.

And so, we are left with nothing short of a fundamental religious faith that leaves us trusting absolutely in neither our moral performances nor our *intellectual concepts and symbols* to save us from divine wrath. Furthermore, this fundamental faith—this back-against-the-wall faith—leaves us free to express forthrightly our doubts about the intellectual concepts of all those prophets and priests who have claimed to be receiving a message hot off the altar of God.

In short, our eternal destiny—if we have one at all—is up to God and seems to be out of our hands. If, of course, there is no God, then we have no need to fear his everlasting punishment. I will not try to summarize the numerous reasons for rejecting the orthodox Christian or Muslim views regarding everlasting divine punishment. The point here is that we may now proceed to live our lives here and now even though we cannot be absolutely certain about even the existence or nonexistence of God.

Nevertheless, following some of the light that we mortals do have, I have tried to explain why some views are definitely too lacking in intellectual appeal to recommend themselves as viable options. The panentheism and the naturalism outlined in earlier chapters were offered (in place of certain other views) as fruitful belief systems worthy of human commitment. What is appealing about these systems is their combination of stability with openness to intellectual growth. It is hoped that this intellectual growth will contribute to moral and emotional growth as well.

Boasting of no infallible oracles from God, the naturalist and the panentheist stand in a favored position to receive new information and stimuli from a world that lies open before them as a horizon of both structure and surging chaos. Somewhere in the vast spread of things we very cerebral mortals find a home and make it ours for at least a little while. Some people might resent the longevity of the stars, but others would prefer living as human beings for a season over existing as glowing gases for aeons.

Various studies in depression indicate that prolonged depression often comes to those who demand from life far more than it seems to offer. To be sure, much of the happiness of humanity comes through finding new ways to enrich the given circumstances through music, art, love, work, and play. But it may not be in our power to find or produce an environment that will guarantee us everlasting happiness. It may well be that such unending bliss is something that we have no right or reason to demand or expect. Hence, in order to avoid both self-deception about our immortality and a grandiose conception of what our rights are in the universe, we might do well to scale down high expectations of life beyond the grave. Many people have learned to live within their mortal span and to do so with a measure of grace, joy, and social responsibility.

This is not, however, to discourage research and experimental inquiry into the possibility that there is life after death. If the evidence shows that there is another life and that it is pleasant, then this will be an added blessing. But to insist that there *must* be another life after the present one is to set oneself up for either possible self-deception or great disillusionment and mental anguish.

KARMA

A brief comment on the doctrine of karma is appropriate here. The notion of karma has its origins in the attempt to explain the rather obvious unfairness of life. Some people are born into happy circumstances and others are born into conditions of great poverty, hopelessness, and deprivation. Why? The doctrine of karma is based on the presupposition that the universe *ought* to be fair and just. Unable to accept the hypothesis that the universe may be simply without concern for human values and interests, those who believe strongly in karma seem to demand that their own vision of fairness be not just a human vision but a *cosmic fact*. Hence, instead of saying that the cosmos has tragedy in it and that it apparently is not run by the principle of fairness and justice, those who believe strongly in karma hold that *the injustice is due to the way individuals have lived in their previous lives*. If they lived wickedly in the previous life, they will not enjoy good karma (circumstances and causes) in the present life. On the other hand, those who lived responsibly in the former life will enjoy good conditions and circumstances in this life. Needless to say, such a doctrine was easily utilized to justify the injustices of the caste system of India for many centuries. Of course, a doctrine of compassion might dictate that those who do well in this life should help those who do not do well. But this raises the question of whether such helpers are to be seen as interfering with the cosmic scheme of fairness and balance. Indeed, who is to say that they are or are not? As was seen in earlier chapters, cosmic visions of what is perfection and balance may vary from culture to culture and from individual to individual.

When the issue of fairness and justice comes to the front, the following question needs to be faced by the proponents of karma and reincarnation. Is it fair and just that a one-year-old child be made to suffer great agony because of the behavior of an adult or animal who lived in a previous life? Furthermore, it seems to stretch beyond intelligibility the notion of "personal identity" when this one-year-old child is declared to be identical with a human adult or a mouse who presumably lived in a previous life. The fact that many people have for centuries professed belief in this doctrine of karma and reincarnation does not show that is is *worthy* of belief. It may show that the so-called rational animal can embrace some very irrational notions.

DEMYTHOLOGIZING KARMA AND REINCARNATION

Gautama the Buddha could not accept the Hindu doctrine of karma because, for him, it fails to acknowledge the impermanence of all things, including persons. Nevertheless, the Buddha seemed to hold to a kind of demythologized version of karma that a naturalist today could accept and panentheists and others could accept with some reservations. According to this demythologized version of karma, there is "the transmission of effects of action from one generation of men to all succeeding generations."[13] Buddha had a profound appreciation of the mutual causal involvement and interrelationship of all things. He was concerned to teach a kind of universal human responsibility to every sentient creature. Each of us has been affected by those who have lived before us, and we in turn affect those with us now and those coming after us. The notion of each individual's own *private* karma is too simplistic, for we human beings are bound in a kind of *common* karma of humanity. Each of us has a responsibility toward the whole. The world of karma (i.e., our inherited world of nature, society, and culture) has formed us and set us on our individual ways. And we in turn are contributing to the collective karma that will continue long after us. Understood in this light, the doctrine of karma becomes a mythologized expression of a profound moral truth to which the Buddha, naturalistic humanists, panentheists, and many theists as well as atheistic existentialists can today subscribe in good faith.[14]

NOTES

1. See Clifford Geertz, *The Interpretation of Cultures: Selected Essays* (New York: Basic Books, 1973), p. 123.
2. Peter L. Berger, "Some Second Thoughts on Substantive Versus Functional Definitions of Religion," *Journal for the Scientific Study of Religion* 13, no. 2 (June 1973): 133.
3. Geertz, *Interpretation of Cultures*, p. 141.
4. Sam Keen is quoting Campbell in "Man and Myth: A Conversation with Joseph Campbell," *Psychology Today*, July 1971, p. 94.
5. See Lucio P. Ruotolo, *Six Existential Heroes: The Politics of Faith* (Cambridge: Harvard University Press, 1973).
6. Martin Heidegger, "What is Metaphysics?" *Existence and Being* (Chicago: Henry Regnery, 1949), pp. 347–349.
7. Geertz, *Interpretation of Cultures*, p. 99.
8. Ibid.
9. See C. W. Smith and A. M. Dale, *The Illa-Speaking Peoples of Northern Rhodesia* (London, 1920), pp. 197 f. This story is quoted in Paul Radin, *Primitive Man as a Philosopher* (New York: D. Appleton & Co., 1927), pp. 100–101.
10. This case may be found in the introduction to Joseph Campbell, *The Masks of God: Primitive Mythology* (New York: Viking, 1959). (This book is the first of a three-volume work entitled *The Masks of God*.)
11. See the conclusion to Joseph Campbell, *The Masks of God: Occidental Mythology* (New York: Viking, 1964).
12. On July 28, 1974, a Roman Catholic priest on a Dallas-Fort Worth television interview was asked about atheists. He replied that a person is intellectually an atheist because of intellectual pride or sin. The priest seemed at first to be making an empirical generalization, but it turned out to be only a tautology, for the priest was *defining* atheism as a sufficient element of intellectual pride or sin. He did not *discover* this to be the case. The trouble with this kind of argument by tautology is that anyone can play the game and thus turn the search for understanding into a battle of stipulative definitions. With equal insensitivity, the fundamentalist atheist Madalyn Murray O'Hair defined 'Christianity' as everything evil and nothing good. These kinds of

stipulative definitions cut off fruitful debate and dialogue, as was seen in the 1975 debate in Dallas between O'Hair and Billy Graham's pastor, W. A. Criswell.

13. J. C. Jennings, *The Vedantic Buddhism of the Buddha* (London: Oxford University Press, 1948), p. xvii. See also John Hick, *Philosophy of Religion*, 2d ed. (Englewood Cliffs, N.J.: Prentice-Hall, 1973), pp. 116 f.

14. See Hick, *Philosophy of Religion*, pp. 116 f.

INDEX

INDEX

Subject Index

(See page 309 for Name Index)

A

Absolute, the, Chap. VII; 146, 164, 268, 294
Angels, 244, 245
Animal magnetism, 220–222
Apocalypse and hatred, 284
Arminianism, 120–129
  critique of, 122–129
Astral travel, 267, 268
  astral clothes, 273
  role of imagination in, 273, 274
Astrology, 276
Atheism, ix, 17, 171, 299
  See Naturalism
Atonement of Christ, theories of, 257–259

B

Baalam's ass, 55, 57
Baptism, Paul's view of, 246
Behavioral sciences, 17, 35, 224
  See Cultural conditions; Natural science; Science
Belief and belief system, 288, 290
  See Myth
Bible, See Scripture
Brainwashing, 28, 29
Buddhism, ix, 226, 230, 241, 242, 299, 300
  See Buddha

C

Calvinism, Chap. VI; 111–121, 131–133, 149, 281
  See Arminianism; Clark, Gordon
"Catch 22" and prayer, 227
  See prayer
Chance, 70, 71, 101, 133, 157
  See Freedom of choice; Free will
Chaos, threat of, 285–287, 292
  See Myth
Christianity
  naturalistic view of, 256
  without Jesus, Chap. XII
  without Paul, 254
  See Christ; God; Jesus of the Early Christians (by G. A. Wells); Classical theism; Scripture; Salvation
Clairvoyance, 276
Classical theism, Chaps. III, IV, V, passim. defined, 61
Common Unconscious, 230
Conversion, 7, 8, 231–236
  "external" conditions of, 232–235
  like marriage vows, 233
  natural and cultural phenomena of, 236
  naturalistic view of, 232–236
  necessary for reform? 235, 236
  See Cultural conditions
Cosmological argument for existence of God, Chap. IV; 190;

definition, 180
dilemma of, 87, 88
contrasted with ontological argument, 100, 101
Courage, 285
Creation of the World, Chap. IV; 53
Cultural conditions, 113, 205–207, 218, 219, 231–236

D

Daniel, Book of, 244, 245, 247
Dead Sea (Qumran) Scrolls, 245, 247
Death, Chap. XIII; 163, 164
consciousness without brain, 275
of Savior-God, 245, 246
spirit with scent, 274
spirit with asthma, 274
See Survival after death
Deism, 61
Dreams
locating, 267–269
objects in, 271, 272
shared, 268–272
See Visions
Dream telepathy, 238

E

Egyptian and Chaldean mysteries, 253, 254
Enoch, Book of, 245, 247
ESP, 270
Essenes, 245
Evangelical Christianity, 22, 23
See Arminianism; Calvinism; Scripture
Evil, problem of, Chap. VI; 114, 115, 155–159
See Brightman, E. S.; Calvinism; Arminianism
Evolution, 70–74, 159
See Darwin, Charles
Existentialism, 52, 299
See Bultmann, Rudolf; Heidegger, Martin; Kierkegaard, Søren

F

Fact and theory, 45
See Hypothesis; Popper, Karl
Faith, 24, 294–296
as natural phenomenon, 218, 219
Paul's doctrine extended, 294–297
Feeling, 12, 13
Freedom, Paul's view of, 246
Freedom of choice, 112–116, 122–126, 158, 159, 163, 289
Free will, 289
See Freedom of choice; Chance

G

Ghost Dance, 281
See LaBarre, Weston
God
and the Absolute, 91, 292
See the Absolute and time, 136
and the universe as one, 94
See Hartshorne, Charles; Panentheism; Pantheism; Spinoza, Benedict
anthropomorphic views of, 134–141
as caused to move, 94, 134, 135
as changing and unchanging, 85–92, 107, 108
as diapolar, 107
See Brightman, E. S.; Hartshorne, Charles
as First Cause, Chap. IV
See Cosmological argument for existence of God
as limited in power, 69, 70, 77, 78, 130
as Unmoved Mover, 86, 88
Bradley's view of, 143, 144, 146
See Bradley, F. H.
Brightman's personalistic view of, 153–159, 162–165
See Brightman, E. S.; Personalism
Hartshorne's view of, 160–165
See Hartshorne, Charles; Panentheism
Hebrew view of, 86, 87
holiness of, 286
immanence of, 90–92
metaphysical v. metaphorical de-

scriptions of, 87
See Geisler, Norman
Necessary Being, Chaps. IV, V
See Thomas Aquinas
objective v. subjective existence of, 11, 12
perfection of, 88, 89, 97–101, 104–108
perishing of, 93
permissive will of, 113
revealed will of, 117, 118
secret will of, 117, 118
setting of, 102, 103
Spinoza's view of, 136–141
See Spinoza, Benedict
the world of nature within, 154, 155
transcendence of, 90
Whitehead's view of, 144–148
See Whitehead, A. N.
See Cosmological argument; Ontological argument; Teleological argument
Guilt, 7–9

H

Healing, supernatural, 219–231
exorcist, 219, 220
See Gassner, Joseph; Roberts, Oral
Heaven, 52, 286
Hebrew Law, Paul's view of, 246, 247, 249
Hell, threat of, 23, 52, 116, 117, 286, 296
as form of human aggression, 125, 126
choice of, 124–126
Christianity without belief in, 129, 130
Jesus's view of, 243
Ramsey's article on, 133
See Ramsey, Ian
Hindu, 226, 230
History, meaning of, 150, 151, 155, 156, 183, 184
Holy Spirit, 233
Humanism, Chap. X; 189, 226, 299
See Naturalism; Morality
Hypothesis (theory) and fact, 17, 27, 171

of the existence of Jesus, 244ff
See Christ; Fact

I

Idolatry, 285
See Saviors and hero-worship; Savior-God
Insiders and outsiders, 30
Ignorance, 277
Ik society, 202
Inner heart, 232, 233, 236

J

Jesus of the Early Christians, 254, 255
See Christ
Justification by faith, 295, 296
See Paul the Apostle

K

Karma, 276, 277, 297–299
presupposition of, 297
reinterpretation of, 298, 299
Killing, 235
See Morality
Kirlian photography, 223, 224

L

Language and revelation
See Scripture
Life after death
See Survival after death
Lourdes, 225

M

Mana, 220, 221
Marxism, ix, 8, 9, 223
Mediums (between the living and the departed), 262, 263, 272, 273
Mass, Roman Catholic, 272, 293
Meaning in life without immortality, 264
See History, meaning of
Messiah

Messiah (*cont.*)
  defined, 245
  Jewish view of, 247
  Paul's view of, 247
Methodology, 177, 178
Might makes right, 119, 120
  See Calvinism; Clark, Gordon;
    Morality
Miracle, Chap. XI
  and laws of nature, 213, 214
  and prayer, 230
  definition and meaning of, 212–
    217
  limited to biblical times, 214, 215
  of conversion, 231–236
  of creation, 92
  of universe without God, 92
  See Naturalism; Supernaturalism
Morality, Chap. X
  and belief in God, 191–193, 195
  and reward of heaven, 195
  and self-interest, 201
  and selfishness, 194, 195, 199,
    200–203
  and threat of hell, 195
  and unselfishness, 203
  autonomy of, 197
  critique of humanistic and natu-
    ralistic view of, 204
  Critique of supernaturalistic view
    of, 196, 197, 204, 207, 209,
    210
  humanistic and naturalistic view
    of, 208, 209
  importance of, 194–197
  justification of, 193, 194
  killing, 209
  motivation for, 53
  supernaturalistic view of, 193–
    197
  Why be moral? 193–197
  Why be selfish? 194, 195
Mormon, Book of, 36, 37
  See Smith, Joseph
Multi-embodiment, 276
Muslim, 18, 63, 111–114, 229, 296
Mystery, 281
Mystical experience, 9, 18, 27, 28
  See Religious experience
Myth, Chap. XII; 53, 54, 287, 288,
    290–293
  and pretending, 291, 292

  See Fact and theory; Hypothesis;
    Popper, Karl

N

Nature, 62, 179, 185, 205, 206, 208
  without beginning, 81–85
Natural conditions and stimuli, 13,
    17
Natural and cultural conditions of
    "spirit locations," 270, 271
Naturalism, Chap. IX; 103, 104,
    286, 299
  as a live option, 293, 294, 296
  and cultural conditions, 248
  and prayer, 229
  critique of, 182–185
  in criticism of supernaturalism,
    242
  religious dimensions of, 185–187
  view of life after death, Chap.
    XIII
  See Cultural conditions; Dewey,
    John; Hook, Sidney; Hu-
    manism; Lamprecht, Sterling
    P.; Miracles; Nielsen, Kai;
    Popper, Karl; Testing hypo-
    theses; Science
Natural sciences, 281
  See Behavioral sciences
Nature
  See Miracles; Cosmological argu-
    ment; Naturalism; Personal-
    ism
Nazi Führer, 282, 283
Necessary Being, Chaps. IV; V
  the universe as, 89, 90, 92
  See Cosmological argument; On-
    tological argument
Neo-Platonism, 105, 106
Nirvana, 108
Nothingness, 285

O

Occultism, 224, 225
Omega Point, 73
Ontological argument for existence
    of God, Chap. V
  contrasted with cosmological
    argument, 100, 101
  definition, 97

logical necessity and factual necessity, 101
problems of, 102–109

P

Pagan and Jewish thought, 253, 254
Pagan literature and Christianity, 248
Panentheism, Chap. VII
as a live option, 293, 294, 296
Brightman's version of, 153–159, 162–165
defined, 152, 153
See Hartshorne, Charles; Personalism
Pantheism defined, 152
Perfection, versions of, 104–108
See God
Personalism, 153–159, 162–165, 286
as live option, 293, 294, 296
See Brightman, E. S.; Panentheism
Pharmakeia, 34
Philosophy
relation to religion, 1–5, 26, 280
relation to theology, 280, 281
Physiology, 20, 21
Polytheism, 63
Pope, 46, 104
Poro, God, 14, 15
Prayer, Chap. XI, 227–230, 277
as miracle, 230
Predestination, 111–128
See Arminianism; Calvinism; Personalism
Presuppositions, 242
See Fact; Hypothesis
Process Philosophy, Chap. VIII, 144–148
See Brightman, E. S.; Hartshorne, Charles; Whitehead, A. N.
Prophets of Baal slaughtered, 263
Prophets and priests in competition, 263
Providence, 61
See History, meaning of; Predestination
Pythagoreans, 220

Q

Qur'an (Muslim Scripture), 3, 36, 58, 206

R

Refutation of All Heresies, 253, 254
Reincarnation, 276
Relationships, 141–148, 201, 202
See Cultural conditions; Natural conditions
Religion
as a sickness, 289
as a perennial phenomenon, 281, 282
relation to philosophy, 1–5
relation to science, 1, 280–282
See Cultural conditions; Naturalism; Supernaturalism
Religious experience
and drugs, 17–21
longing of, 14–17
must be interpreted, 36
referent of, 16
See Mystical experience
Repentance, 234, 235
Resurrection of many, 251
Revelation, Chap. II
a conjecture or hypothesis, 36
always interpreted, 57
See Scripture
Review and Expositor, 59

S

Salvation, 2, 3, 47, 49, 52, 53, 222, 223
Satan, 74–76, 120, 173, 177, 219, 277
Savior-God, Paul's view of, 244–252
Saviors, longing for, 282, 283
Saviors and hero-worship, 282–286
See Idolatry
Science, 69, 221, 222
and inquiry into survival after death, Chap. XIII
and religion, 280–282
study of conditions rather than "intrinsic" nature, 270, 271

See Behavioral sciences, Naturalism, Natural sciences
Scripture, Chap. II
  as interpretations, 154, 155, 207
  as always interpreted, 36
  as a selection of literature, 55–56
  Essential Truth theory of, 44–50, 59, 60
  'inerrant inspiration' defined, 37
  'infallible inspiration' defined, 37
  infallibility of, 45, 46
  Key Images theory of, 50
  partial infallibility assumed, 46, 47–49
  Perfect Meaning theory, 40–44
  Perfectly Worded Document theory, 37–41
  Sacred Encounter theory, 50–55
  Seedbed of Interpretation theory, 55–58
  unity and disunity of, 41–44
  See Revelation; Naturalism; Supernaturalism
Sensory deprivation and/or overload, 21, 22, 28, 29
Shaman, 222
Sin, necessity of, 127
Social Darwinism, 199, 200
Sorcery, 23, 262
Spirits, 178, 179, 248
  asthmatic, 274
  in space, 266–268
  with scent, 274
Subjectivism, 48
Suffering and evil, 77, 78
  See Evil
Superman, 284
Supernaturalism, Chap. X
  as an attitude, 264, 265
  stimuli, 13, 14
  See Miracles; Naturalism
Survival after death, Chap. XIII; 296, 297
  love of life without, 278, 279
  preparation for, 278, 279
  temporary duration only, 272

T

Teacher of Righteousness (Qumran leader), 253

Theological argument for existence of God, Chap. III
  some problems of, 65–76
  wider theological argument, 76–78
  See Tennant, Frederick R.; Bertocci, Peter A.
Teleology, defined, 62
Telepathy, 270, 276
Testing hypotheses, 171–175, 222
  See Naturalism
Testament of Levi, 248
Theism
  See Classical theism; Personalism; Panentheism
Transcendent, the, 281
Transcendental meditation, 228
Transmigration, 277
Trinity, 63

U

Universe
  Big Bang theory of, 93
  See Absolute, the; Cosmological argument; Creation; Personalism; Panentheism; Spinoza, Benedict; Whitehead, A. N.

V

Values, 182
Vibrations, 223, 225
Visions, 25, 57

W

Wider teleological argument for existence of God
  See Bertocci, Peter; Teleological argument; Tennant, Frederick R.
Witches, 272, 276

Z

Zen, 45

Name Index

(See page 303 for Subject Index)

A

Aaronson, Steve, 224
Abelson, Abraham, 32
Anselm, 97–102, 107, 108, 109, 110
Aquinas, Thomas
  See Thomas
Aristotle, 86, 94, 97
Arminius, Jacobus
  See Arminianism
Arnold, Matthew, 109
Atkinson, Basil, 132
Augustine, 35, 99, 100, 109, 200, 217, 237

B

Baillie, John, 10, 32
Barnhart, J. E., 34, 79, 133, 149, 211
Barnhart, Mary Ann, 211
Barth, Karl, 133, 151
Beegle, Dewey, 46, 49, 59, 95
Bennett, Ernest, 279
Berger, Peter, 34, 280, 299
Bergson, Henri, 78
Berkouwer, G. C., 133
Bertocci, Peter A., 77–79
Bird, Admiral, 22
Birdwhistell, Ray L., 237
Braithwaite, R. B., 261
Brightman, E. S., 79, 153, 165, 286, 293

See Personalism; Panentheism
Broad, C. D., 279
Brodie, Fawn, 34, 260
Brown, Patterson, 96
Buddha, 15, 16, 163, 298
Bultmann, Rudolf, 21, 52, 53, 60
Bunyan, John, 7, 21, 183
Burrill, Donald, 96

C

Calvin, John
  See Calvinism
Campbell, Joseph, 284, 292, 299
Carnell, E. J., 58, 59, 132, 133
Castaneda, Carlos, 26, 34
Cavendish, Richard, 35
Christ, 14, 28, 41, 47, 49, 51–54, 133, 175, 177, 209, 213, 222, 227, 231, 233, 235, 239, 277, 282–285
  atonement of, 257–259
  as code name, 16, 17, 52
  as Lord, 250
  as profound myth, 256, 257
  as Suffering Servant, 253
  Jesus as historical figure, Chap. XII; 54, 242–255
  existential view of, 50–54, 255–256
    See Kierkegaard, Søren; Bultmann, Rudolf
  Paul's view of, 244–255

Teaching of Jesus, 252–254
See Jesus; Messiah
Clark, Elmer T., 33
Clark, Gordon, 114, 119, 131, 132, 133, 149, 188
Cole, Sanford H., 211
Cohen, Jack, 181, 189
Cotton, J. Harry, 60
Cuzzort R. P., 260

D

Dale, A. M., 299
Danto, Arthur, 35
Darwin, Charles, 57, 62, 68, 72, 76, 199
Davies, W. D., 260
Davitt, Thomas E., 211
Delgado, Jose, 33
Dewey, John, 205, 206, 210
Diamond, Malcolm, 237
Dionysus, 240
Dohen, Dorothy, 210
Donnelly, John, 210
Dostoevsky, F., 191
Ducasse, C. J., 276, 277, 278

E

Edson, Hiram, 231, 232
Edwards, Jonathan, 19, 113, 131
Einstein, Albert, 57
Eli, 24, 25
Eliade, Mircea, 32, 54, 60
Elijah, 20, 263
Ellenberger, Henri F., 237
Esther, 209
Ewing, A. C., 110

F

Farrar, Austin, 60
Findlay, J. N., 96, 109
Finegan, Jack, 60
Finney, Charles, 8
Ford, Lewis S., 165
Freud, Sigmund, 7, 8, 25, 26, 289
Frost, Frederic, 165

G

Galileo, 57
Gassner, Johann Joseph, 219, 220, 222
Geach, Peter, 94
Geertz, Clifford, 280, 299
Geisler, Norman, 59, 109
Gilson, Etienne, 32, 94
Graham, Billy, 8, 15, 177, 282, 283
Graves, Robert, 60
Guanilo, 109

H

Hammurabi, 56, 57
Hannah, 24
Hanson, Norwood R., 35, 188
Hare, Peter H., 79
Hart, Hornell, 268, 273–275, 279
Hartshorne, Charles, 96, 97, 107, 108, 109, 153, 159–165, 189, 277, 293
See Ontological argument; Panentheism
Heidegger, Martin, 285, 299
Henry, Carl F. H., 238
Hepburn, Ronald, 31, 32, 110
Hercules, 240, 241
Hick, John, 133, 279, 300
Hook, Sidney, 166, 188
Howe, Leroy T., 110
Hume, David, 69, 95

I

Isaiah, the Prophet, 58

J

James, William, 7, 8, 31, 32
Jefferson, Thomas, 192, 193, 198, 199
'Jesus': defined, 247
See Christ
John XXII, Pope, 46
Juan, Don, 26, 27, 34

K

Kant, Immanuel, 69
Keen, Sam, 299
Kierkegaard, Søren, 31, 34, 205, 211, 261
  view of historical Jesus, 255, 256, 261
Koestler, Arthur, 8, 9, 32
Küng, Hans, 59

L

LaBarre, Weston, 22, 23
Lamprecht, Sterling P., 189
Larsen, Caroline, 273, 274
Lewis, C. S., 201, 210
Lloyd-Jones, D. Martyn, 35
London, Perry, 279
Luther, Martin, 68, 74, 115, 131, 132, 286

M

Madden, Edward H., 79
Malcolm, Norman, 109
Mantey, Julius R., 238
Martin, C. B., 9, 10, 11, 32
Martin, Michael, 35
Marx, Karl, 223
Mary, Virgin, 104, 226
Mavrodes, George, 193, 210
Mesmer, Franz Anton, 220–223
Miles, T. R., 189
Mill, John Stuart, 69
Miller, John F. III, 189
Miller, William, 231
Morrison, Frank, 189
Moses, 56, 209, 212, 239
Muhammad, the Prophet
  See Muslim
Muldoon, Sylvan, 178, 273
Mullins, E. Y., 133

N

Nagel, Ernest, 183, 189
Nathan, Peter
  The Nervous System, 19, 20, 23
Newton, Isaac, 57
Nielsen, Kai, 185, 186, 189
Nixon, Richard, 234

O

O'Neil, William F., 210
Ornstein, Robert E., 237
Osiris, 240
Otto, Rudolf, 32, 35

P

Packer, James I., 58
Pailin, David A., 109
Paley, William, 78, 79
Parsons, Howard L., 189
Paul, the Apostle, 7, 21, 23, 68, 69, 178, 209, 260, 294, 295
  cosmology and religion of, 244–252, 260
  See Christ; Savior-God
Pharaoh, 212, 213
Pike, James A., 262
Pike, Nelson, 149
Pinnock, Clark H., 58, 59
Pius IX, Pope, 45, 46
Plantinga, Alvin, 128, 133, 193
Plato, 99, 100, 105, 109, 260
Popper, Karl, 27, 35, 79, 95, 151, 152, 165, 188, 237
Price, H. H., 237, 275, 276, 279
Price, James L., 260
Price, Peter, 275

R

Radin, Paul, 299
Rahab, 209
Ramm, Bernard, 59
Ramsey, Ian, 133
Rand, Ayn, 48, 49, 200, 202, 203, 210, 283
Roberts, Oral, 74, 175, 226
Ruotolo, Lucio P., 299
Russell, Bertrand, 183, 189

S

Samuel, 24, 25, 263
Sankara of India, 200, 201
Sargant, William, 31, 32, 33, 34
Saul, King, 262
Schachter, Michael, 224
Schaffer, Francis A., 264, 279
Scriven, Michael, 110

Settle, Thomas W., 110
Smart, Ninian, 32, 109, 237, 261
Smith, C. W., 299
Smith, Huston, 33
Smith, Joseph, 24, 26, 27, 34, 35,
   239, 240
Spinoza, B., 20, 33, 136–141, 149
Stalin, Joseph, 128
Swinburne, R. G., 79

T

Tanner, Jerald and Sandra, 34
Temple, William, 228
Tennant, Frederick R., 76–79
Thomas Aquinas, 81, 86, 88, 94,
   115, 131
Turnbull, Colin M., 210

V

VanBaalen, Ian Karel, 238

VanTil, Cornelius, 188

W

Warfield, Benjamin A., 131, 132
Weil, Andrew, 33, 175, 189
Wells, Donald, 94
Wells, G. A., 254, 255, 260
Wesley, John, 15, 26
White, A. D., 79
Whitehead, A. N., 144–149, 293
   See Panentheism; Process philo-
   sophy
Wilken, Robert L., 32, 60, 260
Wirt, Sherwood, 238
Witch of Endor, 262

Y

Young, Edward J., 38, 39, 59
Young, Robert, 237

DATE DUE